PRACTICAL
MATHEMATICAL AND
STATISTICAL TECHNIQUES FOR
PRODUCTION MANAGERS

Practical Mathematical and Statistical Techniques for Production Managers

JAMES A. PARSONS

Prentice-Hall, Inc.
Englewood Cliffs, New Jersey

PRENTICE-HALL INTERNATIONAL, INC., *London*
PRENTICE-HALL OF AUSTRALIA, PTY., LTD., *Sydney*
PRENTICE-HALL OF CANADA, LTD., *Toronto*
PRENTICE-HALL OF INDIA PRIVATE LTD., *New Delhi*
PRENTICE-HALL OF JAPAN, INC., *Tokyo*

Library of Congress Cataloging in Publication Data

Parsons, James A.
  Practical mathematical and statistical techniques
for production managers.

  Includes bibliographies.
    1. Industrial engineering--Statistical methods.
2. Operations research. I. Title.
T57.35.P37   658.4'033   72-10579
ISBN 0-13-692830-7

PRINTED IN THE UNITED STATES OF AMERICA

About the Author

James A. Parsons is Group Leader of Management Sciences and Mathematical Services, Lederle Laboratories, a division of American Cyanamid Company. He has been associated with the firm since 1963, specializing in the areas of production planning and inventory control, scheduling, forecasting, financial analysis, as well as market research.

He is the author of *The Use of Mathematics in Business* published by the Alexander Hamilton Institute. The author has written the Operations Research chapter in the Mc-Graw-Hill *Handbook of Business Administration* and the OR Section in the *Encyclopedia of Science and Technology*. In addition, Dr. Parsons is Associate Editor of the *Journal of Systems Management* and serves on the Editorial Board of the *Journal of Industrial Engineering*. He is a frequent contributor to these and other journals in the area of mathematics and operations research.

The author has a B.S. in biochemistry from Hofstra University, and a B.S., M.S., and Ph.D. in mathematics from the Polytechnic Institute of Brooklyn.

Dedicated to my father, Frederick Spencer Parsons

What This Book Will Do for You

This book demonstrates proven mathematical and statistical techniques of great usefulness to anyone who must extract information from numerical data for the purpose of evaluating decision alternatives. How is data best organized and presented? How can various information contents be extracted and summarized? How can two sets of data be compared? How can we find relationships, if they exist, between two or more sets of data, and once found how can we make use of them? These are all questions pertaining to the analysis of numerical data and will be covered, along with other tools from *statistical analysis,* in chapters 1 and 2.

An undeniable characteristic of any forward-looking decision is that it is couched in a certain amount of uncertainty: there is a degree of risk associated with the decision. While no technique can erase risks, there are certain statistical techniques which can be used to measure risks in a realistic way and thus provide a way for integrating them into the estimating and hypothesizing steps which one goes through on the way to the eventual decision. Just how one does this is the subject of chapter 3. The topic is developed in a different way than usually found in most textbooks, for here everything is expressed in terms of a single concept: that of the *confidence interval.* While this is the usual thing for estimating, it is new for hypothesis testing; the result is that the reader has a unified treatment of *statistical decision theory.*

Basic to forward planning decisions is the forecast to which the decision maker is reacting. A method known as *exponential smoothing* has found wide and successful application in manufacturing. It is a short-range forecasting technique. The basic operations of the technique are presented in chapter 4 without the usual mathematical notations which for so long have hidden this very important tool from the nontechnical reader. Some of the modern refinements of the method are also demonstrated along with a different smoothing technique which can be used to uncover patterns in historical data which can then be extrapolated out into the future thereby providing more long-range forecasts.

Certain techniques, usually associated with Operations Research, will be introduced in the final two chapters. These techniques are designed to solve specific decision problems and the aim of the book is to develop in the reader the ability to recognize potential applications on his own, as well as a degree of proficiency in actually applying the techniques.

In chapter 5 the *simplex, distribution,* and *assignment methods* for solving the *linear programming problem* are presented. The simplex method is the most general one, whereas the other two are applicable only if the problem is of a specific type; when applicable these methods are much more efficient. It has been the author's intention to provide the reader with hand computing techniques and for this reason certain approximation methods are introduced. The *Vogel method* is one such method which will very often produce the true optimum solution and if not, the solution most often differs only slightly from the optimum one. The computations necessary to use this method are such that quite large problems can be effectively handled by hand.

Decision problems can very often be formulated as *network problems,* or *network flow problems.* In chapter 6 four general network problems are treated along with the techniques used to resolve them. It is surprising how many real-world problems can be represented by these general prototypes. In addition, a very simple method for developing solution data for *PERT* and *CPM* problems is demonstrated; one designed for hand calculating ease.

In summary, the book will provide the decision maker with a sound understanding of a number of quantitative techniques; a realistic appraisal of their usefulness to him, where best used, and their limitations; along with a degree of proficiency in using them.

James A. Parsons

Contents

2 How to Extract Information from Bivariate Data Sets, *cont.*

3 Statistical Decision Making: How to Estimate and Test Hypotheses Based on Data Set Analyses 73

4 Analysis and Smoothing of Data Sets for the Purpose of Forecasting 121

1

How to Extract Information
from Univariate Data Sets

Underlying each decision-making problem is some sort of process which has either direct or indirect bearing on the alternative choices of action we have to resolve the problem. This might be tangible—such as an assembly line, a chemical process, or a job shop operation—but just as likely it will be an intangible such as the process which creates customer demand, or which regulates the efficiency of operators of machine tools. In any case, in most situations, we already know the connection which exists between the process and our problem, in a general sense, and also the type of information we need to evaluate the alternatives. This "information" is in answer to such questions as: "How much?" How many?" "How often?" "When?" or, "What are the chances?" We find the answers to these questions through the analysis and subsequent interpretation of data, which is either given to us or which we ourselves collect, and which is believed to have this information content. This chapter and the one following will demonstrate certain concepts and techniques of statistics (specifically taken from *descriptive statistics*) which are most useful in exposing and isolating information contents of numerical data.

How do these techniques accomplish the task we have set for them? For the most part by doing the following: *arranging* data so that it is more readily understood; *presenting* data so as to clearly expose its significant features; and, *summarizing* data by means of numerical measures of certain "standard" properties which data has in general and in terms of which we normally frame our evaluations and answer our questions.

Now, of course, we will be working with a quantity of data which is in most instances just a relatively small portion of the output of the process under investigation. In addition, whatever we develop with these techniques can only be directly related to this data. Naturally, we are not interested in *this* set of data, but rather in the process which gave rise to it. To make this step we will need other techniques (from the *theory of statistical inference*) which will enable us to *infer* information *from* our data *to* the process. These will be provided in chapter 3, and as we will see they rest solidly on what is done here.

Types of Variables and Data

To begin we will need certain basic concepts which are useful in classifying the "type" of data we are working with, and so the information content we should expect it to have.

A *variable* may be thought of as simply a symbol, such as *X*, *Y*, or *t*, which can take on any of a prescribed set of values, this set being termed the *domain of the variable*. A *constant*, then, is simply a variable whose domain consists of a single number. The individual pieces of data we are working with can be termed observations, measurements, or attributes, but essentially they are simply values of some variable. It is the variable which is directly associated with the underlying process we are investigating.

Suppose we have the variable, *N*, which is defined as the number of employees in the various departments of a plant. This variable can assume only *certain distinct values,* 0, 1, 15, 20, etc., and so is termed a *discrete variable*. On the other hand, a variable, *S*, which might be the measurements of such things as lengths, weights, or density of objects, can theoretically assume *any value between prescribed limits* and is termed a *continuous variable*.

A variable is more practically categorized according to the particular type of information content which its values have. If these values refer to a measurable magnitude, or enumeration of objects, then the variable, and the data it represents, are termed *quantitative*. If each value tells us only whether or not some object has a certain characteristic or attribute (it is "red," it is "defective," etc.) then the variable and data are termed *qualitative*. Only quantitative data can be statistically "processed," as the techniques require numbers and not descriptions as would be the case with qualitative data. Therefore, if we start with qualitative data, our very first step must be to transform this into some form of numerical, quantitative data. There are standard ways for doing this, which we will demonstrate in this chapter, and they essentially boil down to enumerating all the descriptions of each different type and then processing these counts. We will be seriously limited in what we can extract from this enumeration data as well as what we can infer from it.

A data set can also be classified by the number of variables which are simultaneously represented in it. When each observation of the set refers to a single value of just one variable then the data is termed *univariate*. Thus, the number of hours for which each of 100 machines has been in operation is a univariate data set on the variable *M*, machine age. Suppose that along with the age of each machine we also obtained its present salvage value—values of the variable *S*. Each observation of this data set would be a pair of values of age and salvage value, that is, observations on the pair (*M,S*). These 100 observations constitute a *bivariate* data set as two distinct variables are represented. This concept is extended to *trivariate,* and *multivariate* data sets.

It is important to point out that if we had obtained the 100 age values and then from a different source, independently and without recognition of the machines, the 100 salvage values, we would not be able to construct the bivariate data set; information on how the observations are *paired* is required for this. However, starting with the bivariate data set we could obtain both univariate data sets. This points out the importance of knowing the extent to which we wish to carry our analysis prior to actually collecting the data.

Arranging Data in an Ordered Array

A useful first-step arrangement of a relatively small set of quantitative data is by ascending (or descending) order of magnitude, which gives us the *ordered array* of the data. Certain information can be quickly gained by just looking at the array, but this is rarely the final step in an analysis.

To illustrate, let us suppose that a certain raw material is purchased in fixed amounts from a vendor. The variable, *L,* is the delivery lead time, in days, of this material and a data set on this is as follows (as originally obtained from a file):

> 11, 10, 9, 8, 6, 5, 7, 8, 8, 11, 5, 10, 7
>
> 6, 8, 10, 9, 9, 7, 8, 6, 9, 8, 7, 8

By studying this data we would find that the shortest and longest lead times were 5 and 11 days respectively, but not very much else can be immediately obtained from it.

The ordered array of this data is the following:

> 5, 5, 6, 6, 6, 7, 7, 7, 7, 8, 8, 8, 8,
>
> 8, 8, 8, 9, 9, 9, 9, 10, 10, 10, 11, 11

At a glance we again see the smallest and largest values, but here we also begin to see how the lead times group, or cluster, themselves. There appears to be a clustering between 7 and 9 days, with relatively few lead times shorter than 7 days or longer than 9 days. In addition, we see that 8 days is the lead time which appears more often than any other, that is in this data set.

The array, as indicated, is an initial step and is useful for organizing data when being presented to others. An important thing to note here is that by arranging the data according to magnitude we lose the initial arrangement, that is we no longer know which was "first," "second," and so on. This is probably not pertinent information in this example; however, it would be if these were weekly demand figures where order of occurrence is most important.

Organizing Data by Natural Categories

Arraying numerical data makes use of the inherent order which numbers have whereby one number is either greater than, smaller than, or equal to another number. We lose this feature when working with qualitative data where our observations are descriptions, or words. Transforming qualitative data into quantitative data is affected by organizing it by natural categories, and these are "natural" in the sense that they are indicated to us by the purpose we have for studying the data. To illustrate this procedure we will consider the following example.

Suppose that we performed electrical, mechanical, and visual tests on each of 500 units of a certain appliance, which represents a standard run size. In the latter test we are looking for surface mars which make the unit defective. We find 25 units which are rejected: 15 due to failure of the electrical test; 8 due to failure of the mechanical test; and 2 due to surface defects. This data is conveniently organized into the following table:

A Frequency Table of Qualitative Data

Attribute of Unit (Natural Category)	Frequency of Occurrence, f	Proportion of the Total, p
Nondefective	475	$475/500 = 0.950$
Electrically Defective	15	$15/500 = 0.030$
Mechanically Defective	8	$8/500 = 0.016$
Visually Defective	2	$2/500 = 0.004$
Totals:	500	$500/500 = 1.000$

For this table we have used the four categories which suggest themselves from the data to organize our findings, these being those shown in the first column. In the second column of the table we post the total number of times each category was found in the data, termed "frequency of occurrence," and given the variable symbol f. In the last column each frequency is shown as a ratio to the total number of observations and also in its equivalent decimal proportion, these being given the symbol p. Proportions are normally interpreted as percentages of the total, thus we read 0.030 as 3.0 percent.

Certain obvious information can be drawn from this *frequency table*. For instance, 95 percent of the units are nondefective and so our rejection rate is just 5 percent. In addition, electrical defects occur nearly twice as often as mechanical defects and almost eight times as often as visual ones, and so on.

The analysis of the frequency of occurrence, or *frequency analysis,* is basically all we can do when working with qualitative data. This type of analysis is also performed on quantitative data, but as we will see in subsequent sections, a richer analysis can be achieved.

Frequency tables can be compared to provide us with important information. Thus, we might have another lot of 500 units from some other shift, or work center, and in this case we could compare frequencies and proportions directly to see the differences between the two. If our second lot was of 1,000 units then we cannot directly compare frequencies, but must make the comparison through the proportions. In addition, proportions, as percentages, can be used to estimate what we can expect in a situation which has not as yet happened. For instance, if we are increasing the standard run size to 700 units, with other conditions holding fixed, then we could apply the proportions calculated in the above table against this figure and thus estimate: $0.95 \times 700 = 665$ nondefective units, $0.03 \times 700 = 21$ electrically defective units, $0.016 \times 700 = 11.2$, or 11 mechanically defective units, and, $0.004 \times 700 = 2.8$, or 3 visually defective units as the likely outcome.

Very often our concern will be with a *dichotomous categorization* of our qualitative data. Interpreting this for our example, we would be interested in simply whether a unit is defective or nondefective. Here we would have a frequency table with just two categories. If this is what we do, then our findings will usually lead the way to any subsequent analyses. Thus, we might have started with the two-way classification and then finding 5 percent defectives we might then turn to a study of these defects to highlight problem areas. This would have led us to the table above from which we would conclude that the electrical defects are the dominant ones and perhaps next turn to a further breakdown of these thereby enabling us to see where our effort for improvement should be most logically directed

Perhaps the most common use of qualitative data with a dichotomous categorization is in some form of *acceptance sampling*. Here we select a small part of a delivery lot and inspect each of these objects as to their acceptability (this collection of objects is our *sample,* and our observations on these form our data set) arriving at a proportion, *p,* of nonacceptable, or defective, objects. This proportion is then "processed" through certain statistical techniques (to be covered in chapter 3) which produce an estimate of the proportion of defective objects we should expect are in the total lot. On the basis of this, usually specified in our contract with the vendor, we may reject or accept the delivery. Much of quality control on internal processes is based on this same type of analysis and inferencing procedure, and, in general, we usually work with a two-way categorization.

Organizing Data by Frequency Category

It is natural that we would want to be able to perform a frequency analysis on a quantitative data set; all we need to accomplish this is a substitute for the natural categories. What we use are "numerical" categories which may be defined with a single number or a specifically designated group of numbers. We again produce a *frequency table* (in this context this is often referred to as a *frequency distribution*) which we term *ungrouped* or *grouped* depending upon whether we use a single number or a group of numbers to define our categories.

To illustrate, let us suppose that we have a machine which automatically cuts bar material into preset lengths of shaft. The machine was set to cut lengths of 2.05 inches and the lengths of twenty-five shafts, which were drawn from a day's output on the machine, drawing every tenth shaft, are as follows:

2.02	2.05	2.05	2.08	2.10
2.04	2.06	2.09	2.07	2.03
2.05	2.07	2.05	2.08	2.09
2.06	2.04	2.05	2.06	2.07
2.11	2.08	2.06	2.07	2.04

Let us use each different length in this data as a separate category, thus we are working with ungrouped data, then we would prepare the following (ungrouped) frequency table:

A Frequency Table of Quantitative Data

Length of Shaft (Category)	Frequency of Occurrence, f (absolute frequency)	Proportion of the Total, p (relative frequency)
2.02	1	0.04
2.03	1	0.04
2.04	3	0.12
2.05	5	0.20
2.06	4	0.16
2.07	4	0.16
2.08	3	0.12
2.09	2	0.08
2.10	1	0.04
2.11	1	0.04
Totals:	25	1.00

This has the same format as our previous frequency table except that we have added new names for f and p. The former is usually termed the *absolute frequency,* as it expresses the frequency of occurrences in absolute terms, while the latter is termed the *relative frequency,* expressing the frequency of occurrences relative to the total. Otherwise, our interpretation and subsequent uses of this information are the same as before; we can use it in comparisons, in estimating likely outcomes in the future, and in directing our subsequent studies.

In certain problems we will not care to lose any of the details of the original data, and when this is so, it is probably not wise to prepare a grouped frequency table since by so doing we will lose details. What we gain from grouping is a reduction in the size of the data set with which we have to work, and this is an important advantage when working with hundreds of values. As we already have said, all we need do here is to define our categories as groups of values rather than singles.

To illustrate the basic construction procedure let us suppose that we have obtained the production hours, rounded to the nearest whole hour, required to produce 50 batches of the same material through the same operation. These times are as follows:

16	27	34	38	43	48	51	53	56	57
19	28	35	40	45	48	52	53	56	57
22	28	36	41	45	48	52	53	56	63
23	31	37	41	46	49	52	53	57	63
25	33	37	43	46	50	53	54	57	64

The grouped frequency table for this data, using categories consisting of five values each, is as follows:

A Grouped Frequency Table of Quantitative Data

Production Hours (Category Definition)	Midpoint of Category, X	Frequency of Occurrence, f (absolute frequency)	Proportion of the Total, p (relative frequency)
16, 17, 18, 19, 20	18 hrs.	2	0.04
21, 22, 23, 24, 25	23 hrs.	3	0.06
26, 27, 28, 29, 30	28 hrs.	3	0.06
31, 32, 33, 34, 35	33 hrs.	4	0.08
36, 37, 38, 39, 40	38 hrs.	5	0.10
41, 42, 43, 44, 45	43 hrs.	6	0.12
46, 47, 48, 49, 50	48 hrs.	7	0.14
51, 52, 53, 54, 55	53 hrs.	10	0.20
56, 57, 58, 59, 60	58 hrs.	7	0.14
61, 62, 63, 64, 65	63 hrs.	3	0.06
Totals:		50	1.00

To construct this table we decided on categories with five consecutive values each and then counted the number of data values which fell in each category, posting these counts as the values of f and their proportions to the total number of observations, 50, as the values of p. The new feature in this table is the column listing the midpoint values of the categories, denoted by X. The purpose behind these is that in subsequent computations, in answer to our questions, the categories are discarded and the midpoints are used instead. Here is where we lose the original detail of the data; by using these midpoints as representatives of the actual categories, we are in effect assuming that all values in any given category actually coincided with the midpoint. Thus, in effect, the last three columns of this present table are viewed as an ungrouped frequency table analogous to the previous one for shaft lengths.

Using the midpoints as representatives is merely a convenience and to be more practical (and to gain back some of our lost detail) we should actually use as the representative of a category that value which "best" represents the distribution of actual data within this category. Thus, for example, in the ninth category, 56, 57, 58, 59, 60, our midpoint, 58, was not an actual data point, and in this category we had three 56-hour and four 57-hour observations. Here the 57-hour figure would perhaps be a better value to use as the category representative as it more nearly indicates the "most typical" value being represented.

While there are no set rules to follow in constructing a grouped frequency table, there are these guidelines:

1. In general, do not use less than five nor more than twenty distinct categories.
2. If possible, have all categories of the same "length," and avoid open definitions such as: "300 or more," or "6 or less."
3. Define categories so that there is never a question as to which category a data value belongs. To effect this we might have to use defining values which are written to more decimal places than actually used in the data.

To start we may subtract the smallest value of the data from the largest value and divide this difference by the number of categories we want, this result will roughly indicate the "length" of each category. By laying out categories of this fixed length, in consecutive order, we will cover the range of values with the desired number of categories. Basically, we simply look for a way to subdivide the full range of data values into a convenient number of subgroups each of which covers the same subrange of values. In our example we had 49 values between our lowest data point 16 and the highest 64, which would mean 4.9 values for each of ten categories which we rounded-up to 5 values each. If we had decided to group our shaft length data into five categories, then our calculations would give $(2.11 - 2.02)/5 = 0.018$, or 0.02 as the length of each category. So as not to have any questions as to which category we assign a shaft length, we would define the categories as follows: 2.015 to 2.035, 2.035 to 2.055, 2.055 to 2.075, 2.075 to 2.095, and 2.095 to 2.115. Thus, with our lengths measured to the nearest one-hundredth of an inch, we define our categories with numbers which are midway between these, and so a length can never be equal to any boundary value.

Something which is not a major problem, but does detract somewhat from the overall appearance of the table, is that, due to rounding, the sum of our relative frequencies may not be 1.00 as they should. This may be corrected by multiplying each relative frequency by the factor $1/S$, where S is the actual sum (not equal to 1.00) which we obtain. The resulting frequencies will, in most cases, sum properly.

Organizing Data by Cumulative Frequency Category

Often the information we are particularly interested in is provided from a *cumulative frequency table* which is obtained from the regular frequency table we have thus far shown. Here our interest is not so much with the frequency of occurrence of individual values as it is with the cumulative impact of these. This is the same idea underlying data labeled "Total year to date," as found in business reports. Typical questions are: "How frequently do the data points fall below *this* particular value?" "What value is located in such a way that 45 percent of the other data values exceed this value?" Naturally, we can answer these questions from the regular frequency table by simply accumulating frequencies as is indicated by our particular question. The cumulative frequency table is simply a way of preparing our original data for these types of questions.

The first, second, and fourth columns of this table are those of the regular frequency table, while the third and fifth columns list the cumulative frequency values. These are designated "or less" as they indicate the frequency of occurrence of data values *equal to or less* than that length of shaft value specified in the table. Thus, 10 lengths, or 40 percent of all data values were equal to or less than 2.05 inches. Cumulative frequencies of the "or more" type might be those which best provide the information we seek. These would give us the frequency of occurrence of data values *equal to or more* than each shaft length. To compute these we simply accumulate the frequency values from the bottom of the table upward rather than from the top downward as we did in the table.

The (ungrouped) cumulative frequency table for our shaft length data is as follows:

A Cumulative Frequency Table

Length of Shaft	Absolute Frequency, f	Cumulative Absolute Frequency ("or less")	Relative Frequency, p	Cumulative Relative Frequency ("or less")
2.02	1	1	0.04	0.04
2.03	1	2	0.04	0.08
2.04	3	5	0.12	0.20
2.05	5	10	0.20	0.40
2.06	4	14	0.16	0.56
2.07	4	18	0.16	0.72
2.08	3	21	0.12	0.84
2.09	2	23	0.08	0.92
2.10	1	24	0.04	0.96
2.11	1	25	0.04	1.00

When we construct the cumulative tables for grouped data we must be a little more careful which value we use against which frequencies are accumulated. We have to use the lower boundaries of successive categories for an "or more" table and the upper boundaries for an "or less" table. Of course, if we have the actual data, we can select each category representative and accumulate the frequencies against these; it is only when we just have the grouped frequency table and not the original data that we accumulate against the boundary values. To illustrate, we have the following cumulative frequency table for our production time data, where only the relative frequencies are shown and accumulated.

A Grouped Cumulative Frequency Table

Production Hour Values (lower boundaries)	Relative Frequency Associated with This Category	Cumulative Relative Frequency ("or more")	Production Hour Values (upper boundaries)	Cumulative Relative Frequency ("or less")
16	0.04	1.00	20	0.04
21	0.06	0.96	25	0.10
26	0.06	0.90	30	0.16
31	0.08	0.84	35	0.24
36	0.10	0.76	40	0.34
41	0.12	0.66	45	0.46
46	0.14	0.54	50	0.60
51	0.20	0.40	55	0.80
56	0.14	0.20	60	0.94
61	0.06	0.06	65	1.00

In those cases where we are given a table of frequency data, developed through grouping, but only listing the category midpoints (and not even the length of each category), then to prepare a cumulative frequency table we would have to use these midpoint values to accumulate against.

There do arise cases of qualitative data where the concept of "more than" and that of "less than" have meaning. For instance, if our observations are on the levels of schooling which individuals have completed, grade school, high school, college, and graduate, then there is meaning to such expressions as: "grade school or more," "high school or less," and so on. When this is the case we can construct a cumulative frequency table for our data, accumulating frequencies against the logical natural categories. However, in most instances qualitative data will not have this interpretation characteristic and so cumulative tables are in general reserved for quantitative data.

Charting Frequency Tables

To further aid in comprehending any set of data, we should prepare an appropriate chart of it. The eye can capture the significant characteristics of a set of data much faster when viewing a chart than when having to review a table of numbers.

The chart usually drawn for a regular frequency table is the *histogram*. In Figure 1–1, we have drawn this chart for the production hours example, and to construct it we simply erect rectangles over each category, or midpoint, as is done in this figure, the height of which is proportional to the frequency of the associated category. We can plot either the relative or the absolute frequencies in our charts, and having a chart for one of these we obtain the one for the other by simply changing the vertical scale from one type of frequency to the other; the diagram is the same in both cases.

The best type of graphical presentation of cumulative frequency tables is the *ogive*, illustrated in Figure 1–2 for our production hours example, using the "or less" cumulative relative frequencies. To construct this type of chart we plot the cumulative "or less" (or "or more") frequencies against the upper (or lower) category boundaries, and then connect successive points with straight-line segments.

Essential Interpretations of Frequency Tables

Up to this point we have concerned ourselves with the construction of frequency tables from our original data as well as the charting of the data in these tables. In this section we will turn to the question of how we interpret and otherwise use frequency tables.

Perhaps the most useful aspect of frequency data is achieved when we interpret the relative frequencies as probabilities (chances, odds, or risk levels). Returning to our frequency table of shaft lengths, and recalling that the machine cutting these shafts was set to cut lengths of 2.05 inches, we can see that the probability that any arbitrary shaft will be properly cut is only 20 percent, or 20 chances out of 100. Therefore, the probability that a shaft is either too long or too short is 80 percent, or 80 chances out of 100. Suppose now that if a shaft is between 2.03 and 2.07 inches long it will be acceptable. Looking at our table we see that 4 percent of the shafts can be expected to be shorter than 2.03 inches, and 28 percent of them longer than 2.07 inches, meaning we have the probability of 4 +

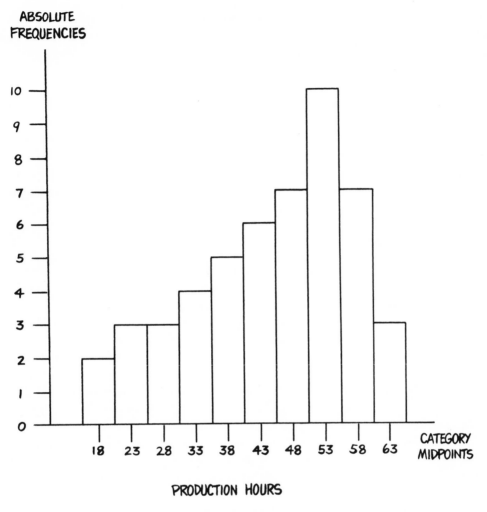

ABSOLUTE
FREQUENCIES

CATEGORY
MIDPOINTS

PRODUCTION HOURS

Figure 1–1

28 = 32 percent, or a little more than 3 chances out of 10, of rejecting any shaft. We can also view this as saying that in meeting these set limits the machine is operating at an effectiveness level of 68 percent. Knowing this we would have grounds for either replacing this machine or spending the money to rebuild it.

The connotation of risk is particularly meaningful in the interpretation of frequency data when this is involved in our forward-looking plans or decisions. To illustrate this let us return to the cumulative table on our production hours example. Suppose that we are making production plans for this production operation and we can only tolerate a 20 percent level of risk of missing our schedules. Here we want to know that value of production time we should include in our plans which will achieve this level of risk. From the table, the "or more" cumulative frequencies, we see that a production time of 56 hours has associated with it a cumulative frequency of 20 percent. This means that there is only a 20 percent risk of actually having a batch produced in 56 hours or more, thus by planning

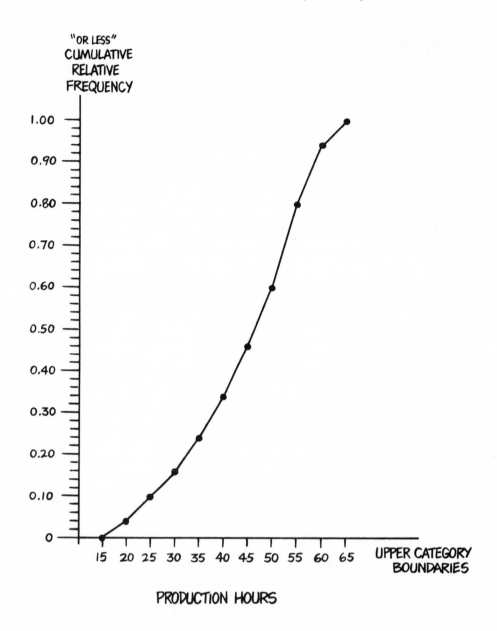

Figure 1–2

with a 55-hour production cycle we can expect to meet our schedules under the specified risk level.

Suppose that we have prepared a cumulative frequency table for two different shops which are capable of producing this same material. Furthermore, let us suppose that our plans call for a batch to be produced in 50 hours or less, and our question is: Which shop should be given the work assignment if our objective is to have the greatest chances for meeting our time requirements? To make this selection we would simply have to enter each shop's cumulative frequency table at the 50-hour value and select that shop whose corresponding cumulative relative, "or less," frequency is greater.

It is very likely that our questions specify values which do not appear in our tables. This is particularly true in the cumulative frequency tables of grouped data which is not available for further analysis, as in this case we can only legitimately make frequency statements for lower or upper boundary values. In such situations the ogive is a useful device for developing estimates of the required values whether these are frequencies or quantity values. We use this chart to interpolate between known data points. For example, suppose that we wish to know the "or less" cumulative relative frequency we can attach to a production time of 42.5 hours. We enter Figure 1–2, on the horizontal scale, with this figure and read up from this point to the ogive, and then across from this point to the frequency scale. We find the 40 percent figure which is then our estimate. In other words, even though we never actually recorded this value, we can expect that 40 percent of the production batches will require a production time of something smaller than, or equal to, 42.5 hours.

In the same way we can enter Figure 1–2 with a given frequency value and locate an estimate of the production hours associated with this value. And, naturally, we can do these same things on an "or more" ogive.

The histogram can also be used to produce estimates corresponding to given values. For this purpose one normally connects the midpoints of the "tops" of successive rectangles with straight-line segments and then develops the needed estimates from the resulting line graph.

Another type of analysis, which we might term a "quantity analysis," can be carried out for quantitative data along with the frequency analysis we have been discussing. Here our concern is more with the information content in our data relating to the "quantity" of our experiences rather than in the frequency with these were experienced. The histogram indicates the major characteristics of this content. The point where the histogram appears to be centered, the manner in which it is spread over the range of values, and the apparent lopsidedness of it are all indicative of significant contents, and ones which we describe with summary "shorthand."

Describing the Average Property

Our first interest in the quantity analysis of data is: around what value do the observations tend to cluster? We might call this the "most typical value," "expected value," but far more often the "average value." Looking at a histogram of some data, we would logically locate the average at the "center" of the diagram. What we are talking about is the *central tendency property* of data, and there are various measures of this property each with its own interpretation of what "average" signifies.

The *modal average,* or simply the *mode,* of a set of values is that particular value which occurs more often than any other single value. This does not mean that it occurs more often than all the other values put together, which is a point to be kept in mind when drawing conclusions from the mode. Working with a frequency table, the mode is that value or category with the highest frequency, as such it may be computed for both qualitative and quantitative data sets.

Sometimes the mode may not exist and often there is so slight a difference between the frequency of the mode value and the one with the next highest frequency that we may not really distinguish the one as the mode. At other times we have data which shows a clustering of values around more than one value, and in sufficient quantities to indicate multiple modes. When this is so we have exposed important information for we may have more than one independent process underlying our data. Thus, for example, if we have two departments which are the heaviest users of some stocked part and each uses a different quantity, then a study of the stock withdrawals of this part would probably show the *bimodal* situation. This would be vital information if we are attempting to control this inventory with a fixed reorder point.

Aside from the fact that the mode is truly the "most typical" value, it also has the advantage of not being affected by the presence of extremely small or large values in the data. Its main disadvantage is that not much, in the statistical sense, can be done with it.

The *median average,* or *median* is another measure of central tendency. It is the middle observation in the ordered array. If we happen to have an even number of observations, then there will be no true middle value, and we take as the median the value midway between the two "middle" values in the array. The median is not overly affected by the presence of extreme values, and in fact is the preferrable average to use when we have such values in the data. Of course, this is only true when we judge that these extreme values are not relevant to the "typicalness" of the overall data. A disadvantage of the median is that it is not that generally familiar, and, as others, we must perform arraying in order to find the median, and like the mode not much statistically can be done with it.

What one usually has in mind when using the word "average" is what statisticians call the *arithmetic average* or *mean value.* This measure is greatly influenced by extreme values because in calculating it we use all the individual observations. To calculate it we sum the individual values in the data and then divide this total by the number of values in the data set.

It is convenient at this point to introduce notation for the arithmetical operation of summation. In this we use the capital Greek letter "sigma" written as $\sum$. If X is our variable symbol, then the composite symbol $\sum X$ indicates the "sum of the X values." If we have n observations in our data set, then the rule for calculating the mean value of these is expressed in the following shorthand:

$$\text{Mean value, } \bar{X} = \frac{\sum X}{n}$$

In this we have used the standard notation "$\bar{X}$" (to be read "X bar") for the mean of X values.

In this rule we have not explicitly indicated "which" values of X to sum, being tacitly taken that we refer to all those values we have in the data set on X. If the situation requires that we be more explicit, then we must first identify each value in the data with a unique symbol and refer to these in our summation notation. For these unique symbols we add subscripts to the variable symbol. Thus, "X_1" (to be read "X sub one") is the symbol for the "first" value of X; "X_2" for the "second," and so on, until with n values, "X_n" is used for the "last" or "nth" value of X. Now, if we only wanted to sum five values, starting with the second, X_2, and ending with X_6, we could indicate this as follows:

$$\sum_{i=2}^{i=6} X_i$$

where the subscript i is used here in the generic sense.

Some of the advantages of the mean value are: we do not have to arrange our data before we can calculate its value; there will always be a mean value, and this will be unique; and, most statistical theory is developed around this particular measure of central tendency.

When our observations are ratios, rates of change, or index numbers, then the *geometric average* is more consistent a measure of central tendency than any of the others. The geometric average of n values is simply the nth root of their product, that is:

$$\boxed{\text{Geometric average,} \quad G = \sqrt[n]{X_1 \cdot X_2 \cdot \,\cdots X_n}}$$

In particular, with just two values, the geometric average is the square root of their product. Logarithms are of great use in calculating this average.

Suppose that the ratings on four performance traits of an individual are: 50, 85, 6, and 1.8. The highest rating possible on these traits are: 50, 100, 10, and 2.0 respectively. The mean of his four ratings would not be a proper measure of the "average" rating of this individual as they all have different bases of reference. We must first put each on a comparative basis by dividing each by its base value. Doing this would give us the ratios: 1.00, 0.85, 0.60, and 0.90. Since these are ratios, the average of them is best measured by their geometric average, which we compute as:

$$G = \sqrt[4]{(1.00)(0.85)(0.60)(0.90)} = \sqrt[4]{0.4590}$$
$$\log G = \tfrac{1}{4} \log (0.4590) = \tfrac{1}{4}(-0.33819) = -0.08455$$
$$G = 0.82 \text{ (rounded off from 0.8230)}$$

The mean of these four ratios is 0.84, and, while this does not differ greatly from the geometric average, this certainly need not be true in general. The geometric average will always be smaller than the mean value, being actually equal to it only when all numbers are the same.

The geometric average is not very well known and is relatively difficult to calculate, furthermore, it may not be computed if one of the values is *zero* nor when the product of all values is a negative quantity.

When our observations are rates of some kind (such as production rates, travel speeds, or purchase prices) the so-called *harmonic average* may be more appropriate to use. This average for a set of n numbers is the reciprocal of the arithmetic average of the reciprocals of the numbers. An easier rule to use is:

$$\boxed{\text{Harmonic average,} \quad H = \dfrac{n}{\sum \dfrac{1}{X}}}$$

It is necessary to recall here that the sum of the $(1/X)$ values is not the same as "1" divided by the sum of the X values.

To illustrate the need for this average, let's suppose that a production line produced 2,000 units of an item, with the first 1,000 units produced at the rate of 100 units per hour, and the second 1,000 at the rate of 200 units per hour. These two different rates might be due to different machines being used, different workshifts, operators, etc. Our question: "What is the average rate of production for these 2,000 units?" The mean value of these two rates $(100 + 200)/2 = 150$ units per hour, is incorrect, and to see why let's take the problem apart.

The first 1,000 units were produced at a rate of 100 units per hour and so the total length of time required was $1,000/100 = 10$ hours. The second 1,000 units required a total time of $1,000/200 = 5$ hours of production time. Thus, 2,000 units were produced in 15 hours, or at the overall rate of $2,000/15 = 133\text{-}1/3$ units per hour. This is our correct answer and it is also the harmonic average of the two rates as the following computation shows:

$$H = \frac{2}{\frac{1}{100} + \frac{1}{200}} = \frac{2}{\frac{3}{200}} = \frac{400}{3} = 133\frac{1}{3}\text{units per hour}$$

Suppose that the conditions under which these 2,000 units were made were, for some reason, standard. Then if we had been given only the 150 units per hour figure, then for the "next" 15-hour period we would be led to expect to see $150 \times 15 = 2,250$ units produced rather than the same 2,000 units.

We must have a test by which we can choose between the two averages, and so that this is kept as general as possible let's make the identification of all "rates" with the following formula:

$$\text{Rate} = \frac{\text{Distance}}{\text{Time}}$$

In each situation involving rates we will identify something with the "Distance" term in this formula, and something else with the "Time" term. For example:

Working with This *Rate*	Identify This with *Distance*	Identify This with *Time*
Production rate in: units per hour	Total number of units produced	Total production hours used
Cost rate in: dollars per piece	Total number of dollars spent	Total number of pieces purchased
Travel speed in: miles per hour	Total miles traveled	Total hours of travel

In our example the total number of units produced under each rate was 1,000 and these are identified with "Distance." The production hours, 10 hours and 5 hours, are identified with "Time."

The selection rule is this: (1) if, for the rates being averaged, we find that the quantity identified with *Time* is the same for each rate, then use the *mean value*; whereas, (2) if the factor identified with *Distance* was the same for each rate, then use the *harmonic average*.

According to the selection rule, the harmonic average was the proper choice since 1,000 units were produced under each rate and this was identified with the Distance term.

The illustration just given showed that the difference between the mean value and harmonic average can be quite large, and, what is more, this difference is likely to be greatly amplified in our subsequent evaluations or manipulations involving the average figure. As rates are very common in manufacturing problems, it becomes important to always go through this selection rule before we calculate an average rate.

Suppose that the unit manufacturing cost for a product is $1.50, $2.00, and $3.25 depending upon whether the production is done in Plant A, B, or C, respectively. It would not be realistic on our part to say that the average manufacturing cost per unit, over all plants, is the mean value of these, which is $2.25. To be consistent with reality we must take into consideration the volume of production done at each site, and over a specified length of time. Looking at a yearly figure, if the annual productions of this unit at the three plants are respectively 10,000, 25,000, and 5,000 units, then a better average figure would be obtained from the calculation:

$$\frac{10,000 \times \$1.50 + 25,000 \times \$2.00 + 5,000 \times \$3.25}{10,000 + 25,000 + 5,000}$$

which computes to be $2.03 per unit.

What we have done here is to judge that the three plants differ in relative importance with respect to the information we are seeking, and so to put them on an equal basis we have weighted each cost rate with the respective annual productions. We refer to the procedure as calculating the *weighted average* of the costs. In general we determine a weighting factor, W, for each figure being averaged, and multiply each value by its weighting factor, sum all these products, and then divide this total by the sum of the individual factors. In a formula we have:

$$\boxed{\text{Weighted average, } \bar{X} = \frac{\sum W \cdot X}{\sum W}}$$

In this calculation the X values may be averages themselves, or any other quantity for which an overall average is desired. In certain situations the weighting factors will be obtained from judgment or opinion rather than from actual data. At other times the X values are judgmental, possibly coming as forecasts from different sources. In this case the weighting factors might reflect the accuracy in past forecasts or some other relevant attribute such as familiarity with the product, its uses, and its market.

From knowledge of the circumstances surrounding our data, we should be able to decide if a geometric, harmonic, or weighted average is needed. But to select from among the mean value, median, and mode, we must review just what the "average" means in our particular problem. The mode is probably what we have in mind if we are asking, "Which product does our *average* customer buy?" Here the connotation being most popular. If we are looking for a "middle of the road" value, one for which an actual observation is just as likely to be larger than as it is to be smaller, then the median is appropriate as the average. And, as previously cited, the median is appropriate if we do not want an extreme value in our data to overshadow the other values. The mean value includes the information content of every piece of data and for this reason it is preferrable in certain situations. The mean is also that measure of central tendency for which most of statistics is developed, and for this reason we will often use it as the average even when we would like to avoid its weakness of being sensitive to extreme values. Certainly, it does no harm to calculate all three averages and so compare their different points of view (as will be seen, doing this will provide us with a quick insight into the skewness of our data), it is just that we must be careful which one we carry on into subsequent evaluations and our ultimate decision actions.

Describing the Variability Property

Regardless of which average value we use, there will be a natural dispersion of the data about this value. It is in fact to "smooth" out this variability in the data that we sought the average value. As such averages only give us a partial picture, and if the data is widely scattered its value may mean nothing at all. As averages are used to measure central tendency, there are descriptive numbers calculated to measure the *variability property*, and in any practical situation we should look at both properties.

Perhaps the easiest measure of variability to understand, and certainly the easiest to compute, is the *range value*, or simply the *range*. To calculate it we just subtract the smallest observation from the largest. Although the range gives us an important piece of information on our data, it is the least satisfactory measure of variability. On just the intuitive level we would expect this to be so since the range only uses the information content of but two observations.

The next step up from the range is to divide the ordered array of the data into four parts, separating each by a *quartile*. The first quartile, Q_1, is located in the array with 25 percent of the values below it and 75 percent above it. The *second quartile, Q_2,* is simply the median. The *third quartile, Q_3,* has 75 percent of the values in the array falling below it and the other 25 percent above it. Quartiles are located in the same way medians are and they effect a positional measure of variability.

As a very simple illustration we consider the data: 1, 2, 3, 4, 5, 6, 7, 8, 9, 10, 11, 12. The quartiles are located as shown in the following display:

$$1 \quad 2 \quad 3 \mid 4 \quad 5 \quad 6 \mid 7 \quad 8 \quad 9 \mid 10 \quad 11 \quad 12$$
$$Q_1 = 3.5 \quad Q_2 = 6.5 \quad Q_3 = 9.5$$

Between Q_1 and Q_3 are one-half of the observations and under most circumstances this central half of the array tends to be fairly typical. The *interquartile range* is the difference between these two values, that is:

$$\boxed{\text{Interquartile range} = Q_3 - Q_1}$$

and it measures the absolute variability in the data. A small interquartile range indicates a large degree of uniformity, while a large interquartile range indicates a lesser degree of uniformity. The *semi-interquartile range* is simply $(Q_3 - Q_1)/2$, and it is probably better known as the *quartile deviation*. It affords us a way of measuring the "average" distance of each quartile from the median; the median plus or minus the quartile deviation will contain roughly 50 percent of the cases.

We may also choose to divide our array into ten equal parts with the use of nine *deciles* P_1, P_2, . . ., P_9. These are often referred to as *percentiles*. The *decile 1–9 range*, also termed the *10–90 percentile range* is $P_9 - P_1$ and is analogous to the interquartile range except that now 80 percent of the array is included in this range. The calculation of the deciles is similar to that of the quartiles, and both may be performed directly on the *ogive* of our data set (see Figure 1–2).

The most popular measure of variability is a descriptive number called the *standard deviation*. It measures the scatter of data in terms of differences from the mean value. As such it affords us with a quantitative measure of variability rather than the positional measures of the various range values. The units of a standard deviation will be those of the original observations which is a definite advantage.

In the process of calculating the standard deviation, we first determine the so-called *variance*, which itself is a measure of variability and in certain situations is preferable to the former. If X is the variable and we have n observations on its values, then the variance, denoted by s^2, is computed according to the following rule:

$$\boxed{\text{Variance, } s^2 = \frac{\sum(X - \bar{X})^2}{n}}$$

This rule says that we are to subtract the mean value of the data from each individual observation, square these differences, sum all of them, and then divide this total by the number of observations involved. A rule we may use to find s^2 which does not require that we find these differences is the following:

$$\boxed{\text{Variance, } s^2 = \frac{\sum(X)^2}{n} - (\bar{X})^2}$$

Here we simply sum the squares of all observations, divide this total by n and subtract from this result the square of the mean value of the data.

In calculating the mean value we must perform a division and normally we will round off the answer. By so doing we are introducing *round-off errors*. When this is a serious problem, the following rule should be used to calculate the variance:

$$\text{Variance, } s^2 = \frac{n\sum(X)^2 - (\sum X)^2}{n^2}$$

This is obtained from the previous one by simply substituting $\sum X/n$ in place of $\bar{X}$ and simplifying the result.

The standard deviation is just the positive square root of the variance, and logically denoted by s. So that we have actual rules for reference we list these for the three variance rules:

$$\text{Standard Deviation, } s = \sqrt{\frac{\sum(X - \bar{X})^2}{n}} = \sqrt{\frac{\sum X^2}{n} - (\bar{X})^2} = \frac{\sqrt{n\sum X^2 - (\sum X)^2}}{n}$$

At this point we should introduce a modification to the above calculations which has to do with the fact that for certain purposes the value we would calculate from the above rules, for the variance and standard deviation, would in a sense be "biased." As long as we are talking about the data set itself, then the rules given above apply. It is when we wish to assign the data variance, or standard deviation, over to the underlying process giving rise to the data that we must introduce a correction factor which will correct the bias. We simply multiply the variance as calculated with the above rules by the quantity $n/(n-1)$, or, the calculated standard deviation by the factor $\sqrt{n/(n-1)}$. When n is fairly large the bias will be slight, and usually we do not use the factor when n is something greater than 30. The factor won't be used in subsequent calculations, but again, by so doing we will be concentrating our attention on the original samples. In chapter 3 this point will be raised again in its proper context.

There are those times when we need a quick look at the standard deviation, and would be willing to use an approximate value of it. If we know the range of the data, then in a "pinch" we can divide this by 6 and use the result as the standard deviation. Better approximations are achieved by dividing the range by the appropriate divisor as found in the following table.

For These Limits on n	1–10	11–32	33–100	101–500	500 or more
Divide the Range by This	$\sqrt{n}$	4	5	6	6.5

Describing the Skewness Property

Whenever our data is not symmetrically located around the mean value we say it is skewed. This was the "lopsidedness" we referred to in Figure 1–1, where the data appeared to fall on the left side of the mode midpoint of 53 hours more often than on the right side. This is an example of data *skewed to the left,* or *left-handed skewness.* If the data tended to the right of the mode we would have had data *skewed to the right,* or *right-handed skewness.*

Needless to say, when our data is significantly nonsymmetrical we will not know the whole story with just the average and standard deviation values for we will not know the "direction" of the variability.

In the section on ordered arrays an example was given of lead times, and if we calculate the mean value, median, and mode for this data we would find that all three are equal to 8 days. If next we computed these values for the production-hours example we would find: mean value of 44 hours, median value of 47 hours, and mode value of 53 hours. Whenever these three values are equal then the data is symmetrical (skewness of zero), but when they are not, skewness is present. Thus, the lead times are symmetrical whereas the production hours are not. We may also determine from these averages the direction of our skewness, for the mean value will always lie on the same side of the mode as the direction of skewness, with the median value somewhere in-between. The production-hours data is thus skewed to the left, as has already been stated.

Naturally, we can have a difference between these three average values but yet have only "slight" skewness, it depends on how much variability is in the data. To account for the variability we can calculate a measure of skewness from any of the following rules:

$$\text{First Coefficient of Skewness} = \frac{\bar{X} - \text{Mode}}{s}$$

$$\text{Second Coefficient of Skewness} = \frac{3(\bar{X} - \text{Median})}{s}$$

$$\text{Quartile Coefficient of Skewness} = \frac{Q_3 - 2Q_2 + Q_1}{Q_3 - Q_1}$$

The second coefficient of skewness is perhaps more preferable as it avoids the need of the existence of a mode value. With left-handed skewness this coefficient will be a negative number, whereas it will be positive for right-handed skewness. Furthermore, if the computed value is between ± 1.0 and ± 3.0, the skewness may be judged "high;" between $\pm \frac{1}{2}$ and ± 1.0 it is "moderate;" and, between 0.0 and $\pm \frac{1}{2}$ it is "low."

The standard deviation of our production-hours data would be computed to be 12 hours (rounded to the nearest hour). With this value we would calculate the second coefficient of skewness as: $3(44 - 47)/12 = -0.75$, from which we could conclude that this data has "moderate" left-handed skewness. From this we could judge this production operation to have a tendency toward the shorter production times which is useful information for planning and scheduling through this operation.

Describing Total Variables

There are many situations where the variable of primary interest is a sum, or total, of a certain number of other variables. Thus, for example, lead time demand is the sum of a certain number of daily demands, the sum being determined by the number of days in the lead time. From the knowledge of the mean value and standard deviation for each separate variable we would like to develop these values for the *total variable*.

To illustrate, let us suppose that our total variable, T, is the sum of the three variables X_1, X_2, and X_3 (these might be the production times for three consecutive operations working on the same order, but one after another); that is, $T = X_1 + X_2 + X_3$. Suppose also that the mean values and standard deviations of these three variables are respectively $\bar{X}_1, S_1$; $\bar{X}_2, S_2$; and $\bar{X}_3, S_3$. The mean value of the total variable, $\bar{T}$, is given by:

$$\bar{T} = \bar{X}_1 + \bar{X}_2 + \bar{X}_3.$$

The standard deviation of the total variable, denoted by S_T, is developed as follows for the case where the X's are *independent variables*:

$$\text{Variance of } T: \qquad S_T{}^2 = S_1{}^2 + S_2{}^2 + S_3{}^2$$

and so,

$$\text{Standard Deviation of } T: \qquad S_T = \sqrt{S_1{}^2 + S_2{}^2 + S_3{}^2}$$

By "independent" we roughly mean that the values which any of the summed variables takes on is not influenced by, nor do these themselves influence, the values which the other variables have. If we again view our total variable as lead time demand we might have the situation where customer demand on any given day is influenced by the previous day's demand, and also influences the next day's demands; if yesterday's demand were high, today's will be low. In this case the variables in the total are *correlated,* and *dependent* rather than independent. For this situation we use the same rule for $\bar{T}$, but a different one for S_T (one which will be given in the next chapter where one of its terms, *covariance,* will be introduced).

It is most important to remember that the variance of the total is equal to the sum of the variances of the independent variables, and then the standard deviation is found by square-rooting this. The standard deviation of the total is *not equal* to the sum of the standard deviations of the individual variables, and if this is in fact the way one calculates this, his errors in subsequent calculations will be large.

To illustrate, suppose a certain tool is manufactured by passing through operations A, B, and C of a shop, and the mean values and standard deviations of these operations' processing times (in hours) are: $\bar{X}_A = 2.1$, $\bar{X}_B = 4.2$, $\bar{X}_C = 2.5$, $S_A = 0.50$, $S_B = 1.10$, $S_C = 0.75$. Therefore, assuming independent operations, the total processing time through this shop, T, for each of these tool units has mean time $\bar{T} = 2.1 + 4.2 + 2.5 = 8.8$ hours and a variance of $(0.50)^2 + (1.10)^2 + (0.75)^2 = 2.0225$, and so a standard deviation S_T given by $\sqrt{2.0225} = 1.42$ hours. Note the sum of the individual standard deviations is 2.35 hours.

Next suppose we are scheduling time for the next 25 of these tools and we wish to know the mean and standard deviation of the total processing time for all 25 units. We are therefore asking about another total variable, one which by definition is equal to 25 of our previous T variables. The mean value of this new total is thus just 8.8 hours added 25 times and its variance is 2.0225 added also 25 times. These two sums are respectively 220 hours and 50.5625 hours. By square-rooting the latter we have for the standard deviation of this new total variable 7.11 hours. Note here the incorrect standard deviation, being $25 \times 1.42 = 35.5$ hours, is radically off from this correct value of 7.11 hours.

Using the wrong value for the standard deviation of a total can be particularly costly when we set up controls on our process based on this value as is usually done in setting safety stock levels to carry us through replenishment cycles. As the incorrect value is larger we will thus incorporate false variability in our process which will usually mean we under-control, or overprotect, the process.

Descriptive Numbers Useful for Making Comparisons

To compare the average property of two variables (or more) we can compare their mean values directly, as we would ordinary numbers. We can use the standard deviations to compare their variabilities only if the two variables have the same mean value. As this is likely not the case, the *coefficient of variation* is normally used here. We have:

$$\text{Coefficient of variation, } V = \frac{s}{\bar{X}}$$

The drawback of V is that it is not defined when $\bar{X} = 0$, and may be unwieldly if the mean is very close to *zero*. Usually we express the value of this coefficient as a percent rather than as a decimal, thus we speak of a coefficient of variation of, say, 23 percent rather than 0.23.

Suppose that lead time data has been collected on four material "types" purchased from the same vendor, and our calculations produced the following:

Material Type	Mean Value of Lead Time	Standard Deviation	Coefficient of Variation
A	2 days	0.42 days	21
B	9 days	1.68 days	21
C	20 days	4.20 days	21
D	90 days	18.90 days	21

From this information we would conclude that even though the mean lead times and standard deviations differ considerably, there is in fact no difference in the "relative" amount of variability in the lead times of the different materials. This we certainly would not have concluded without the coefficient of variation.

If we have developed the quartiles for our data, then the *coefficient of dispersion* may be calculated and used in the same way as the coefficient of variation. We calculate it as follows:

$$\text{Coefficient of dispersion} = \frac{Q_3 - Q_1}{Q_3 + Q_1}$$

Often we will want to compare two or more individual observations, which may or may not come from the same data set. Calculating the *standardized value,* or the *z value,* for these observations allows us to make direct comparisons. All we do is express an observed value X_o in terms of its deviation from the mean value of the data from which it came, relative to the data standard deviation. That is:

$$\text{Standardized value of } X_o, \text{ its } z \text{ value} = \frac{X_o - \bar{X}}{s}$$

To illustrate, let's suppose that we are again working with the lead time data on the four materials A, B, C, and D, referred to in the above table. A delivery of a standard order quantity for material A has just taken 4 days, while that of material B took 10 days. Our question: Which of these deliveries showed the better performance? Using the values in the above table, we would compute the standardized values of these two lead times to be: $(4 - 2)/0.42 = 4.8$ for material A, and $(10 - 8)/1.68 = 1.2$ for material B. So, relatively speaking, the vendor showed better performance in delivering material B than A since the z value of the former was smaller than that of the latter.

Calculations with Frequency Tables

When working with data which has already been organized into an ungrouped frequency table, we can save time in calculating our descriptive measures by using the frequencies, f, with which the different values, X, occur. Thus, if the value 4 occurs ten times in our data then instead of adding 4 ten times, we would add into our sum of value the quantity $10 \times 4 = 40$. Stating the rules in terms of the frequencies f_i, the corresponding values X_i, and number of observations n, the rules of computation are those shown in Table 1–1.

$$\text{Mean value, } \bar{X} = \frac{f_1 X_1 + f_2 X_2 + \ldots + f_n X_n}{n} = \frac{\sum f_i \cdot X_i}{n}$$

$$\text{Variance, } s^2 = \frac{\sum f_i (X_i - \bar{X})^2}{n} = \frac{\sum f_i (X_i)^2}{n} - \bar{X}^2$$

$$\text{Harmonic average, } H = \frac{n}{\sum f_i \cdot \left(\frac{1}{X_i}\right)}$$

$$\text{Geometric average, } G = \sqrt[n]{(f_1 X_1)(f_2 X_2) \ldots (f_n X_n)}$$

Table 1–1

If our data is organized into a grouped frequency table then we will normally not be able to use our previous rules since we will no longer know the original observations. In such cases we identify the midpoint, or whatever other representative we are using for the category, with the X_i term in the above rules, and the corresponding category frequency with the term f_i, then we proceed as the rules indicate.

To calculate the median and mode from grouped data we could locate the median category or modal category and use the midpoints of these as the required values. In those cases when we wish to have a more refined values of these two averages, we must use special procedures, which are listed and illustrated below.

$$\text{Median} = L + \left[\frac{\frac{1}{2}n - (\sum f)}{f_{med}}\right] c$$

where:

L = the lower category boundary of the category containing the median

n = the number of observations in the data set

$(\sum f)$ = the sum of the frequencies of all categories below the median category

f_{med} = the frequency of the median category

c = the size of the median category

Recalling our production-hours example we had 50 observations and so the median will be found in that category which contains the 25th value in the array. Referring back to the table on page 19 we find this to be the "46–50 hours" category. Thus $f_{med} = 7$, $L_1 = 46$, and $(\sum f) = 23$. The value of n is 50 and $c = 5$. The median is thus computed as: $46 + (25 - 23/7) \cdot 5 = 47.4$ hours.

For the mode computation we have:

$$\text{Mode} = L + \left[\frac{D_1}{D_1 + D_2}\right] c$$

where:

L = lower category boundary of the modal category

D_1 = the excess of the frequency of the modal category over the frequency of the next lower category

D_2 = the excess of the frequency of the modal category over the frequency of the next higher category

c = the size of the modal category

Also from the production-hours example we would find: modal category is "51–55 hours," frequency of this is 10, so $L = 51$, $D_1 = 10 - 7 = 3$, $D_2 = 10 - 7 = 3$, and $c = 5$. Thus the modal value is: $51 + (3/3 + 3) \cdot 5 = 53.5$ hours.

We have already used the fact that the true median and mode of this data are 47 and 53 hours respectively. These agree quite well with the values we have just computed, the difference is due to our grouping operation in which we lost the original details.

A comment is in order with regard to the value of c used in these two procedures. There is a necessary distinction to be made between a *continuous category* and a *discrete category,* both of which may be used in grouping data. If we define our categories by specifying a particular set of values for each, then these are discrete categories, and the size, *c,* is simply the number of values we specify for the categories. This is what we did in grouping the production hours with each category having five specified values, which is why we set *c* equal to 5 in the above calculations. If, on the other hand, we specify a category by giving its lower and upper boundary values, and include all values in-between then we have a continuous category. In this case, the value for *c* is taken as the "length" of the category, which is the upper boundary value minus the lower one. This type of category was suggested for our shaft lengths example where the category length, and so the value of *c,* was 0.02 inches.

CONCLUSION

This chapter has provided ways for organizing, describing, and charting data sets which represent the values of a single variable. Both quantitative and qualitative data have been considered and the various kinds of questions we may logically ask about each have been indicated. Most of this material will be extended to the bivariate data set in the next chapter, and then used in the analysis methods presented in chapter 3.

REFERENCES

Freund, J.E. *Elementary Business Statistics: The Modern Approach.* Englewood Cliffs, N.J.: Prentice-Hall, Inc., 1964.

Hoel, P. *Introduction to Mathematical Statistics.* New York, N.Y.: John Wiley & Sons, Inc., 1961.

Springer, C.H., et. al. *Mathematics for Management Series.* Homewood, Ill.: Richard D. Irwin, Inc., 1965.

Wallis, W.A., and H.V. Roberts. *Statistics: A New Approach.* New York, N.Y.: The Free Press (Macmillan Co.), 1965.

2

How to Extract Information
from Bivariate Data Sets

A bivariate data set is one whose observations are pairs of values, one each of two different variables. As such each observation gives us two facts, one on each variable. The data set as a whole, on the other hand, gives us a new type of information content, namely, information on how the two variables "pair up" as each takes on particular values in its respective range. The exposure of this information content is almost always the purpose for which bivariate data is analyzed. One often expresses his question of interest as: "Will a change in one variable produce a change in the other one, and if so, in what direction, and by how much?" Whenever a change in one variable can be expected to produce (or accompany) a change in the other variable, we say that the two variables are *associated* with each other. Perhaps the most relevant question a manager will have is: "Will I be better able to predict the value of one of the variables if I know the value which the other variable will have?" And accompanying this one is: "What is the best rule or formula through which such a prediction should be made?" In answer to this last question we will have to construct an estimate of the precise structural *relationship* between the variables.

Various aspects of the problem of measuring the degree to which two variables are associated and that of actually demonstrating the most likely relationship between them will be the subject of this chapter. To illustrate what an analysis is capable of producing we consider the following situation.

The number of man-hours required to assemble successive units of some large appliance, such as a refrigerator, have been recorded. Our data set consists of, say, n observations (N, H), where N is the (variable) number of the unit in this succession, and H (also variable) is the number of man-hours required for this particular unit. Our interest is most likely in the "learning-curve" effect on this operation, and our general question is: "How are the man-hours required to do this job influenced by the number of times the same job has been performed?"

By applying certain analysis procedures we might be able to show (based on the collected data) that as a reasonable estimate of this "cause-and-effect" relationship we could use the formula: $H = 100 (N)^{-0.4}$. This would be the equation of the *learning curve* for this particular job and product. The ways in which such a formula could be used immediately suggest themselves. For example, we could cost-out future production lots, set delivery dates which are more meaningful, and establish wage incentive plans. By substituting for N in the formula the unit number in the succession, and performing the arithmetic indicated, we would obtain an estimate of the number of man-hours, H, which will be required to produce this unit.

In the following it will be useful for us to think of the "degree" to which two variables are associated as a property of bivariate data in general. By recalling the way in which we described the average and variability properties of univariate data, it is natural to expect that we will describe this new property with various numerical measures which are computed from the data. This is precisely what we do, and these numbers are termed *correlation coefficients,* or *indices of association.*

Joint Frequency Tables

The first step in the analysis of any bivariate data set should be the cross-classification of its members, and one way to achieve this is to construct the *joint frequency table* for the data set. This is an extension of the frequency table constructed for univariate data, and we start by defining the categories into which our observations will be grouped. Since we are now working with two variables, we must first categorize the values of each variable separately and from these form the bivariate categories.

As an illustration, suppose that 215 production lots are reviewed as to their actual delivery dates compared to their scheduled due dates. There are three different products, A, B, and C, and production performance for each lot is rated Late, On-Time, or Early depending upon whether the actual delivery date exceeded the due date, met it exactly, or was finished production prior to it. In this example both variables—product type, T, and production performance, P—are qualitative. Some actual observations might be: (B, Late), (A, On-Time), (A, Early), and so on.

There are three natural categories for T (A, B, and C) and also three for the variable P, therefore, there will be nine categories (or *cells*) into which our bivariate observations (T, P) will be grouped. The frequency associated with each of these bivariate categories is the number of times its "pair" was seen in the data. Suppose that we organized these frequencies into the following joint frequency table:

Product Type	Production Performance			Row Totals
	Late	On-Time	Early	
A	30	40	10	80
B	35	25	15	75
C	25	30	5	60
Column Totals	90	95	30	215

The nine figures in the center of this table are the joint frequencies, thus 40 indicates that the observation (A, On-Time) appeared forty times in the data set.

The "column totals" row gives the frequencies with which each of the production performances was observed; these constitute the frequency table for the variable P. Likewise, the "row totals" column is the frequency table (univariate) for the variable T.

This particular table (in the bivariate case) does not supply us with very much information; because there were a different number of lots for each product we cannot make meaningful comparisons between two rows term-by-term. The table which is designed to allow such comparisons is the *relative joint frequency table,* in which the count frequencies are expressed as relatives. The individual cell frequencies may be expressed relative to the total of the row they are in, or to the total of their column, or else to the total of all frequencies. There are therefore three kinds of relative joint frequency tables which may be constructed; Tables 2–1, 2–2, and 2–3 are these for our present example. It is good practice to construct all three since each will impart a different information content.

In Table 2–1 each count frequency has been divided by the row total of the row it is in, hence, the figures in each row (which should be thought of as percents) indicate how the total number of production lots associated with the product for this row are distributed among the three production performances. If we compare two of these rows we are comparing *between* two products *with respect to* production performance. We see, for example, that products A and C have the same likelihood of being On-Time, whereas product C is more likely to be Late than is product A.

In Table 2–2 each entry is the corresponding count frequency divided by the total frequency in its column. We are thus seeing how each production performance is distributed among the product types. If we compare one column against another we are comparing *between* production performance *with respect to* product type. It is seen from this table that an Early production lot is more likely to be one for product B than either of the other two products, and this same statement is also true for Late deliveries.

There are naturally other questions we can pose and answer with the information in each table, as well as with both tables together. For example, we may conclude from Table 2–1 that lots of product B are least often Early, but from Table 2–2 we may also say that most of the Early deliveries are due to lots of product B. These are not conflicting statements, and they illustrate the type of confusion which may develop if one does not continually keep in mind just what each table is expressing.

Table 2–3 is constructed by dividing each count frequency by the total (215) of all production lots. This table, like the original one giving the counts, does not expose much information of a comparative nature except how all observations distribute themselves into the nine categories. Two pieces of information we do extract from it are worth mentioning. The first is that the *modal category* can be determined, this being (A, On-Time) which has a greater frequency than any other category. The second piece of information we get from Table 2–3 is that the "row totals" column and "column totals" row are the relative frequency tables for the variables P and T respectively.

Product Type	Production Performance			Row Totals
	Late	On-Time	Early	
A	37.5	50.0	12.5	100.0 (80)
B	46.7	33.3	20.0	100.0 (75)
C	41.7	50.0	8.3	100.0 (60)

Table 2–1   As Percentages of the Row Totals

Product Type	Production Performance		
	Late	On-Time	Early
A	33.3	42.1	33.3
B	38.9	26.3	50.0
C	27.8	31.6	16.7
Column Totals	100.0 (90)	100.0 (95)	100.0 (30)

Table 2–2. As Percentages of the Column Totals

Product Type	Production Performance			Row Totals
	Late	On-Time	Early	
A	14.0	18.5	4.7	37.2
B	16.3	11.6	7.0	34.9
C	11.6	14.0	2.3	27.9
Column Totals	41.9	44.1	14.0	100.0 (215)

Table 2–3. As Percentages of Table Total

Two charts which may be useful in communicating the information in these tables are illustrated in Figures 2–1 and 2–2. Figure 2–1, constructed for Table 2–1, simply shows three rectangles—one for each product—which have been subdivided into three parts in proportion to the relative frequency for the three values of P. A rectangle would be used for each production performance if we were to construct this type of chart for Table 2–2.

Figure 2–2 has been constructed for Table 2–2 and what we have done is to erect a vertical rectangle for each product type, in groups for each production performance, erecting these so that their heights are proportional to their relative frequencies.

Whenever we have both variables being qualitative, we are usually limited to working with the tables just discussed, and the types of charts indicated for them above. However, when one of our variables is quantitative (which applies also to the case when both are quantitative), or when one of the qualitative variables is such that there is a meaningful interpretation of "or more" and "or less," then we may construct a *cumulative joint fre-*

quency table, in which we may accumulate either the count frequencies or relative frequencies.

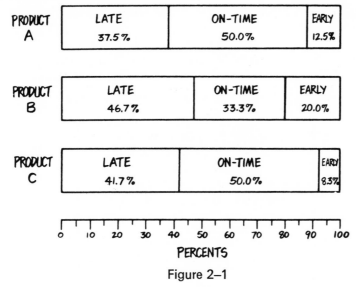

Figure 2–1

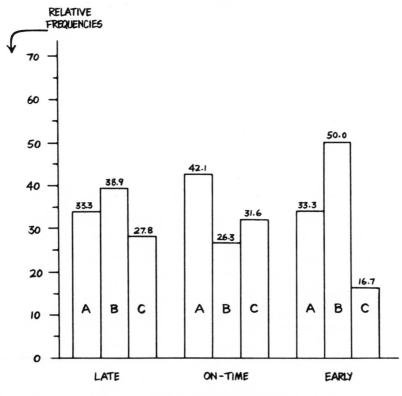

Figure 2–2

By way of illustration, let's suppose that we have further investigated those production lots which were Late and determined for each of them the number of days they were late. Let this variable be N. Suppose further, that the following is the joint frequency table for this bivariate data set (T, N):

Joint Frequency Table

Product Type	Number of Days Late				Row Totals
	1	2	3	4	
A	5	5	10	10	30
B	10	7	8	10	35
C	10	8	7	0	25
Column Totals	25	20	25	20	90

No lot was ever more than 4 days late, as is indicated in this table.

Since N is our quantitative variable, we must accumulate frequencies across this variable, that is, across columns within rows. This in turn means that the only comparisons we will be able to make will be between product type with respect to number of days late. Thus, the relative joint frequency table analogous to Table 2–1 is what we must construct next. This table is:

Relative Joint Frequency Table

Product Type	Number of Days Late				Row Totals
	1	2	3	4	
A	16.7	16.7	33.3	33.3	100 (30)
B	28.6	20.0	22.8	28.6	100 (35)
C	40.0	32.0	28.0	0.0	100 (25)

Suppose that we are interested in comparisons based on a certain number of days late "or more," then the following *cumulative joint relative frequency table* is indicated—relative frequencies accumulated from right-to-left in the one above.

Cumulative Joint Relative Frequency Table

Product Type	Number of Days Late			
	1 or More	2 or More	3 or More	4 or More
A	100.0	83.3	66.6	33.3
B	100.0	71.4	51.4	28.6
C	100.0	60.0	28.0	0.0

Developing this cumulative table, as we did, from the general type of table illustrated by Table 2–1 means that we compare between rows with respect to columns. Interpreting the figures in a row is the same as for univariate cumulative tables. Thus, for example, from the cumulative table we see that, when Late, product A is consistently "later" (on the average) than either of products B or C, and that product B has this same relationship to product C.

Again, many interesting facts develop by interlacing two or more tables. For instance, even though from the cumulative table we may say that product A, when Late, has the tendency to be later than product B, from Table 2–2 we see that most of the Late lots tend to be due to product B, and also from Table 2–1, most of product B production lots are Late.

When one of our variables is quantitative, we begin to get more flexibility in the type of chart we may prepare for the data. One such chart is illustrated in Figure 2–3, drawn for the cumulative joint relative frequency table above. The idea is to construct a univariate-type graph for each value of the qualitative variable, which, in our example is product type. The distinct advantage of this type of graph is that it allows us to interpolate between values. Another is that we are able to draw quick comparisons between the graphs, either vertically or horizontally.

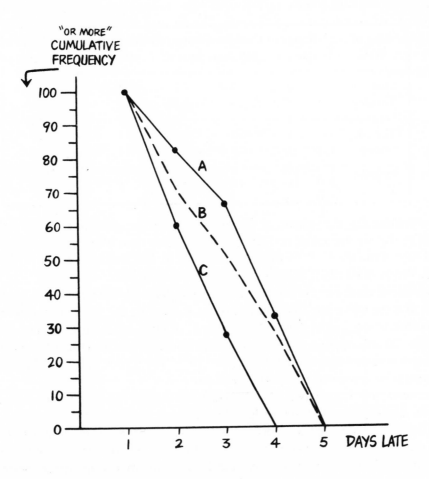

Figure 2–3

The Index of Prediction Error Reduction

Because we are normally investigating bivariate data sets to enhance our predictions of one variable, it is important for us to know what benefits may be expected from using knowledge about the second variable. The variable whose value we will know is termed the *prior variable* since it must logically occur "prior" to the one being predicted. We could, of course, simply collect a univariate data set on the variable being predicted, and from information gained from the analysis of this data go ahead and make our predictions. In so doing, as with any predicting, we can expect to make errors of prediction. It is through knowledge of some "second" variable that we hope to reduce these errors. The *index of prediction error reduction* indicates the average proportion of total errors of prediction we can expect to eliminate by knowing the value of the prior variable, and basing our predictions on this knowledge. This index then, and in a very practical sense, measures the degree of association between the two variables.

As an illustration, let's suppose that we have reviewed the number of customer orders filled daily by our order-filling department, established ranges on these and tabulated the number of actual daily amounts falling within each range. Assume that the joint frequency table on 10 weeks' data is this:

Day of Week	Range of Customer Orders Filled Daily				Row Totals
	100–200	200–300	300–400	400–500	
Monday	6	2	1	1	10
Tuesday	2	4	3	1	10
Wednesday	2	3	4	1	10
Thursday	1	3	5	1	10
Friday	3	5	1	1	10
Column Totals	14	17	14	5	50

It is assumed also that the volume of customer orders is the same for each day (or otherwise adjusted) so that we are seeing performance here rather than what was actually possible to fill. The day of the week, D, is the prior variable in this example, while R, the range of customer orders filled daily, is the variable we wish to predict.

Suppose we close our eyes to the information given by the variable D, that is, all we will look at is the univariate frequency table on R given by the "column totals" row. With just this information, our best guess for the range of filled orders, for any day, is the modal range, 200–300 orders. If we follow this prediction we will be in error each time one of the other ranges occurs, which accounts for $14 + 14 + 5 = 33$ out of a total frequency of 50, or our prediction error will be 33/50 or 66.0 percent.

If we were told that today is Monday we could look at this row in the above table, and predict its modal range, 100–200 orders. By so doing we will be in error $2 + 1 + 1 = 4$ out of 10 times, or our prediction error will be 40 percent. Knowing that it is Tuesday we wish to predict for, our prediction range would be 200–300 orders, and our percent error 60 percent. For Wednesday, Thursday, and Friday our predictions would be respectively the ranges 300–400, 300–400, and 200–300, and our respective percent errors of prediction would be 60 percent, 50 percent, and 50 percent. Using the information on our prior variable and allowing this to guide our prediction will mean that our prediction error overall will be given by the weighted average of these five percentage errors, where the weights used are the relative frequencies with which each day is likely to be experienced. For a different problem we may have to determine these frequencies from additional data, but for our case, assuming that each day occurs with the same frequency, each weight will be 1/5. Therefore, by using the knowledge of "which day it is" our prediction error is expected to be: $(1/5) (40 + 60 + 60 + 50 + 50) = 52$ percent.

The proportion of errors eliminated by taking account of the day of the week we are predicting for is $(66—52)/66 = 0.212$, or 21.2 percent. This 21.2 percent is the value of the *index of prediction error reduction.*

We denote this index by $I_{X/Y}$ (to be read "index of X given Y") where Y is the prior variable. In the situation where X is the column variable and Y the row variable (as is so for our example with R being X and D being Y), the following procedure is used to evaluate this index: (1) find the largest frequency in each row and sum these (in our example we get: $6 + 4 + 4 + 5 + 5 = 24$); (2) subtract from the total thus found the largest frequency in the "column totals" row (for our case $24 - 17 = 7$); (3) subtract this same largest frequency figure from the total of all frequencies in the table (for our case $50 - 17 = 33$); and then, (4) divide the result of Step 2 by that of Step 3, the result being the value of $I_{X/Y}$ (so in our example we compute $7/33 = 0.212$, or 21.2 percent).

It is just as likely that we will want to compute $I_{Y/X}$ where X, the column variable, is now the prior variable. To make these computations we follow the above procedure for $I_{X/Y}$ only interchange the words "row" and "column" in *every* place they appear in the procedure.

If we compute a value for the index, say $I_{X/Y}$, of 0.0 percent, then there is no association between X and Y, while at the other extreme, an index value of 100.0 percent signifies perfect association. Comparing our 21.2 percent figure against this range of possible values, we would most likely judge our association as "fair." However, although such judgments are useful in a summary sense, we should rest our final evaluations on the level of prediction error we can work with in our subsequent decision-making. If a given prior variable does not produce the needed level of error reduction it must be discarded; this particular index is very useful in making selections from among a list of possible prior variables.

The Contingency Coefficient

The *contingency coefficient, C,* is computed for situations involving two qualitative variables. To compute it we must have the joint frequency table (count frequency) and may not use the relative frequency table. If this is in fact what we are given, our first step must then be to convert it back to its original form.

To facilitate our exposition we will work with the following very simple joint frequency table; however, for the general $n \times m$ (n rows and m columns) table the general procedure is the same. Another piece of statistical jargon worth mentioning here is that these tables, in this particular context, are most often called *contingency tables.*

Machine Type	Type of Defect		Row Totals
	A	B	
BB–1	75	25	100
BB–2	65	35	100
Column Totals	140	60	200

For the context of this data let's suppose that a standard production batch was processed on each of two machines, a BB-1 and a BB-2, and for each we counted the number of produced units with Defect A and those with Defect B. The resulting counts are the frequencies presented in the above contingency table.

Our question of interest is: "Can we say that one machine tends to produce, on the average, more of one type of defect than the other does?" Or, more generally, "Is there any association, or dependency, between the two possible classifications of defective units— by machine-type producing them or by defect-type?" The value of C is a measure of this association (dependency, or contingency). A large value of C will mean a high degree of association between the two classifications, and will indicate an answer of "yes" to both questions.

A quantity used in the rule for computing C is the *Chi-square* (denoted by the square of the Greek letter χ, pronounced "ky"), and as we will see in subsequent chapters, it has some other important uses. To give the rule for computing the χ^2 we must first discuss the concept of *expected frequencies*.

The four frequencies 75, 25, 65, and 35 of our table are termed "observed" frequencies to distinguish them from the "expected" frequencies. The expected frequency of a cell in the table is simply that frequency we would have expected to find if there were in fact no association between the two variables. To illustrate let's look at the 140 type-A defects observed. If no association exists in our data then we would expect these 140 A-defects to be distributed between the BB-1 and BB-2 machines in the same proportion as the "row totals" frequencies. That is, evenly divided in proportion 1-to-1, which would mean the expected frequency for (BB-1, A) and (BB-2, A) are respectively 70, and 70. Similarly, the expected frequency for (BB-1, B) and (BB-2, B) should be 30, and 30 respectively. The contingency coefficient, C, measures the discrepancy between these expected frequencies and those frequencies observed in the data.

We need a simple rule for computing the expected frequency of any cell in the table, and the following is such a rule: (1) for the particular cell multiply the value in the "row totals" column in the same row as is this cell, by the value in the "column totals" row under the column which corresponds to the cell; and then, (2) divide this product by the total table frequency. Applying this rule to the (BB-1, A) cell, we find (100) (140)/200 = 70 as the expected frequency.

Letting O_i and E_i denote the observed frequency and expected frequency of the ith cell in our contingency table, and for the rule assuming we have n such cells, we compute the value of χ^2 as follows:

$$\text{Chi-square,} \quad \chi^2 = \sum_{i=1}^{n} \frac{(O_i - E_i)^2}{E_i}$$

The rule simply says to subtract the expected from the observed frequency and square this difference, then divide this square by the expected frequency, and add all these quotients for the different cells in the table.

Applying this rule to the contingency table we have introduced would result in the following:

$$\chi^2 = \frac{(75-70)^2}{70} + \frac{(25-30)^2}{30} + \frac{(65-70)^2}{70} + \frac{(35-30)^2}{30} = 2.38$$

The rule for computing the contingency coefficient is the following:

$$\text{Contingency Coefficient,} \quad C = \sqrt{\frac{\chi^2}{N + \chi^2}}$$

where N stands for the total table frequency. The value of C for our example is therefore: $\sqrt{(2.38)/(200 + 2.38)} = 0.108$.

The precise evaluation of this value (and C values in general) is postponed until chapter 3 since certain concepts of hypothesis testing must be introduced if the proper connection is to be achieved. Suffice it to say at this time that this value shows very little association between our two variables, so that we do not have evidence in our data to conclude that the two machines are not performing "equally" with respect to defect type production. In other words, neither machine has a greater tendency to produce one type of defect over the other.

Whenever we compute a measure of the degree of association we would like to also be able to compare such measures when they come from different sources. It might be that we have measured the association between X and each of the variables Y and Z, and by comparing our measures we would like to determine which of these variables has the "greater" association with X. In another situation we might have two different sets of variables but still wish to compare their associations. We can effect such comparisons by comparing the values of the two contingency coefficients only if both contingency tables are the exact same size.

It might be handy to calculate the *correlation coefficient of attributes*, r_a, for each data set and compare these as ordinary numbers. We can calculate this only for "square" tables, that is with n rows and n columns, and the formula we use is the following:

$$r_a = \sqrt{\frac{\chi^2}{N(n-1)}}$$

The value of r_a calculated for our present example would be $\sqrt{\frac{2.38}{200(2-1)}}$ or 0.109.

The value of r_a is always between *zero* and *one*, where the former value indicates no association, and the latter perfect association. Based on just this range of values, we would judge 0.109 as indicating little association; again, the more important use of this measure is to effect comparisons.

Most of the contingency problems we work with develop into $2 \times k$ contingency tables, where we have just 2 rows and an arbitrary number of columns, k. As this is so, it is convenient to have a shortcut formula for calculating the value of χ^2 for such tables.

To present the rule let us suppose that our table is that shown in Table 2–4, in which subscripted symbols are used as the table entries. In terms of these symbols the rule for calculating the Chi-square is as follows:

$$\chi^2 = \frac{N}{N_A} \cdot \left[\frac{a_1{}^2}{N_1} + \frac{a_2{}^2}{N_2} + \ldots + \frac{a_k{}^2}{N_k} \right] + \frac{N}{N_B} \left[\frac{b_1{}^2}{N_1} + \frac{b_2{}^2}{N_2} + \ldots + \frac{b_k{}^2}{N_k} \right] - N$$

The Rank Correlation Coefficient

In some situations we will have to work with numbers which do not have very much precision and for this reason we would not wish to process this data through a statistical procedure whose accuracy requires a high level of data precision. At other times the observations may have different relative importance on some basis (this can be true for quantitative as well as qualitative data). In such cases we normally assign *ranks* to the individual observations which in our judgment express their relative importance. Measuring the degree of association between the two variables in a bivariate data set where both variables have had their observed values ranked may be accomplished with the *rank correlation coefficient,* r_{rank}.

First there are certain questions pertaining to the assigning of ranks which must be covered. If we have n observations, then our ranks will be taken from the numbers 1, 2, 3, . . ., n. Which observation gets which rank number? This is up to the individual doing the ranking but the assignment should reflect the relative importance of each observation. Often, we just look at the value of each observation and rank them in ascending importance with the smallest observation getting the rank number 1, the next largest getting number 2, and so on with the largest observation getting the rank number n assigned to it.

In ranking we rank the "next" observation with the "next" rank number, and this may lead to giving two observations of the exact same value two different ranks. Ranking the set: 20, 20, 30, 35 would mean that we would assign the respective rank numbers 1, 2,

	1	2	3		k	Row Totals
A	a_1	a_2	a_3	. . .	a_k	N_A
B	b_1	b_2	b_3	. . .	b_k	N_B
Column Totals	N_1	N_2	N_3	. . .	N_k	N

Table 2–4

3, 4; the two 20's have different ranks—the first has 1 while the second has 2. This is inconsistent. How do we correct this problem? Simply by assigning to each of the "tied" observations the mean of their ranks. Following this rule we would assign both 20's the rank of: $\frac{1}{2}(1 + 2)$, or 1.5.

Suppose we have run eight production batches through a particular machine and observed two variables: S, the "speed" at which the machine was set for each batch, and Q, the "quality" of the resulting production. Suppose further that our observations were as follows:

(62, good)	(63, fair)	(64, good)	(65, fair)
(66, fair)	(67, poor)	(67, poor)	(69, poor)

The general observation, (S, Q), takes on eight values and so the rank numbers: 1, 2, 3, 4, 5, 6, 7, 8 will be used to rank the 8 values of each variable. Averaging of rank numbers will be needed, and the initial and final ranks are shown in the following display.

S	62	63	64	65	66	67	67	69
Initial Ranks	1	2	3	4	5	6	7	8
Final Ranks	1	2	3	4	5	6.5	6.5	8
Q	good	fair	good	fair	fair	poor	poor	poor
Initial Ranks	8	6	7	5	4	3	2	1
Final Ranks	7.5	5	7.5	5	5	2	2	2

In this we have put the S values into an arrangement of increasing magnitudes and the corresponding value of Q observed in the data underneath. We must always pair up the rank numbers as their associated observations were paired in the data.

For each pair of ranks we next compute the difference between them, denoted generally by D. Each of these differences is squared, giving D^2, and then we sum all these squares, giving us $\sum D^2$. The rank correlation coefficient is computed with the following rule:

$$\text{Rank Correlation Coefficient, } r_{rank} = 1 - \frac{6 \cdot \sum D^2}{n^3 - n}$$

where n is the number of bivariate observations in the data set.

The computations involved in our present example are indicated in the following display, the first two rows of which are filled in with the paired rank numbers produced in the previous display.

Ranks on S:	1	2	3	4	5	6.5	6.5	8
Ranks on Q:	7.5	5	7.5	5	5	2	2	2
Values of D:	−6.5	−3	−4.5	−1	0	4.5	4.5	6
Values of D^2:	42.25	9.00	20.25	1.00	0.0	20.25	20.25	36.00

From which we easily compute:

$$\sum D^2 = 149.00$$

$$r_{rank} = 1 - \frac{6(149.00)}{8^3 - 8} = -0.774$$

The negative sign in this value indicates that we have an "inverse" correlation between the variables S and Q. This simply means that on the average as we increase one variable we will see a decrease in the other variable. If we have a positive algebraic sign on a correlation coefficient we have a "direct" correlation in that we expect both variables to increase simultaneously. What we see here in this particular example simply illustrates that as we increase the speed at which our machine operates, the quality of production goes down.

The numerical part of this coefficient, the 0.774, indicates that there is quite a high degree of correlation (or association) between S and Q. Again, we must postpone to chapter 3 the more precise statement of evaluation on this particular coefficient.

The Linear Correlation Coefficient

The *linear correlation coefficient, r*, is used as a measure of a certain type of association, namely, the *linear* (straight-line, or proportional) association between X and Y. By the word "linear" we mean that the formula expressing the nature of the relationship between X and Y is that of a straight line, which is $Y = A + BX$. In this formula A and B are constants whose actual numerical values are determined from the observations and certain rules of computation. In other words, we take the position that this formula in fact expresses the relationship between X and Y, and in this context the linear correlation coefficient measures how well this assumption holds up in the light of the bivariate data set on these two variables.

One very often speaks of "fitting" a straight line to the data when computing the particular values of A and B, and, in this sense the value of r indicates how well the line $Y = A + BX$ "fits" the data.

In order that r may be computed, both X and Y must be quantitative variables. And, whenever we suspect the existence of a linear relationship between the variables, the first step is to compute the value of r. If this resulting value indicates that in fact such a relationship may exist, our next step would be to compute the values of A and B—there are easy rules for doing this which require that we know only r, along with the arithmetic average and standard deviation of both X and Y.

When should we suspect a linear relationship? Our first clue is found in the *scatter diagram* drawn for the observations (X, Y) of our data set. In Figures 2–4, 2–5, and 2–6 we have illustrated scatter diagrams, which are constructed by simply plotting the observations (X, Y) on appropriately scaled axes.

In Figure 2–4, the plotted points appear to "cluster" around a straight line; naturally, due to the variability in both variables the points will never fall exactly on a line. In this particular diagram the line would slope upward since as we increase X the Y also increases. An *upward* or *positive slope* means that the value of B, in the formula $Y = A + BX$, will be a positive quantity; *B* is the *slope of the line*. Also in these instances the value of *r* will be positive, indicating a *positive linear correlation*.

When the slope of the line is downward, or negative, both the value of *B* and *r* will be negative, indicating *negative linear correlation*. This is what we should expect for the data plotted in Figure 2–5.

Figure 2–6 has been presented to indicate what the scatter diagram is likely to look like when there is *no* linear correlation in our data, or *zero linear correlation*. Normally, our diagram will be somewhere between these extremes.

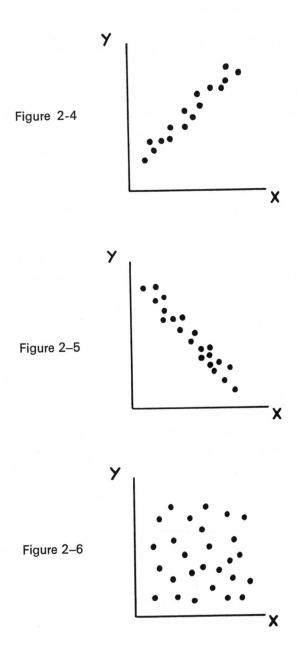

Figure 2-4

Figure 2–5

Figure 2–6

Given a bivariate data set of n observations on the pair of variables (X, Y) the definition of the linear correlation coefficient is the following:

$$\text{Linear Correlation Coefficient, } r = \frac{n\sum(X\cdot Y) - \sum X\cdot\sum Y}{\sqrt{n\sum(X^2) - (\sum X)^2}\cdot\sqrt{n\sum(Y^2) - (\sum Y)^2}}$$

To calculate r with this rule we need the values of the following: $\sum X$, $\sum X^2$, $\sum Y$, $\sum Y^2$, $\sum XY$, and n. Other rules may be used and some of these will be introduced subsequently.

The square of the correlation coefficient, r^2, is termed the *coefficient of determination.* This should be read as a percent, thus, we would read a value of 0.85 as 85 percent. This particular measure of association is of importance in that we can attach a practical meaning to it. Before we discuss this, let us illustrate the calculations.

Suppose that a certain quality control test is performed on a finished item and for various reasons a different number of determinations may be required for this test. We are interested in determining if there is an association between the number of minutes required to perform the determinations and the number of these. Let X be the number of determinations and Y the number of minutes required to perform these tests, our data set is shown in the first two columns of Table 2–5 where also are shown the calculation steps of the linear correlation coefficient r. Figure 2–7 presents the scatter diagram of the data.

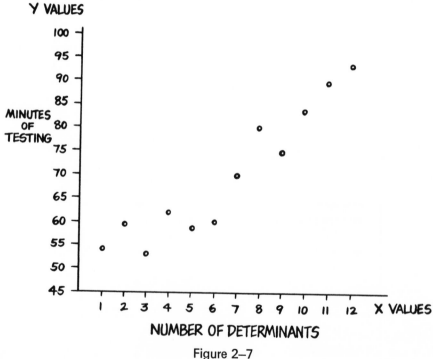

Figure 2–7

Our correlation coefficient is found to be 0.945. In chapter 3 there will be presented a method for testing the "significance" of this value which will enable us to evaluate the degree of association on an objective basis. However, for a subjective evaluation we can use Table 2–6. Locating the value $r = 0.945$ in this table we judge that we have a Very

Computing Linear Correlation Coefficient				
Number of Determinations X	Minutes of Testing Y	Values of X^2	Values of Y^2	Values of $X \cdot Y$
1	54	1	2916	54
2	59	4	3481	118
3	53	9	2809	159
4	62	16	3844	248
5	58	25	3364	290
6	60	36	3600	360
7	70	49	4900	490
8	80	64	6400	640
9	75	81	5625	675
10	84	100	7056	840
11	90	121	8100	990
12	94	144	8836	1128
78	839	650	60931	5992

$$\sum X = 78 \qquad \sum Y = 839 \qquad \sum X \cdot Y = 5{,}992$$
$$\sum X^2 = 650 \qquad \sum Y^2 = 60{,}931 \qquad n = 12$$

$$r = \frac{n\sum X \cdot Y - \sum X \cdot \sum Y}{\sqrt{n\sum X^2 - [\sum X]^2} \cdot \sqrt{n\sum Y^2 - [\sum Y]^2}}$$

$$= \frac{12(5992) - 78(839)}{\sqrt{12(650)-(78)^2}\sqrt{12(60931)-(839)^2}} = \frac{6462}{\sqrt{1716}\ \sqrt{27251}}$$

$$= 0.945$$

Table 2–5

Numerical Value for r	Evaluation of the Linear Correlation
1.0	Perfect
0.9 to 1.0	Very High
0.8 to 0.9	High
0.6 to 0.8	Moderate
0.5 to 0.6	Poor
0.0 to 0.5	Very Poor
0.0	None

Table 2–6

High degree of association between testing time and number of determinations.

In Table 2–6 we have listed only positive values of r but the same evaluations hold for negative values which have the same *numerical* values as shown.

As our linear correlation coefficient is $r = 0.945$, then the coefficient of determination is $r^2 = 0.893$, or 89.3 percent. What this says is that if we go ahead and find the straight line $Y = A + BX$ which fits this data, then 89.3 percent of the variability in the Y values can be attributed to, or explained by, the X variable through this linear relationship. Thus, r^2 has a very practical interpretation of linear association. Knowing this we can therefore expect to find $1.00 - 0.893 = 0.107$ or 10.7 percent of the variability in Y as unexplained. This can be viewed as the level of "error" we face in using X as a predictor or lead variable for Y.

The Covariance Between Variables

Another measure of the association between X and Y is the so-called *covariance between X and Y*, denoted as $s_{x,y}$. The rule we use to calculate this measure is:

$$\text{Covariance, } s_{x,y} = \frac{\sum(X \cdot Y)}{n} - \bar{X} \cdot \bar{Y}$$

Here we are instructed to multiply each X value by its corresponding Y value, add these and divide the sum by n, and then subtract from this the product of the two mean values. Looking at the rule we see that $s_{x,y} = s_{y,x}$ (and this is also true for the correlation coefficient). This is what we should expect since this measure is looking at the association between the two variables without distinguishing between them in any way.

Another way to calculate $s_{x,y}$ which will tend to reduce our round-off errors is with the following rule:

$$s_{x,y} = \frac{n\sum(X \cdot Y) - \sum X \cdot \sum Y}{n^2}$$

Using this rule we do not introduce the error in our mean calculations.

If we know the covariance and the standard deviations s_x and s_y for our two variables, then a convenient way to calculate the correlation coefficient, r, is as follows:

$$\frac{\text{Linear Correlation}}{\text{Coefficient, } r} = \frac{s_{x,y}}{(s_x) \cdot (s_y)}$$

In the previous chapter it was shown how the standard deviation of a variable which was the sum of a number of independent variables could be calculated. Thus, if T is defined as $T = X + Y + Z$, then the standard deviation of T, s_T, is determined from the standard deviations of these variables s_x, s_y, and s_z, according to the following rule:

$$s_T = \sqrt{s_x^2 + s_y^2 + s_z^2}$$

When our variables are independent, the covariances among them will be zero, that is $s_{x,y}$, $s_{x,z}$, and $s_{y,z}$ will equal *zero*. The opposite is not true. That is, zero covariance does not imply independence. A zero covariance implies that the variables are *uncorrelated*, which is not as strong a condition as independence, however, in practice we can react as if it were.

When our calculated covariances are significantly different from zero, they must be included in the calculation of the standard deviation of a total variable. The general rule for calculating the standard deviation s_T is:

$$s_T = \sqrt{s_x^2 + s_y^2 + s_z^2 - 2 \cdot (s_{x,y} + s_{x,z} + s_{y,z})}$$

It should be clear from this how we extend the rule for an arbitrary number of variables.

The Least-Squares Method of Curve Fitting

The so-called *method of least squares* is a computational method by which an equation form is fitted to numerical data to represent the structural relationship between the variables. To get to the heart of the objective of this method let us look at Figure 2–8. Here we have redrawn the scatter diagram of Figure 2–7, but with the straight line $Y = 45.5 + 3.76X$ superimposed—this line is the one we would fit to the data in Table 2–5, its equational form is $Y = A + BX$.

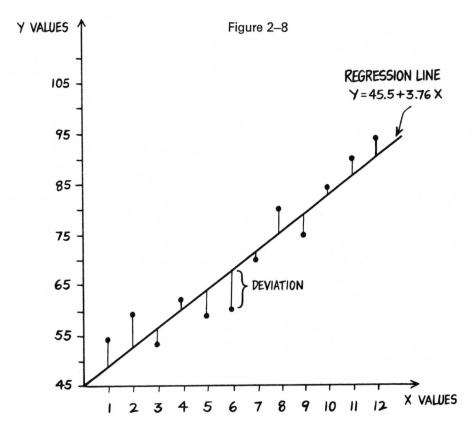

Figure 2–8

In Figure 2–8 we have drawn a vertical line from each data point to the least-squares line. The length of each line measures the *deviation* of this point from the line, or roughly speaking, by how much the line misses going through the point. Points below the line have negative deviation, while those above have positive deviation; the line overstates and understates these points respectively. If we square each deviation and add these, we will have an indication of "how well" the line fits through the points. The method of least squares is geared to produce that line for which this sum of squared deviations is minimum, hence the term "least squares."

Letting Y_i and X_i represent the ith Y value and the ith X value in the data (we assume we have n such pairs), then Y_i is an actual observation while the quantity $A + BX_i$ is an estimate of Y_i according to the line equation. Thus, the deviation at the point (X_i, Y_i) is $(Y_i - A - BX_i)$. To find the least-squares line we would simply have to solve the following problem in calculus: find the values of A and B which minimize this sum:

$$\sum_{i=1}^{n}(Y_i - A - BX_i)^2$$

Following the usual procedure, we would set the first derivative of this sum with respect to A equal to zero, and also the first derivative with respect to B. We would thus produce two equations which when solved for A and B would give the required values for these, which in turn would produce the line $Y = A + BX$. The two rules which are perhaps the most convenient to use in calculating A and B are the following:

**Rules for Calculating A and B
in the Least-Squares Line:**
$$Y = A + BX$$

$$B = \frac{n\sum(X \cdot Y) - \sum X \cdot \sum Y}{n\sum X^2 - (\sum X)^2}$$

$$A = \frac{\sum Y - B \cdot \sum X}{n}$$

Where, in the rule for calculating the value of A, we use the value calculated for B by the first rule.

To illustrate the calculations, let us use the data in Table 2–5 again. We should note that the numerator of the B rule is the same numerator in the rule for calculating the linear correlation coefficient, r. In Table 2–5 we find this to be equal to 6462. In addition, the term in the denominator of the B rule is the term under the first square root in the denominator in the r rule, and again, from Table 2–5, we find this value to be 1716. Therefore, the value of B is immediately found to be:

$$B = \frac{6462}{1716} = 3.76$$

This is the slope of our least-squares line.

To calculate the value of A we again use the data of Table 2–5 and we find here that:

$$A = \frac{839 - (3.76)(78)}{12} = 45.48, \text{ or } 45.5$$

The least-squares line which fits our data is thus:

$$Y = 45.5 + (3.76)X$$

and as our linear correlation coefficient of $r = 0.945$ is directly associated with this line we can judge that it is a Very Good fit to the data.

Our purpose for developing the least-squares line is to serve as a means for us to estimate values of Y corresponding to values of X which were not in our data, or to serve as "standards" in the sense of the "expected value of Y." When we are using the line for this purpose, we refer to it as a *regression line*. With what has been developed for our example we would most likely be quite willing to use the regression line $Y = 45.5 + 3.76X$ to estimate testing time, Y, for a given number of determinants X. We could interpret this line as saying that there is a "fixed" amount of time required for testing regardless of the number of determinations being made. This is the 45.5 minutes figure. With each additional determination there is a "fixed" increment in testing time, which is 3.76 minutes per determination. In some cases we will produce a negative value for A which has no practical interpretation as a "fixed" amount. Such situations arise simply because the least-squares method requires a negative value for A to fit the data as its objective necessitates. What this means in our interpretation is that we cannot attach a meaning to A at the point where $X = 0$.

If we interchange X and Y everywhere in our rules then the resulting values of A and B would be those for the least-squares line $X = A + BY$. This equation can be solved for Y, the result would be the equation $Y = (-A/B) + (1/B)X$. It is important to realize that the value we find for $-A/B$ will in general not be equal to the least-squares value for this line, nor will $1/B$ be equal to the value of the slope we obtain from least squares. Each equation must be fit individually and, while this type of shortcut is tempting, it is incorrect.

Some other rules which can be used to calculate the values of A and B are shown in Table 2–7. Whether or not these will be convenient will depend on what data has already been developed in previous analyses.

Other Rules for Calculating A and B for $Y = A + BX$
$A = \dfrac{\sum Y \cdot \sum (X^2) - \sum X \cdot \sum (X \cdot Y)}{n \sum (X^2) - (\sum X)^2}$
$A = \bar{Y} - B\bar{X}$
$B = \dfrac{r \cdot s_y}{s_x}$
$B = \dfrac{s_{x,y}}{(s_x)^2}$

Table 2–7

The least-squares method can be used to fit equational forms other than the straight-line form. We would simply set the problem up as a problem of minimization, solve the resulting calculus problem and use the rules thus produced to evaluate the constants in the form from the data.

As the fitting of a straight line to his data is probably as far into this theory as the manager should go—and often as far as he *need go* to obtain the answers he seeks—unassisted by a technician, we will not dwell further on the subject. However, there are certain nonlinear curves which are extremely important to the manager, and particularly to the manufacturing manager since they are used to describe such things as sales trends, learning curves, and continuous discounting of cash flows, which can be fit to data with the use of the A and B rules presented for the straight line. Appropriate transformations of the original data, and then using this transformed data in the rules is all that is needed. The four most important of these curves, and the required transformations, will now be presented.

The formula $Y = a(b)^X$ is called the *exponential curve*, where a and b are the constant terms. Depending on the values of the constants, the graph of this curve will appear roughly as shown in Figure 2–9. The reader with an engineering background is probably more accustomed to seeing this equation form written as $Y = a(e^{cX})$ where e is the base 2.71828, shown to five decimal places. One often uses the expression $exp(cX)$ in place of e^{cX}. As $e^{cX} = (e^c)^X = (b)^X$, where $b = e^c$, we see that there is no real difference between the two equations.

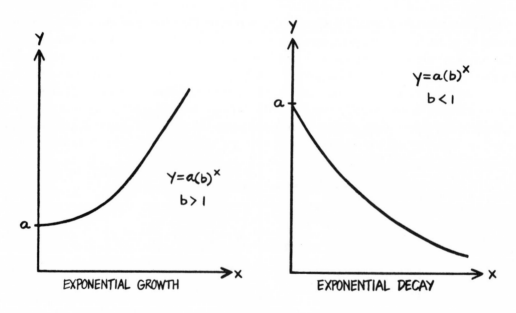

Figure 2–9

If we were to draw a scatter diagram for a given data set, but instead of plotting the values of Y against those of X we plotted the logarithms of the values of Y against the values of X (a log Y versus X plot), and if this diagram indicated a linear pattern, then the exponential curve should be considered as a possible representation of the relationship between X and Y. If we use *semilog graph paper*, we accomplish this plotting without the bother of computing the logarithms of the Y values.

To find the values of the constants a and b we do the following: (1) compute the values of A and B using the rules for the straight-line formula, but, instead of using the Y values in the summations, use the logarithms of the Y values; then, (2) the a in $Y = a(b)^X$ is the antilogarithm of the value of A computed in step (1), and the b is the antilogarithm of the computed B value.

The exponential curve is often found to fit certain short-term sales trends, especially when working with a new product or one for which a new use has been found. It is also useful in describing the accumulation of money under interest compounding, depletion of resources, and for describing the learning curve of hand operations.

The formula $Y = a(X)^b$ is the *geometric* (or *power*) *curve*, which is again an example of a nonlinear curve involving just two constant terms. If we wish to consider this as a possible representation for the relationship between Y and X, we may again start with the scatter diagram. This time we plot the logarithms of the Y values against the logarithms of the X values (a log Y versus log X plot), and again look for the straight-line pattern in this graph. Time will be saved by using *log-log graph paper* here.

To actually find the least-squares values of a and b we do the following: (1) compute the values of A and B with the rules provided for the straight-line fit, but instead of the X and Y values, use the logarithms of these in the rules; then, (2) the a in $Y = a(X)^b$ is the antilogarithm of the computed A value, while b is equal to the computed B value.

Typical curves of the geometric formula are presented in Figure 2–10. Again note how the shape of these curves radically changes depending on the particular values of a and b.

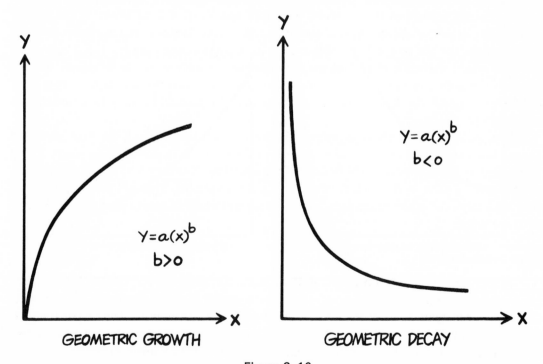

Figure 2–10

It is very often the case that due to the basic variability in our data it is a "tossup" between the exponential and geometric curves. In these cases one may find help in choosing one of them by computing the linear correlation coefficient for each (using the transformed data as called for) and selecting that curve with the larger value of r.

Two other nonlinear curves which may be fit to data through the use of the rules for computing A and B for the line are the *regular hyperbola*, $Y = A + B(\frac{1}{X})$, and the *regular parabola*, $Y = A + BX^2$. In the hyperbola, X is related to Y through its reciprocal values (so it is an *inverse relationship*), whereas in the parabola we are relating X through its square (hence a *quadratic relationship*).

To test the merits of each of these curves for fitting our data we again draw scatter diagrams, but plot Y versus the values of $1/X$ for the hyperbola and versus the values of X^2 for the parabola. Again, we look for linear patterns. We also make use of the A and B rules for the line to fit these two curves, where the values of $1/X$ and X^2 are used in these in place of the X values for the hyperbola and parabola respectively. Figures 2–11 and 2–12 illustrate typical hyperbolas and parabolas.

These two curves find use in describing relationships existing between costs and volumes, or prices and volumes since these may arise from either a production or purchasing environment. However, there are certain limiting characteristics of each which will not usually allow us to use them over the full range of X values. For instance, the Y values computed from the hyperbola equation will approach infinity as X approaches the value 0. This will also happen in the parabola if X is allowed to approach infinitely large negative or positive values. While this is the nature of the curves, it will almost never be the situation as far as we are concerned when describing a data set arising from a manufacturing environment. Another feature of these curves, but more specific to the parabola, is the rate at which they grow, or decay. Again, manufacturing data seldom match these rates. A characteristic specific to the hyperbola is that as X approaches infinity, Y will approach (but not reach) the value of a. This may or may not be the real-world situation. All this means to us is that in using these curves we will normally have to restrict the range of X values over which the hyperbola or parabola may be justifiably used to describe our relationships.

The trick employed above in fitting nonlinear curves to data with the rules provided for the line may not be extended to equations of the form: $Y = A + B(XY)$, where Y, the dependent variable, appears on both sides of the equation. Nor may it be used for equations of the form: $Y = A + BX + CZ$, where Z is a third variable. This last equation takes us into the analysis of multivariate data, on which we will make selected comments at the end of this chapter.

Time Series Analysis

A *time series* is simply a bivariate data set with, say, general observation (X, T), where the T values are the "times" at which the corresponding X values occurred. By the word "time" we can mean either of two things: (1) the *order of occurrence*, where we distinguish one X value as the "first one," another as the "second one," and so on; or, (2) the actual clock or calendar time of occurrence as measured from a fixed point in time.

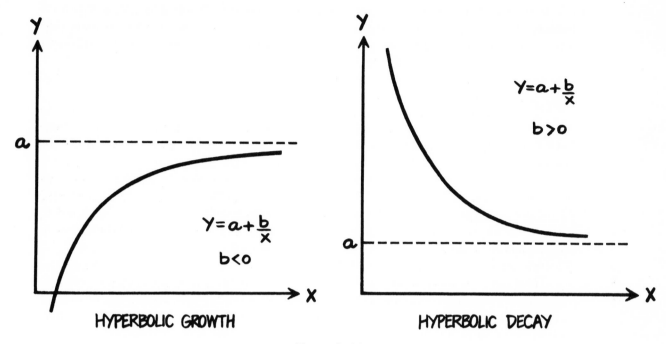

Figure 2–11

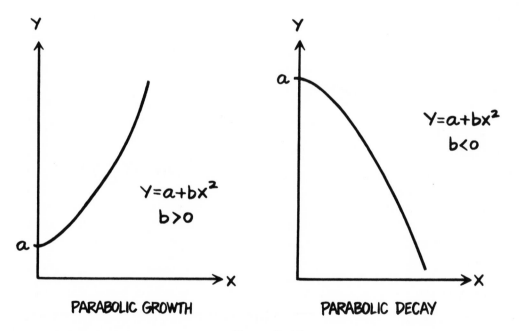

Figure 2–12

The analysis of a time series is almost always associated with our interest in forecasting, or controlling, the X variable. Thus, for example, if X is the monthly demand for an item, then our interest centers around forecasting these demands at future points in time. On the other hand, if the X values are yields of, say, a chemical process as found in successive runs (where T as a time variable has our first interpretation as given above), then most likely our interest is in the control of this process. Through the analysis of this time series we will know what to expect under "normal" operating conditions, and therefore also know when we should interpret an occurrence as indicating the loss of process control.

The average value of the X values, averaged over time, is an important factor in our analysis, but often more important is the *trend* which the X values follow over the course of time. By trend we mean the growth or decline occurring in the X values over time, and this would be seen in a scatter diagram of the data as the general direction in which the graph appears to be going. To quantify a trend movement, we can often find an adequate model in the straight-line equation $X = A + BT$. At other times one of the curves we have discussed will have to be used for a correct representation of trend (and these would be referred to as *trend curves*, as opposed to *trend lines*). The least-squares fitting method is most useful in developing these characterizations of trend.

To illustrate, let us suppose that we have the weekly demand for a product which was first available in week number 1; our observations on (D, T) are shown in Table 2–8 where we have let $T =$ week number, and $D =$ weekly demand. In this display are shown the steps required to fit the line $D = A + BT$ to the original data in the first two columns.

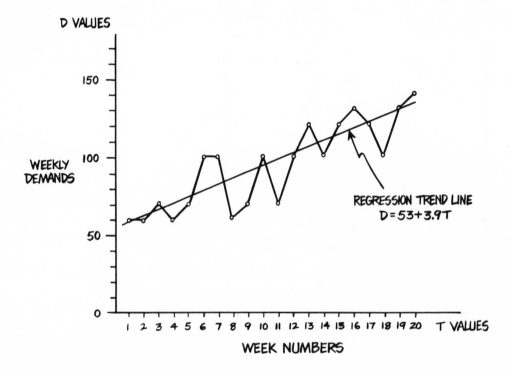

Figure 2–13

The scatter diagram for this time series is shown in Figure 2–13 along with the regression line we have just quantified, $D = 53 + 3.9T$. From this figure we get the im-

Week Numbers T	Weekly Demands D	Values of T^2	Values of D^2	Values of $T \cdot D$
		Estimating Trend in Weekly Demands with Line $D = A + BT$		
1	60	1	3,600	60
2	60	4	3,600	120
3	70	9	4,900	210
4	60	16	3,600	240
5	70	25	4,900	350
6	100	36	10,000	600
7	100	49	10,000	700
8	60	64	3,600	480
9	70	81	4,900	630
10	100	100	10,000	1,000
11	70	121	4,900	770
12	100	144	10,000	1,200
13	120	169	14,400	1,560
14	100	196	10,000	1,400
15	120	225	14,400	1,800
16	130	256	16,900	2,080
17	120	289	14,400	2,040
18	100	324	10,000	1,800
19	130	361	16,900	2,470
20	140	400	19,600	2,800
210	1,880	2,870	190,600	22,310

$$\sum T = 210 \qquad \sum D = 1,880 \qquad \sum T \cdot D = 22,310$$
$$\sum T^2 = 2,870 \qquad \sum D^2 = 190,600 \qquad n = 20$$

$$r = \frac{n\sum T \cdot D - \sum T \cdot \sum D}{\sqrt{n\sum T^2 - (\sum T)^2} \cdot \sqrt{n\sum D^2 - (\sum D)^2}} = \frac{51,400}{\sqrt{13,300} \cdot \sqrt{277,600}} = 0.846$$

$$B = \frac{n\sum T \cdot D - \sum T \cdot \sum D}{n\sum T^2 - (\sum T)^2} = \frac{51,400}{13,300} = 3.865, \text{ or } 3.9$$

$$A = \frac{\sum D - B \cdot \sum T}{n} = \frac{1,880 - (3.865)(210)}{20} = 53.4, \text{ or } 53.$$

Table 2–8

pression that the trend line indicates the general direction of demands, and as $r = 0.846$, then $r^2 = 0.716$, or roughly 72 percent of the variability in weekly demands may be attributed to the trend movement as represented by the trend line. From this we would perhaps be willing to assume that our weekly demand pattern consists of a trend movement with random "noise" on top of this.

To visualize this random movement we could pick off the trend values for each week from the graph, but as a rule it is better to use the equation to find these. Thus, the trend part of the 10th week's demand is 53 + 3.9 (10) = 92 units. The actual demand for this week was 100 units and the difference, 100 − 92 = 8 units, is due to the random movement (that is, this is due to the movement in our demand pattern which is left unexplained by the trend we have isolated). We could continue finding these differences, and for our example we would find that the average (mean) value of these is *zero*, and their standard deviation is 14.07 units.

In chapter 3 there will be presented methods for incorporating the random movement into our forecasts for future demands (using confidence intervals), but for now let us only consider the trend movement forecast. To forecast the trend for a future week we also use the equation but here we use week numbers which were not part of our historical data. Thus, we would forecast the trend part of the demand in the 25th week as 53 + 3.9 (25) = 150.5, or 150 units. Of course, in so doing we are making the critical assumption that the demand pattern in the future will continue to have a dominant trend and this will be represented there as it is in our data by the line $D = 53 + 3.9T$. One should always question this assumption as it will rarely hold for extended future periods, such as over a ten-year period. As a rule we should never extend our forecasts for a period of time greater than the length of time covered by our data and even this is likely to be too long.

If our data had showed a changing slope, then the straight line would not be a very good representative of trend. We would also receive an indication of this in a low value of *r*, and also when we computed our errors; we would reach a point beyond which our errors were either all positive or all negative. In these cases one of the curves introduced in this section could be considered.

Another basic movement we should look for in a time series is a *seasonal* or *periodic movement*. This is seen in the line graph of the series as identical, or almost identical, patterns of highs and lows which the graph appears to follow during corresponding calendar times, or at points in time located a fixed time-interval apart. Usually we refer to this pattern as a seasonal movement when we are working with demand or sales data, and a periodic movement otherwise. The length of time it takes before the pattern starts to repeat itself is termed the *period* of movement.

In Figure 2–14 we have plotted two time series, the bottom one depicting an exact seasonal movement and the one at the top indicating what we might actually see in real demands. Although a seasonal pattern is evident in both graphs, these are "level" in that they move across time without an obvious trend growth or decay. If a trend movement was also present, these graphs would have a general direction upward or downward while still showing their seasonal movements.

To characterize a seasonal movement, or for that matter any periodic movement, we do not have to separate it from the time series data. We can instead calculate *seasonal indices* as the characterization. These are just a set of numbers which show the relative importance of our data at the different points of time over which the series is given. If we are working with monthly demands, then for each month we would have a seasonal index which would indicate the relative weight to be attributed to this month's demand as compared to some fixed base value.

The most common type of seasonal index is that calculated by the *average percent method*. To illustrate, let us suppose that we have monthly demand data for some item

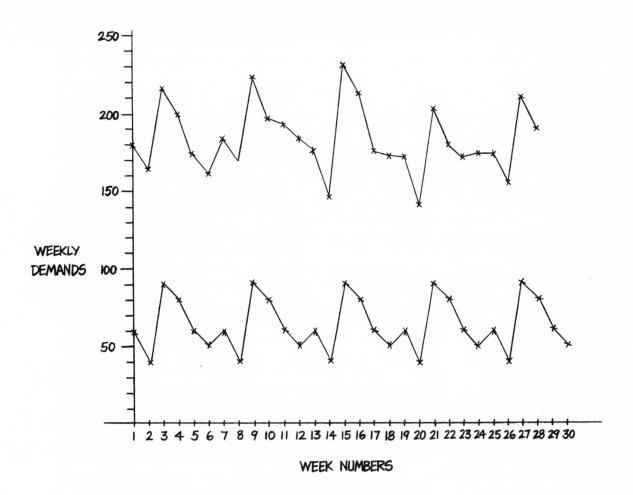

Figure 2–14

over a period of three years. Our first step is to calculate the mean value of demand for each year. Taking this value for the first year we divide each monthly demand figure by this, and we then do this for the other two years dividing each monthly figure by the average value calculated for its year. At this point we would have thirty-six percent-values, twelve for each year, one for each month. These are initial estimates for the seasonal indices. We now average these percent-values for corresponding months of the three different years, which will give us twelve percent-values which are our final estimates for the monthly seasonal indices. In taking averages here if there are extreme values we should use the median average. A final adjustment may be needed in our twelve indices since we must have these total to 12.0. If instead they total to some other value, say, to S, then we multiply each index by the factor $(12/S)$ which should in most cases (except when round-off errors do not allow it) effect this adjustment.

If our demand pattern does not have a seasonal movement, then these indices we have just calculated should be equal to 1.00. Due to normal rounding-off errors the indices may not be exactly equal to 1.00, but they should be quite close to this before we judge demand as nonseasonal.

This method for calculating these indices is termed "average" percent method since the mean value of yearly demand is used as the base value; that is, this is the value we divide by and relative to which our individual monthly demands are expressed. Actually, this technique is only appropriate when our demand has no trend present, and when this is not the case, we should calculate our indices via the *trend percent method*. This method starts by our calculating the trend part of each month's demand (using a trend equation previously quantified). We then divide the demand in each month by its estimated trend part. This step will produce initial estimates for the indices and by averaging these for corresponding months in our different years we will produce the final twelve seasonal indices—these must also be adjusted when necessary.

Another type of index is developed by the *link relative method*. In this we divide the demand in each month by the demand in the previous month and through these indices we "link" each month to the preceding one. An appropriate average of the link indices for corresponding months is then taken. An application of these indices is found when we wish to predict the daily demands likely to arise in the next week when we only know the actual demand which occurred on Monday of this week. Here, if we multiply the link index calculated for Tuesday by the demand on Monday, we will have an estimate of Tuesday's demand. This value multiplied by Wednesday's index will produce the estimate for Wednesday's demand, and so on.

Suppose that we have calculated the monthly seasonal indices. If we now go back through our original demand values and divide a monthly figure by the index for this month, the result will be the *deseasonalized demand* for this month. Doing this for every month will give us the complete picture of deseasonalized demand. This operation will not delete any trend movement which may be present.

When it comes to forecasting a seasonal demand, we start with a base forecast which will be our overall mean monthly demand or our extrapolated trend line depending on whether our demand does or does not have a trend. In either case, we will be able to produce an estimate for the base demand in each future month, and if we multiply these by their corresponding seasonal indices we will have the finished forecast.

If for some reason we want to actually see that portion of each month's demand which may be attributed to the seasonal movement, we can find these by subtracting the deseasonalized demand values from the original ones.

It cannot be overemphasized that our underlying assumption in preparing forecasts from a time series analysis of past demands is that this same demand process will continue in the same fashion into the future. As this is hardly ever the actual situation, we should use these forecasts as general guidelines to our subsequent decision-making, rather than follow them as pure truth.

When we suspect a seasonal or periodic movement present in a time series, a graphical display of the data may not immediately reveal to us the period of this movement—without this we cannot start to calculate seasonal indices. The correlation coefficient is a convenient tool which can be used here to help us select the proper period. To illustrate the steps, let us suppose that our time series has n values in it which are coded as follows:

$$X_1, X_2, X_3, X_4, X_5, \ldots, X_n$$

We are proposing that we calculate the correlation coefficient for the following bivariate data set:

$$(X_1, X_5), \ (X_2, X_6), \ (X_3, X_7), \ (X_4, X_8), \ldots, (X_{n-4}, X_n)$$

Here we have paired a value with a previous value which has occurred in the time series *four* periods earlier. The correlation coefficient we would thus calculate would be associated with a *period of 4*. We would then repeat this same procedure only now on a different pairing data set, say where X_1 and X_6 were paired up; this would provide us with a correlation coefficient associated with period 5. This would be repeated until we could no longer produce any more pairings. That period with the largest correlation coefficient would be our best estimate of the period of our seasonal (or periodic) movement.

This procedure is termed *autocorrelation* and is particularly useful in the analysis of forecast errors, lead time demands, or any other set of data which may have a dependence between the value of one variable and the value of some preceding one. This is a lengthy process if we are performing the calculations by hand, so we should do our best to start with a pretty good estimate of the period. Having this estimate we would calculate the correlation coefficient associated with it and then those for periods on either side of this one, and then make our final choice on the basis of the values we find for the r's.

The Analysis of Multivariate Data

Each observation of a multivariate data set gives the values of three or more distinct variables. Thus, "Department 34, Day Shift, Operator" might be an observation of a data set consisting of each employee's department, work shift, and job title.

Just as in the study of bivariate data, along with our describing each variable separately, our interest in multivariate data is mainly in the degree and the structural relationship existing between the variables involved. For example, we might be interested in determining how T, the time required for drilling holes in a machined part, relates to D, the density of the material of which the part is made, and to W, the depth of the hole to be drilled, and also to N, the number of separate holes to be drilled in the part. In this case the data set to collect and analyze would consist of observations (T, D, W, N).

Describing the nature of multivariate relationships is analogous to that which is done for bivariate data, that is, with equations such as this one: $T = a + bD + cW + dN$, which might be used for the hole-drilling example (the constants a, b, c, d, being determined from the data collected). To measure the degree of association, or the "goodness of fit" of a relationship formula to the data, we compute a *multiple correlation coefficient*, which is a natural extension of the linear correlation coefficient. Again, when our relationship formula is to be used to estimate one variable from given values of the others, we term it a *multiple regression equation*, and the general topic is *multiple regression analysis*.

It is also possible to set up *multiple frequency tables* for multivariate data sets, which is most often the way we proceed when one or more of the variables is qualitative. The construction of such tables merely requires that along with major categories we also create subcategories and list the observation frequencies in each cell thus defined. The example given in the first paragraph of this section may, for example, give us this table:

Sex	Department A		Department B		Row Totals
	Day Shift	Night Shift	Day Shift	Night Shift	
Male	10	5	20	10	45
Female	4	3	3	0	10
Column Subtotals	14	8	23	10	55
Column Totals	22		33		55

The approach to interpreting these (and their relative frequency counterparts) is the same as for joint frequency tables, but obviously such interpretation is more involved owing to the greater number of interactions to be considered.

The scope and complexities of multivariate analysis immediately suggest themselves, and for our purposes only certain basic concepts will be treated. Selecting those parts of the theory to be demonstrated was guided by their relative importance to the manager's needs. These will be illustrated for the case where just three variables are involved, for which the subscripted symbols X_1, X_2, and X_3 will be used.

The linear correlation coefficient plays a vital role in multivariate analysis; for the most part, multivariate coefficients and multiple regression equations may be determined from these measurements. For the linear correlation coefficient between X_1 and X_2, between X_1 and X_3, and between X_2 and X_3, we will use respectively the symbols r_{12}, r_{13}, and r_{23}. Again, a bar over the symbol will indicate its arithmetic average and s_1, s_2, s_3 will denote the three standard deviations.

The geometric extension of the line into three dimensions is the plane. The equation form for the line was $Y = A + BX$, and that for the plane is $X_1 = A + BX_2 + CX_3$. Our essential requirement being that each variable is included to its first power (not as X_2^3, or X_3^4, etc.), and there are no cross-product terms (such as $X_1 X_2$). The equation for the plane we have just given is set up so that X_2 and X_3 are the prior or independent variables, with X_1 as the predicted or dependent variable. The equations for the other planes we could consider are obvious.

To determine the constant terms of this plane equation we may use the following rules:

$$B = \frac{s_1 \cdot (r_{12} - r_{13}r_{23})}{s_2 \cdot (1 - r_{23}^2)}$$

$$C = \frac{s_1 \cdot (r_{13} - r_{12}r_{23})}{s_3 \cdot (1 - r_{23}^2)}$$

$$A = \bar{X}_1 - \bar{X}_2 B - \bar{X}_3 C$$

For this plane the *linear coefficient of multiple correlation* $R_{1(23)}$ measures the degree of association between X_1 and the *combined* effects of X_2 and X_3, as is expressed by the plane $X_1 = A + BX_2 + CX_3$. In the curve-fitting terminology, $R_{1(23)}$ measures the "goodness of fit" of this plane to the given data. We compute this coefficient as follows:

$$\boxed{\begin{array}{ll} \text{Linear Coefficient of} \\ \text{Multiple Correlation, } R_{1(23)} \end{array} = \sqrt{\dfrac{r_{12}{}^2 + r_{13}{}^2 - 2r_{12}r_{13}r_{23}}{(1 - r_{23}{}^2)}}}$$

This coefficient lies between 0.0 and 1.0, and the closer its value is to 1.0 (perfect linear correlation), the better the linear relationship between the variables; while the closer it is to 0.0 (no linear correlation), the poorer the linear relationship. We are stressing the "linear" aspects of correlation here as this is related to the plane equation describing the relationship, however, there are nonlinear equations which could be considered, and the nonlinear correlation is not being measured by $R_{1(23)}$. It is to be noted that even though one type of correlation does not exist between a set of variables, this does not say that the other type may not exist.

By interchanging the roles of the variables in our plane equation, and making the same interchanges of their subscripts in the cited formulas of computation, we are able to determine the other two planes as well as the coefficients $R_{2(13)}$, and $R_{3(12)}$.

The *coefficient of multiple determination*, $R_{1(23)}{}^2$ has the same interpretation in the multivariate situations as it does in the bivariate case, which is: the percent of variability in X_1 accounted for by the *combined* influence of X_2 and X_3.

Although X_1 is being related to the combined influence of the two variables X_2 and X_3, it is natural for us to inquire as to what proportion of this combined influence may be attributed to each variable separately. This is of particular interest when many independent variables are being considered and where circumstances require that we choose from these only the most critical. The *partial correlation coefficients* are used for this purpose. The partial correlation coefficient $r_{(12)3}$ measures the influence of X_2 on X_1 with the influence of X_3 on X_1 being held fixed. The coefficient $r_{(13)2}$ measures the influence of X_3 on X_1, but now holding X_2 fixed. To compute these two measures we have the following rules:

$$\boxed{\begin{array}{l} r_{(12)3} = \dfrac{r_{12} - r_{13}r_{23}}{\sqrt{(1 - r_{13}{}^2)(1 - r_{23}{}^2)}} \\[3ex] r_{(13)2} = \dfrac{r_{13} - r_{12}r_{23}}{\sqrt{(1 - r_{12}{}^2)\,(1 - r_{23}{}^2)}} \end{array}}$$

Looking at the first of these rules, let's suppose that X_3 is unrelated to X_1 and X_2. This will require that r_{13} and r_{23} are both 0. But, resulting from this we find that $r_{(12)3} = r_{12}$ which is the linear correlation coefficient between X_1 and X_2. This fact may often be of assistance when evaluating the dependency of one variable on a list of others.

The rule for computing $R_{1(23)}$ involves the coefficient r_{23}, which means that as part of our correlation of X_1 between X_2 and X_3 we have included the correlation between X_2 and X_3—that is, between the two prior variables themselves. Thus, for example, if X_1 is the number of hours required by a job coordinator to coordinate large construction jobs, X_2 is the estimated total cost of the job, and X_3 is the estimated number of days to do the job, then we might be interested in measuring the correlation between coordinating hours and total cost with the influence of length of job "taken out" of total cost. In symbols we want here the correlation between X_1 and X_2 with X_3 partialled out of X_2. This restricted correlation may be measured by the *part correlation coefficient* $r_{1(2/3)}$ given by

$$r_{1(2/3)} = \frac{r_{12} - r_{13}r_{23}}{\sqrt{1 - r_{23}^2}}$$

It is to be noted that $r_{1(2/3)} = \sqrt{(1 - r_{13}^2)} \cdot r_{(12)3}$, and also for the other case $r_{1(3/2)} = \sqrt{(1 - r_{12}^2)} \cdot r_{(13)2}$.

There are instances, usually due to the origins of the variables involved, where illegitimate or *spurious correlation* may arise. One type arises when X_1 is a total of other variables one of which is, say, X_2, which is being correlated to X_1. That is $X_1 = X_2 +$ other variables, and we compute r_{12}. The fact that we find a correlation between X_1 and X_2 is naturally due to the fact that X_1 "includes" X_2, so we are partly seeing the correlation of X_2 with itself. Another type of spurious correlation arises when we are correlating two (or more) indices each of which has a common variable denominator. For example, correlating X_1 and X_2 where X_1 is Y/X_3 and X_2 is Z/X_3 (Y and Z being other variables). Here again, we will have the correlation of $1/X_3$ to itself included in r_{12}.

Spurious correlation does not necessarily mean we have gained nothing. For example, in case of a very high correlation coefficient r_{12} in our total example above, regardless of the spurious correlation we would be justified in using X_2 in place of the total variable X_1 as a prior variable in some other regression problem. As long as one is aware of the spurious nature of his correlation and makes his subsequent evaluations accordingly, most problems can be controlled. It is the ignorance of this type of correlation which usually leads to the spurious decision.

CONCLUSION

This chapter has attempted to provide the reader with those tools for analyzing bivariate data sets which expose the dependency of the variables involved. The accompanying methods for testing the "significance" of this information have been referred to chapter 3, however, in any investigation the two work together as complements. Certain general concepts have been demonstrated from the area of analysis of multivariate data sets. Those topics actually discussed should enable the reader to follow and contribute to any study involving multiple regression analysis, regardless of the number of variables involved or the particular context.

REFERENCES

Acton, F. S. *Analysis of Straight-Line Data.* New York, N. Y.: John Wiley & Sons, Inc., 1959.

Freund, J. E., and F. J. Williams. *Modern Business Statistics.* Englewood Cliffs, N. J.: Prentice-Hall, Inc., 1958.

McNemar, Q. *Psychological Statistics.* New York, N. Y.: John Wiley & Sons, Inc., 1969.

Wallis, W.A.. and H.V. Roberts. *Statistics: A New Approach.* New York, N.Y.: The Free Press (Macmillan Co.), 1965.

3

Statistical Decision Making: How to Estimate and Test Hypotheses Based on Data Set Analyses

Perhaps the three most important uses for statistics in the general area of decision-oriented management are: (1) to extract the essential meaning of the information content of data; (2) to establish and measure the significance of relationships existing among variables affecting a problem or a situation; and, (3) to evaluate the risk involved in decisions due to the uncertainty (variability) inherent in the data bases used. In the previous chapters, descriptive measures and various analysis methods have been demonstrated and these provide us with the basic tools with which we perform these tasks.

So far in our presentation, we have applied our tools to data sets which are but relatively small parts of larger "wholes," and it is with these larger sets of "like" data wherein our true interest lies. Thus, although we calculate the average lead time as found in, say, fifty material orders, our interest is in the overall set of lead times and not just these fifty values. In other words, we are interested in gaining knowledge on the delivery *process,* and this we hope to get by making inferences based on what we find in the selected data set. How we can bridge this gap will be the subject of this present chapter, and there are two basic approaches we can follow depending upon whether or not we have any prior information regarding the process or phenomenon under investigation. Before we discuss these, the concepts of a *sample* and a *population* are needed.

Roughly speaking, a *population* is that collection of "objects" in which our true interest lies and which we would like to study in detail, whereas, a *sample* is a relatively small part of the population and is that set of "objects" we actually do study. Thus, any data set is a sample, while the larger whole from which it was somehow selected is the population.

At the start of any investigation, we almost always begin with a population of people or physical objects such as customers, employees, units of product, equipment, and so on. However, for analysis we must replace these populations of "objects" with ones consisting of observations of measurement or attribute, one value of which is associated with one person or object of the original population. As we measure the length or weight of an object, say from the population of production output of some item, we are making this object-to-number conversion. While we operate in the realm of numerical populations we always back-interpret our findings into the object populations.

Our first type of question arises in a situation where we have no prior information concerning a population and we are seeking numerical descriptions of its membership. This is the same type of question we posed for data sets in our previous chapters, where we asked for such things as the average value, a measure of variability, the degree of association between two distinct data sets, and so on. Here, however, we are posing the questions for the populations. The methods found in the theory of *statistical estimation* are those which are applied to answer these questions.

The second basic question we have is basically a true-false question. It arises when we have sufficient information concerning our population to form a hypothesis as to what we believe actually exists in the population. From a study of a sample drawn from this population we hope to uncover evidence which will be sufficient for us to either reject or accept this hypothesis. The methods of *statistical hypothesis testing* are those which are applicable here.

Statistical estimation and hypothesis testing together form what is termed the *theory of statistical inference*, which along with the methods of *descriptive statistics* (the subject of the previous chapters) represent a general classification of all statistical theory. It is to this general topic of statistical inference which we address ourselves in this present chapter.

The Normally Distributed Population

Although we usually have rather incomplete knowledge on a population, in order to legitimately apply certain techniques we will have to make some assumption concerning its basic nature. The assumption we have in mind is what the relative frequency distribution is which governs the occurrence of the distinct values in the population. The relative frequency table we construct from the sampled data set should give us some clues as to the nature of the population distribution, and in fact we can set up a hypothesis in this regard and test this with our sampled distribution.

By far the most convenient type of population we can work with is one which is distributed in accordance with the *normal distribution law,* or as more commonly stated, one which is *normally distributed.* The normal distribution law is essentially just a special type of frequency table and one which is completely specified by the mean value and standard deviation of the values being distributed. This theoretical distribution has a mathematical formula which can be used to calculate the relative frequency to be associated with each data value, however, we need not concern ourselves with this formula since for most practical purposes we always refer to a table of values of the normal distribution and not the mathematical equation.

Figure 3–1 shows a typical plot of a normal distribution with a population mean of M, and a population standard deviation S. The peak of the normal distribution curve is always located above the mean value, and the curve is symmetrical about a line erected vertically at this point. The points of inflection of the curve are located a standard deviation away on either side of the mean value. In this figure the horizontal axis is the scale on which the data values are located (that is, the population X values), while on the vertical axis are located the relative frequency values. Approximately 68 percent of the population values will fall between $M - S$ and $M + S$, 95 percent between $M - 2S$ and $M + 2S$, and 99 percent between $M - 3S$ and $M + 3S$. In the first case, with 68 percent between $M \pm S$, we will therefore have 32 percent of the X values falling outside of these boundaries, with 16 percent below $M - S$, and the other 16 percent above $M + S$. These statements hold true for any normal distribution.

For a different mean value the normal curve would have the exact same shape, but would be centered at a different location on the horizontal axis. However, keeping the same mean value but changing the standard deviation will produce a change in both the "peakedness" and "width" of the normal curve. A larger S value would give a "flatter and wider" curve, while a smaller S value would produce "sharper and thinner" curves. Naturally, as we change S we will change the relative frequencies associated with a particular X value, which does not happen with changes in just the mean value where we keep the same frequencies but change the X values with which these are associated.

As each different value of the mean, as well as the standard deviation, produces a different normal curve, then if the normal law is to be of any practical use to us we must have a means for identifying all distributions with just a single normal curve (or table). The device we use to accomplish this is the standardized, or z value which was first introduced in chapter 1.

Given a population with mean M, and standard deviation S, then the z value for any particular value, say X_0, is calculated as: $z_0 = (X_0 - M)/S$. This expresses X_0 as plus or minus some multiple of standard deviations from the mean value. There is only one normal table for a normally distributed population of z values, and by standardizing the values of X for an original population we can thus identify it with this table. Naturally, as we come back from the z values to the original population, we will find different X values for the same z value for populations with different mean values and standard deviations. The relative frequency which we located in our table to be associated with a given z value will in turn be associated with the original X value which produced this particular standardized value. This is the key in using the standardized normal distribution.

Figure 3–2 shows the normal curve shown in Figure 3–1, but now with z values in place of the X values. We note how the standardization process locates the curve over the 0, z value, and that both positive and negative values are involved. Furthermore, we see that the standard deviation of the z values is 1, and as just indicated the mean value of the X's goes into the 0, z value.

In the methods of estimation and hypothesis testing we are interested in cumulative relative frequencies associated with X values rather than the individual frequencies. That is, we are more interested in knowing with what relative frequency we can expect the population X values to exceed a particular value rather than the relative frequency with which we can expect to see this particular value. With this particular viewpoint in mind, the normal distribution is tabulated as shown in Table 3–1. Here, in the first column, we list selected z values of the normal distribution with additional digits of these listed across the top of the table as column headings. The numbers in the body of the table are the relative frequencies with which normally distributed z values will exceed those with which we enter the table.

For example, suppose that we have a normally distributed population with mean

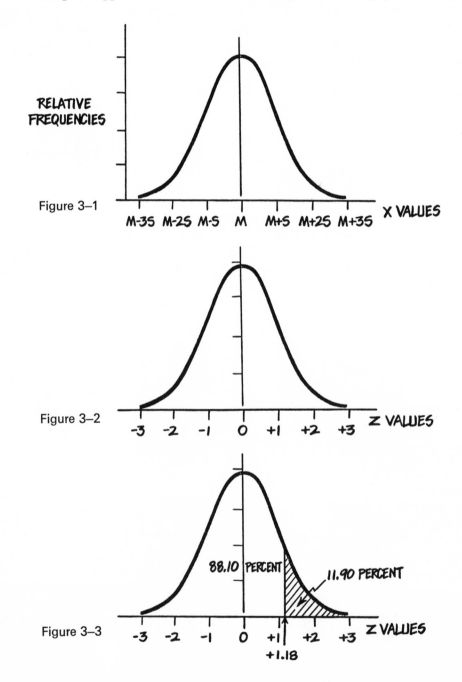

Figure 3–1

Figure 3–2

Figure 3–3

Normal Variable	0	1	2	3	4	5	6	7	8	9
0.0	.5000	.4960	.4920	.4880	.4840	.4801	.4761	.4721	.4681	.4641
0.1	.4602	.4562	.4522	.4483	.4443	.4404	.4364	.4325	.4286	.4247
0.2	.4207	.4168	.4129	.4090	.4052	.4013	.3974	.3936	.3897	.3859
0.3	.3821	.3783	.3745	.3707	.3669	.3632	.3594	.3557	.3520	.3483
0.4	.3446	.3409	.3372	.3336	.3300	.3264	.3228	.3192	.3156	.3121
0.5	.3085	.3050	.3015	.2981	.2946	.2912	.2877	.2843	.2810	.2776
0.6	.2743	.2709	.2676	.2643	.2611	.2578	.2546	.2514	.2483	.2451
0.7	.2420	.2389	.2358	.2327	.2296	.2266	.2236	.2206	.2177	.2148
0.8	.2119	.2090	.2061	.2033	.2005	.1977	.1949	.1922	.1894	.1867
0.9	.1841	.1814	.1788	.1762	.1736	.1711	.1685	.1660	.1635	.1611
1.0	.1587	.1562	.1539	.1515	.1492	.1469	.1446	.1423	.1401	.1379
1.1	.1357	.1335	.1314	.1292	.1271	.1251	.1230	.1210	.1190	.1170
1.2	.1151	.1131	.1112	.1093	.1075	.1056	.1038	.1020	.1003	.0985
1.3	.0968	.0951	.0934	.0918	.0901	.0885	.0869	.0853	.0838	.0823
1.4	.0808	.0793	.0778	.0764	.0749	.0735	.0721	.0708	.0694	.0681
1.5	.0668	.0655	.0643	.0630	.0618	.0606	.0594	.0582	.0571	.0559
1.6	.0548	.0537	.0526	.0516	.0505	.0495	.0485	.0475	.0465	.0455
1.7	.0446	.0436	.0427	.0418	.0409	.0401	.0392	.0384	.0375	.0367
1.8	.0359	.0351	.0344	.0336	.0329	.0322	.0314	.0307	.0301	.0294
1.9	.0287	.0281	.0274	.0268	.0262	.0256	.0250	.0244	.0239	.0233
2.0	.0228	.0222	.0217	.0212	.0207	.0202	.0197	.0192	.0188	.0183
2.1	.0179	.0174	.0170	.0166	.0162	.0158	.0154	.0150	.0146	.0143
2.2	.0139	.0136	.0132	.0129	.0125	.0122	.0119	.0116	.0113	.0110
2.3	.0107	.0104	.0102	.0099	.0096	.0094	.0091	.0089	.0087	.0084
2.4	.0082	.0080	.0078	.0075	.0073	.0071	.0069	.0068	.0066	.0064
2.5	.0062	.0060	.0059	.0057	.0055	.0054	.0052	.0051	.0049	.0048
2.6	.0047	.0045	.0044	.0043	.0041	.0040	.0039	.0038	.0037	.0036
2.7	.0045	.0034	.0033	.0032	.0031	.0030	.0029	.0028	.0027	.0026
2.8	.0026	.0025	.0024	.0023	.0023	.0022	.0021	.0021	.0020	.0019
2.9	.0019	.0018	.0018	.0017	.0016	.0016	.0015	.0015	.0014	.0014
3.0	.0013	.0013	.0013	.0012	.0012	.0011	.0011	.0011	.0010	.0010

Table 3–1. Relative Frequencies with Which a Given Standard Normal Variable Will Be Exceeded

value 20 and standard deviation 10. And, suppose further that we are interested in determining the relative frequency with which the X values of this population will exceed the value 31.8. First we calculate the z value for this value, which is: $(31.8 - 20)/10 = 1.18$. Entering Table 3–1 at the row "1.1" and reading across to the "8" column, we locate the figure 0.1190. This should be read as 11.90 percent. We interpret this as saying that 11.90 percent of the normally distributed z values will be *larger than* 1.18, but more importantly, that this percentage of the X values will be *larger than* 31.8. This situation is depicted in Figure 3–3.

Due to the symmetry of the normal distribution, Table 3–1 is used for both positive and negative z values. Thus, for a standardized z value of -1.18 we would say that 11.90 percent of the other z values will be *smaller than* this value. Back into the X population, this means that 11.90 percent of these values will be *smaller than:* $(-1.18)(10) + 20 = 8.2$, which is found from the rule: $X = z \cdot S + M$.

Combining our two results we can say that *between* -1.18 and $+1.18$ will fall $100.00 - 2(11.90) = 76.20$ percent of the z values, that is to say this percentage of the original X values will fall somewhere between 8.2 and 31.8.

These three uses of the normal distribution table illustrate the extent to which we will be using Table 3–1 in subsequent discussions.

The techniques presented in this chapter will be based on the assumption that the underlying population has a normal distribution. This is a major assumption and should be tested in any refined analysis. Often the particular entity we are working with will have a normal distribution governing its values under very mild conditions. However, in other situations the normal distribution is not legitimate and in these instances certain adjustment rules will be provided which when applied will make the normal distribution a very reasonable approximation to the true distribution involved.

Random Samples and Sampling Schemes

When a statistician says that his sample of n observations is *random,* or has been *randomly selected,* he does not mean that it has been haphazardly selected, but rather very precisely selected so that every possible combination of n observations in the population had the same chance of being the sample he actually drew. Thus, "random" is descriptive of the manner in which the sampled observations were drawn from the population and not of the actual observations themselves.

One immediately associates the ideas of a "fair" or "unbiased" representation of the population with the reason for randomizing a sample selection. These are certainly important and correct, but the fundamental reason for using random samples is that in statistical inferencing certain laws of probability will be applied which simply do not hold without the random quality in the data.

How do we select a random sample? To start we return to the object population in most cases. If the population is such that each of its members can be distinguished from every other member then one way to achieve randomness in a sample of size n would be to: assign a unique number to each object in the population; write these numbers on separate slips of paper; put these into a hat; and, withdraw n of them, thoroughly mixing the slips before we start and also before each subsequent drawing. Those objects which correspond to the selected numbers constitute the random sample, and the measurements or attributes we observe in these constitute our numerical sample (that is the data set).

After making the assignments of numbers to objects, we could, in place of the hat device, use the last three digits of telephone numbers in a county directory, selecting any n distinct numbers. The point here being that these digit triples are already randomized. Perhaps the easiest device to use, when one is available, is a *table of random numbers.* This is simply a table of numbers listed in one or more digits and which has been constructed so that whatever sequence of numbers we select from it, these will be randomly organized.

To assign numbers to objects it is not necessary that we can actually collect a population membership in front of us. It is on the conceptual level that we assign the code numbers. For example, tomorrow's scheduled lot of 5,000 subassemblies can be coded today with the use of the first five thousand integers. In another situation we might have 10 file cabinets each containing 4 drawers in each of which there are 100 folders and in each of these are 10 invoices. Our population would consist of $10 \times 4 \times 100 \times 10 = 40,000$ invoices. We could use the integers from 1 to 40,000 in this case or some scheme such as the following. Code each file cabinet with the integers 0 to 9, the drawers in each cabinet with the integers 1 to 4, the folders within each drawer with numbers 0 to 99, and each invoice within each folder with the code numbers 0 to 9. To select an invoice for our sample we would need a one-digit number, a number from 1 to 4, a two-digit number, and another one-digit number, each being randomly selected. These would respectively specify the cabinet, drawer, folder, and invoice within the folder to be selected.

There are various schemes we can follow in selecting a random sample which take advantage of the natural organization of the population members. It may happen that our population is in a "one-after-another" arrangement, such as the output of an assembly line, or records in a drawer, and we judge that the particular characteristic we are looking for does not depend on the position of the objects in this serial order. In other words, the objects are randomly arranged with respect to the characteristic of interest even though they are serially ordered as objects. In these circumstances *systematic sampling* is most useful. In this we randomly select the very first object to select, but from this point on we select, say, every twentieth object until we have the sample size we want.

The use of *stratified sampling* is appropriate in those instances where we know that the population is composed of distinguishable levels, or stratas, which can be accounted for as sampling is performed. This would be the case if our population consisted of maintenance craftsmen which fall into such stratas as painters, electricians, carpenters, machinists, and so on. Here we are basically subdividing the population into a number of distinct *subpopulations,* and in each of these we can perform random sampling on an individual basis. Normally, it is sound practice to allocate our sample requirements to the stratas in the same proportion as these are to the total population. Thus, for example, if the painters represent 10 percent of the craftsmen, we would select 10 percent of our sample from this strata, and so on for the other groups.

There will arise in practice those populations which cannot be conceptually listed. For example, the population of a certain species of fish in a lake, the population of cubic feet of air over the plant, and the patients suffering from the common cold who seek treatment from their doctors. There is no formal procedure to follow in these instances which will guarantee randomization, however, whatever method we choose it is important for us to build into it some form of "blindfolding."

Independent Samples

For certain problems we will have to select more than one sample in our study. These may be taken from the same population or entirely different ones. In such cases it is important that we select *independent samples,* which means that we select each sample with absolutely no reference to the make-up of any previous sample. Thus, for example, if in a sample from the population of plant employees we find that we have selected in our first sample predominantly males, then in the second sample we should not "force" our selection to increase the likelihood for selecting females. For, by so doing, we are producing a sample which will probably not represent the true composition of the employees. A reason for this type of sampling is that it helps eliminate personal bias, but again, there is a more basic reason which has to do with the probability laws underlying our subsequent inferences.

Finite and Infinite Populations

A question we must answer at the start of our investigations is whether our population is *finite* or *infinite* in size. This is a crucial question since it will determine which rules we should use in estimating methods.

If by repeatedly taking samples it is possible to exhaust the population, then we must consider it as finite in size, otherwise it is infinite. In a finite population, because a sample is a substantial part of it, we will produce a substantially different population once we take the first sample out. The subsequent samples will thus be taken from different populations and so are not on a comparable basis. A correction factor is introduced into our methods to account for this situation.

Let us suppose that our population is definitely finite, but as we select an object from it we measure or classify its characteristic of interest and then replace it back into the population before we make the next selection. This type of selection is termed *sampling with replacements*. Following this procedure we can select any number of samples, of any size we want, without ever exhausting the population, and so for all practical purposes we can view this population as being infinite. Naturally, before we follow this type of sampling, we must decide whether or not we would want to allow the same object to appear more than once in our sample, since this is a definite possibility. Although working with infinite populations is preferable, the necessary correction factor is not so difficult to calculate and use to cause us to ignore the distinction.

Parameters and Statistics

In our previous chapters the descriptive measures introduced were applied to samples, and our interest was in such things as averages, standard deviations, coefficients of correlation, and so on. In each case there was a definite rule of procedure to follow in the calculation of the measure. We refer to these descriptive measures as *statistics* when they apply to the sample, and as *parameters* when they apply to the population. In general we will not calculate a parameter with any set rule since we will rarely have the total population of numbers to process through it. This is where the methods of estimating come in and through the use of these we *postulate* the value of a parameter based on the sample values of certain statistics.

It is convenient to have unique symbols to distinguish between a statistic and a parameter, and it is customary to use lower-case Greek letters to represent the latter. The standard symbols used here are the following:

Descriptive Measures	Symbol for the Statistic	Symbol for the Parameter	Name
Mean Value	$\bar{X}$	μ	mu
Standard Deviation	s	σ	sigma
Proportion	p	π	pi
Linear Correlation Coefficient	r	ρ	rho

Sampling Distributions

The most important concept in the theory of statistical inferencing is that of the *sampling distribution of a statistic.* We have one of these for the mean value statistic, another for the standard deviation statistic, and in fact we have one for each statistic whose corresponding parameter we can estimate. The underlying theory of sampling distributions involves a high level of mathematics and it is not necessary to know anything about these to be able to apply the rules. However, with a basic understanding of sampling distributions one will be in a better position to more fully understand what is actually happening when applying the procedures and for this reason a brief sketch of the theory will be given.

The trick we use in developing a sampling distribution is to assume we completely know the population from which we will be taking samples. Knowing this and setting our sample size at *n* observations, we construct all the different samples of size *n* which we could in fact obtain from this known population. In the case of the *sampling distribution of the mean,* our next step is to calculate the mean value for each sample we have constructed and we view this collection of sample means as a new, *derived population* which is the sampling distribution of the mean for samples of size *n*. Thus, the sampling distribution of the mean is just another population but whose members are means, including all the means that we could possibly get from the original population using samples of size *n*.

To illustrate, suppose that we have a population with members 1, 2, 3, 4, and 5. The mean and standard deviation of this population (which would be calculated according to the rules of chapter 1) are: $\mu = 3.0$, and $\sigma = \sqrt{2.0}$ respectively. We should note that in calculating this standard deviation, even though we have but five figures, we do not use the corrected rule where we would divide by 4, but instead we divide by 5. We do this since we are working with the population and not a sample from it.

Next we construct all the *different* samples of, say, size 2, that we could draw from this population. Figure 3–4 presents a logical development of these samples. There are twenty-five samples and for each the arithmetic average has been calculated and these are also shown in the figure; these are the *sample means*. Now we view these twenty-five sample means as members of a derived population, the *sampling distribution of the mean* for this population and *using samples of size two.*

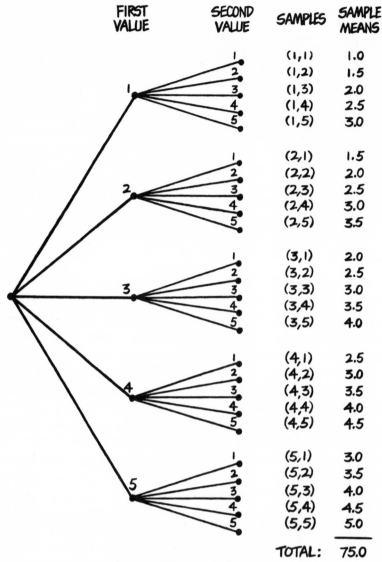

FIRST VALUE	SECOND VALUE	SAMPLES	SAMPLE MEANS
1	1	(1,1)	1.0
	2	(1,2)	1.5
	3	(1,3)	2.0
	4	(1,4)	2.5
	5	(1,5)	3.0
2	1	(2,1)	1.5
	2	(2,2)	2.0
	3	(2,3)	2.5
	4	(2,4)	3.0
	5	(2,5)	3.5
3	1	(3,1)	2.0
	2	(3,2)	2.5
	3	(3,3)	3.0
	4	(3,4)	3.5
	5	(3,5)	4.0
4	1	(4,1)	2.5
	2	(4,2)	3.0
	3	(4,3)	3.5
	4	(4,4)	4.0
	5	(4,5)	4.5
5	1	(5,1)	3.0
	2	(5,2)	3.5
	3	(5,3)	4.0
	4	(5,4)	4.5
	5	(5,5)	5.0
		TOTAL:	75.0

Figure 3–4

Since the sampling distribution is a population we can calculate its mean value and standard deviation, again with the usual rules, and again without the correction in calculating the latter measure. These values for our example would be found to be respectively: $\mu_{\bar{x}} = 3.0$ and $\sigma_{\bar{x}} = 1.0$. Here we use the symbol $\mu_{\bar{x}}$ to represent the mean value of the sampling distribution of the mean and $\sigma_{\bar{x}}$ to stand for the standard deviation (the "$\bar{X}$" is used to signify that we are referring to the distribution of the "mean").

Let us compare the mean value of the original, parent population with that of the sampling distribution. We see that, in symbols, $\mu = \mu_{\bar{x}}$. Or, in words, *the mean of the sampling distribution of the mean is equal to the mean of the original population.*

Next let us look at the two standard deviations. Here we find that we have $\sigma_{\bar{x}} =$

$\sigma/\sqrt{n}$. Or, in words, *the standard deviation of the sampling distribution of the mean is equal to the standard deviation of the original population divided by the square root of the sample size used.*

These two results are not merely coincidental, but rather the general relationships which exist between the orginal and derived populations. However, in order for us to take them as true, we must be selecting *random samples* from an *infinite population*. They hold for our example's population since we were obviously sampling with replacements (which is why the sample (1,1) was allowed), which means that this population of five elements could be viewed as infinite. While we can in fact correct for the finiteness of a population, we cannot assume these relationships if random samples are not taken.

It is also true that the sampling distribution of the mean is approximately normally distributed, where the approximation becomes increasingly more accurate as the sample size, *n*, gets larger. Thus, in summary we have:

For Sample Distribution of the Mean
for an Infinite Population

---

1. $\mu_{\bar{x}} = \mu$

2. $\sigma_{\bar{x}} = \dfrac{\sigma}{\sqrt{n}}$

3. The sampling distribution of the mean is approximately normally distributed with mean $\mu_{\bar{x}}$ and standard deviation $\sigma_{\bar{x}}$

In the analysis of a problem it is very important that we know whether we are talking about an original population or a sampling distribution derived from this. Perhaps the most important difference is in the variability which is present in each. From Statement 2 above, we see that the standard deviation of the sampling distribution will be less than that for the original population—by a factor of $1/\sqrt{n}$. An illustration of where this difference has practical significance is the following.

A company synthesizes a granular material which it sells to chemical companies. This material is automatically filled into containers which are claimed to have 200 ounces per container. The filling machine used has a range of possible fill weights to which it may be set, and once set, the actual fill weights produced will be distributed normally with mean value equal to the setting and a constant standard deviation of 4 ounces. In this situation our original "object" population consists of all containers filled on this machine at a particular setting, whereas our numerical population is comprised of the actual weights of these containers. The mean value of this latter population is $\mu =$ *fill-weight setting,* and the standard deviation $\sigma = 4$ ounces.

There are two "types" of customers which buy this material, and these are distinguished by the way in which they test a delivery lot of containers for its acceptability. The first type randomly selects *one* container from the lot, weighs its contents, and accepts the entire lot if this value is 200 ounces or more; otherwise it refuses delivery. The second type of customer randomly selects *nine* containers, weighs the contents of each, and accepts the lot only if the average of these nine weights is 200 ounces or more. We thus see that the first type of customer is sampling from the original population of fill-weights, whereas the second type of customer is sampling from the sampling distribution of the mean derived from this original population using a sample size of $n = 9$.

Our question is: Could a different fill-weight setting be used for the two types of customers if for each we only want to run a 10 percent risk of having a delivery lot ever refused?

First we ask: What is the standardized normal value which will have 10 percent of the other values falling below it? To find this particular value we look in Table 3–1, looking in the body of the table for the value 0.1000, and we find as our closest value to this 0.1003 corresponding to the z value of 1.28. This says that approximately 10 percent of the other z values will fall above 1.28, which means, due to the symmetrical nature of the normal distribution, that 10 percent of the values will fall below $z = -1.28$. We must therefore identify the 200-ounce value with this particular z value to maintain the desired risk level; we do this since this is the value against which both customers are testing.

The first type of customer samples from our original population of fill-weights and so the mean of the population he works with is μ and its standard deviation is 4 ounces, thus the standardized value of 200 ounces in this population would be: $(200 - \mu)/4$. We want this to be equal to -1.28, which gives us the equation:

$$\frac{200 - \mu}{4} = -1.28$$

The value of μ which makes this equation a true statement is $\mu = 205.12$ ounces, and this is the machine setting we must use to achieve the desired level of risk with deliveries going to the first type of customer.

The second type of customer selects samples of nine container weights and so he is working with the sampling distribution of the mean of sample size 9; the mean of this population is thus $\mu_{\bar{x}}$ (the as yet unknown machine setting) and its standard deviation is $\sigma_{\bar{x}} = \sigma/\sqrt{n} = 4/\sqrt{9} = 4/3$ ounces. The equation we have for this case is the following:

$$\frac{200 - \mu_{\bar{x}}}{(4/3)} = -1.28$$

which has the solution $\mu_{\bar{x}} = 201.71$ ounces. This machine setting would deliver the same 10 percent risk of refusal when dealing with the second type of customer.

Both machine settings will produce a population of fill weights whose central tendency is a value over the 200-ounce container claim, thus both would be aimed at meeting the claim. However, there is a difference of 3.41 ounces between the two settings which indicates the amount of overage we will *tend* to put into containers for the first type of customer as compared to that for the second type to meet the same 10 percent risk of refusal. Depending upon the value of this material as opposed to such costs as machine resetting, scheduling two types of production runs, attendant paperwork, etc., it may or may not be economically advantageous to use the two settings. Certainly, in some situations, the gains being illustrated by this example will be definitely to our advantage.

Sampling Distribution of the Proportion

An extremely common situation in manufacturing, especially in quality control, is where we are working with qualitative data which has a dichotomous classification. For example, each object may be classified as *defective* or *nondefective* according to some measurable attribute. The usual procedure is to select a random sample of the "objects," say, n of them, and count the number of defective units, X, in this sample. The most commonly used statistic is the *proportion* of defective units in the sample, which is $p = (X/n)$. Naturally, we are interested in the proportion, π, of defective units in the total population of objects from which this sample was taken.

A *sampling distribution of the proportion*, based on a specific sample size n, can be derived from the original population of objects. The mean value of this derived distribution, μ_p, and its standard deviation, σ_p, are also related to these parameters for the original population. The rules are:

For Sample Distribution of the
Proportion for an Infinite Population

---

1. $\mu_p = \pi$

2.* $\sigma_p = \dfrac{\sqrt{\pi(1-\pi)}}{\sqrt{n}}$

3. The sampling distribution of the proportion is approximately normally distributed with mean μ_p and standard deviation σ_p

---

*The standard deviation parameter of the parent population is $\sqrt{\pi(1-\pi)}$.

Again random sampling is required. A *sufficient condition* for expecting a good approximation by the normal distribution is that both $n\pi$ and $n(1-\pi)$ be something larger than 5. This is not a *necessary condition* since good approximations are realized without its holding. In general, a value of π between 0.3 and 0.7, with n at least as great as 30 is indicative of a good approximation.

To summarize a bit, the sampling distribution of the proportion is a population of proportions calculated from samples of size n. The average value of all these proportions is μ_p, and the standard deviation of this population of proportions is σ_p. A sample proportion is in effect drawn from this distribution.

In the analysis of a problem we will again be using z values, now based on proportion values, taken from Table 3–1. In calculating these standardized values there is a refinement which, while not entirely necessary for practical results, should be included for more precise answers. We simply add or subtract the quantity $(1/2n)$ to the proportion value we are standardizing, and which operation we perform depends on which type of relative frequency we are looking for. If we are calculating the z value of a proportion p to find with what frequency other z values will exceed p, then we should use the formula:

$$z = \frac{p - (1/2n) - \mu_p}{\sigma_p}$$

While, if we are looking for the frequency of z values falling below p, we should use the refined formula:

$$z = \frac{p + (1/2_n) - \mu_p}{\sigma_p}$$

To illustrate the use of this sampling distribution, let us suppose that it has been found that 3 percent of the tools produced by a certain machine are defective. A customer order of 400 of these tools has just been finished and we ask: What is the level of risk associated with finding 16 or more defective units in this lot?

As far as the original population is concerned, that is, the one consisting of all this type of tool produced on this machine, we have $\pi = 0.03$, and so it follows: $\sqrt{\pi(1 - \pi)} = 0.1706$.

For the sampling distribution of the proportion, of sample size $n = 400$, we have: $\mu_p = 0.03$, and $\sigma_p = 0.1706/\sqrt{400} = 0.00853$.

Regarding the sample we have the correction factor $(1/2n) = 0.00125$, and since both $n\pi = 12$, and $n(1 - \pi) = 388$ are greater than 5, we can expect a good approximation with the normal distribution. Furthermore, the sample proportion we are testing our risk level against is: $p = 16/400 = 0.04$.

Our first step is to standardize this p value using the parameters of the sampling distribution and the correction factor (subtracting this since we are interested in the relative frequency with which we will exceed p). The calculation is:

$$z = \frac{p - (1/2n) - \mu_p}{\sigma_p} = \frac{0.04 - 0.00125 - 0.03}{0.00853} = 1.02$$

Using this z value we find in Table 3–1 the corresponding relative frequency value of 0.1539, or 15.39 percent. Thus, there are roughly 15 chances in 100 that a randomly selected sample of 400 tools will have 16 or more defective units.

More definite information will be added to our analysis if we vary our question a little. For example, if we asked for the risk level associated with finding 20 or more defective tools in this order we would find the odds to be roughly 1 chance in 100 (the z value found would be 2.20). Combining both results we could say that while it is likely to find 16 or more defective tools, it is rather unlikely that we will find 20 or more. In most instances of this type we would perform a 100 percent inspection on our customer orders. By knowing how many defective units we can expect to find, we would know how many "extra" units to make so that an additional run would not be necessary to produce the replacements. Of course, we would most likely look at the balancing of the cost of this small extra run against that of carrying a possible inventory of tools which may develop due to our actually finding less defective units than expected.

Sampling Distribution of the Difference of Means

A manufacturing problem which frequently arises is that of comparing two different methods for doing the same job, or testing conditions "before" and then "after" some change has been installed into an operation. For these problems the *sampling distribution of the difference of means* might be useful. Of course, it will be useful only when our comparisons are being made on the respective mean values of the two situations.

How is this distribution constructed? Essentially it is constructed just as with that of the sampling distribution of the mean. We imagine we know both populations, selecting samples of size n_1 from the "first" and of size n_2 from the "second"; we calculate the mean values for all such samples and record the difference between these means for every possible combination of samples.

We will have two distinct sampling distributions of the mean. One will be derived from our "first" population and will have mean value $\mu_{\bar{x}1}$ and standard deviation $\sigma_{\bar{x}1}$, and the second, derived from our "second" population, will have mean and standard deviation $\mu_{\bar{x}2}$ and $\sigma_{\bar{x}2}$. The sampling distribution of the difference of means will be derived from these two mean distributions and it will have a mean value μ_d and a standard deviation σ_d.

If we let μ_1 and μ_2, and σ_1 and σ_2 denote the mean values and standard deviations of the two original populations (say the "before" and "after" populations), then the relationships we have among all these parameters are:

For Sample Distribution of the
Difference of Means for an Infinite Population

---

1. $\mu_d = \mu_{\bar{x}1} - \mu_{\bar{x}2} = \mu_1 - \mu_2$

2. $\sigma_d = \sqrt{(\sigma_{\bar{x}_1})^2 + (\sigma_{\bar{x}_2})^2} = \sqrt{\dfrac{(\sigma_1)^2}{n_1} + \dfrac{(\sigma_2)^2}{n_2}}$

3. The sampling distribution of the difference of means is approximately normally distributed with mean μ_d and standard deviation σ_d

---

In these, Statement 2 might appear rather involved and its meaning perhaps hidden. The arithmetic is in fact straightforward (requiring us to square each mean distribution standard deviation, add these, and take the square root of the result). To assist in understanding the logic behind the rule, let us recall our previous treatment of the sum of two independent variables (chapters 1 and 2). We have previously said that if $T = X + Y$, and X and Y are independent variables, then the variance of T is equal to the sum of the variances of X and Y. This statement is also true for the difference of two independent variables, that is, for the variable $T = X - Y$. In our present situation we are working with a variable $d = \bar{X}_1 - \bar{X}_2$ and applying what we have just said, the variance of d is equal to the variance of $\bar{X}_1$ plus that of $\bar{X}_2$. This is Statement 2, only in words.

To illustrate the rules, let us suppose that a certain component, call it Component A, of a piece of equipment has a mean lifetime of 500 hours with a standard deviation of lifetime of 50 hours. Component B, which is a substitute for this component, has a mean lifetime of 600 hours with a standard deviation of 75 hours. These are the parameter values (μ_1, σ_1 and μ_2, σ_2) for our two parent populations. As part of their promotion program the manufacturer of Component B claims to have tested 125 components of each type, randomly selected from distributor shelves, and has found that their unit had a mean lifetime of 120 hours or more longer than did Component A. Our question is: What are the odds for finding these results?

For the sampling distribution of the mean derived with sample size $n_A = 125$ from the Component A population we will have a mean value of $\mu_{\bar{x}_A} = 500$ hours and a standard deviation $\sigma_{\bar{x}_A} = 50/\sqrt{125}$ hours. For the mean distribution for Component B with sample size $n_B = 125$ we will have $\mu_{\bar{x}_B} = 600$ hours, and $\sigma_{\bar{x}_B} = 75/\sqrt{125}$ hours. From these values, and Statements 1 and 2 above, we calculate the following mean value and standard deviation for the sampling distribution of the difference of means:

$$\mu_d = \mu_{\bar{x}_B} - \mu_{\bar{x}_A} = 600 - 500 = 100 \text{ hours}$$

$$\sigma_d = \sqrt{(\sigma_{\bar{x}_B})^2 + (\sigma_{\bar{x}_A})^2} = \sqrt{\frac{(75)^2}{125} + \frac{(50)^2}{125}} = 8 \text{ hours}$$

We are testing the difference value $d = 120$ hours and asking for the relative frequency with which we can expect to find a randomly selected value from the difference sampling distribution equal to or greater than this value. With the normal distribution approximation our first job is to standardize this value against the mean value $\mu_d = 100$ hours, and the standard deviation value $\sigma_d = 8$ hours. The resulting z value is: $(120 - 100)/8 = 2.50$.

Entering Table 3–1 with this value, we find that the relative frequency with which we can expect z values to exceed this particular value is 0.0062, or something less than 7 chances in 1,000. These are also the odds for finding the results which the manufacturer of Component B claims to have found, and odds which would most likely lead us to reject their claim, or else conclude that they realized a truly rare event.

If the manufacturer had claimed a difference of lifetime of 100 hours or more, we would have found the odds for this event to be 50:50—a claim we would probably accept as possible.

Standard Errors

The standard deviation of a sampling distribution of some statistic is usually called the *standard error* of the statistic. This name has been given to this parameter due to the role it plays in statistical inferencing, where it is used as the expected amount of error we will make in using a sample statistic to estimate the corresponding population parameter. In the last three sections we have seen how the mean of the sampling distribution and the standard error can be used to formalize "what to expect" in random samples. Either before or after the fact, we can use this information to evaluate "what we actually found" in a sample. If the normal distribution is applicable, then our evaluations would be developed just as before for mean values, proportions, and differences of mean values. We start by calculating, from what is given, the mean of the sampling distribution we are interested in (which in most cases is just the value of the corresponding parameter of the parent population), and also the standard error. With appropriate standardization, and Table 3–1, we find the relative frequency (which is also viewed as a level of risk or a probability) with which the event we are testing for can be expected to occur in our random sample.

In this analysis we need the relationships which hold for the sampling distribution and for the more common types these are shown in Table 3–2. Also in this table are shown the restrictions on when the relationships hold and conditions under which the sampling distribution is approximately normal—underlying these are again the assumptions of random sampling and an infinite population; or, sampling from a finite population with replacements.

To illustrate, let us suppose that the standard deviation of the diameters of a very large historical population of a certain fabricated part is 0.0500 inches. Manufacturing lots of 200 parts each are run for economy reasons (these are thus the samples in the problem) and for control purposes the standard deviations of the diameters of each lot are computed. What percentage of the lots can be expected to have a standard deviation of between 0.0501 inches and 0.0503 inches?

From Table 3–2 we calculate that the mean and standard error of the sampling distribution from which the *lot-standard deviations* are in effect drawn are respectively,

Sampling Distribution of the	Mean Value of Sampling Distribution	Standard Deviation of Sampling Distribution	Restrictions on Underlying Parent Population	Conditions for Approximately Normal Sampling Distribution
Means	$\mu_{\bar{x}} = \mu$	$\sigma_{\bar{x}} = \dfrac{\sigma}{\sqrt{n}}$	for all populations	$n \geq 30$
Proportions	$\mu_p = \pi$	$\sigma_p = \dfrac{\sqrt{\pi(1-\pi)}}{\sqrt{n}}$	for all populations	$n \geq 30$
Variance	$\mu_{s^2} = \sigma^2\left(\dfrac{n-1}{n}\right)$	$\sigma_{s^2} = \dfrac{\sigma^2}{\sqrt{n/2}}$	only if a normal population	$n \geq 100$
Standard Deviation	$\mu_s = \sigma$	$\sigma_s = \dfrac{\sigma}{\sqrt{2n}}$	only if a normal population	$n \geq 100$
Median	$\mu_{med} = \mu$	$\sigma_{med} = \dfrac{1.2533\sigma}{\sqrt{n}}$	only if a normal population	$n \geq 30$
First and Third Quartiles	μ_{Q_1} and μ_{Q_2} equal to pop'n 1st and 3rd quartiles	$\sigma_{Q_1} = \sigma_{Q_2}$ $= \dfrac{1.3626\sigma}{\sqrt{n}}$	only if a normal population	$n \geq 30$
Coefficient of Variation	$\mu_V = v = \dfrac{\mu}{\sigma}$	$\sigma_V = \sqrt{\dfrac{v^2 + 2v^4}{2n}}$	only if a normal population	$n \geq 100$
Coefficient of Correlation	$\mu_r = \rho$	$\sigma_r = \dfrac{1 - \rho^2}{\sqrt{n}}$	only if a normal population	$n \geq 30$

Table 3–2 Standard Deviation

$\mu_s = \sigma = 0.0500$ inches, and $\sigma_s = \sigma/\sqrt{2n} = 0.0500/\sqrt{400} = 0.0025$ inches. The z value corresponding to 0.0501 inches is $(0.0501 - 0.0500)/0.0025 = 0.04$, and that corresponding to 0.0503 inches is $(0.0503 - 0.0500)/0.0025 = 0.12$.

Consulting Table 3–1, entering with the z value 0.04, we find the percentage 48.40 percent. This percent of our lots will have a standard deviation greater than 0.0501 inches. Now entering Table 3–1 with the z value 0.12, we find the percentage value 45.22 percent. This percent of our lots will have a standard deviation greater than 0.0503 inches. The difference between these two percentages, that is, $48.40 - 45.22 = 3.18$ percent, will be the percent of our manufactured lots whose standard deviations will be some value between 0.0501 and 0.0503 inches, which is the figure asked for in the problem.

Adjusting Standard Errors for Finite Populations

The size of the population, N, from which we are sampling also has an effect on the standard error of a derived population. For large populations this effect is slight, and it is zero for truly infinite populations. In those situations where we must view our parent population as finite, we should multiply the standard error as would be calculated with our previously given rules by the *finite population correction factor*. For a population of size N and sample size n this factor is calculated as follows:

$$\frac{\text{Finite Population}}{\text{Correction Factor}} = \sqrt{\frac{N - n}{N - 1}}$$

As an approximation to this factor we can use: $1 - (n/2N)$.

Thus, the adjusted rules for calculating the standard error of the mean, the proportion, and the difference of means are as follows:

Standard Errors for a Finite Parent Population
Standard Error of Mean $\sigma_{\bar{x}} = \dfrac{\sigma}{\sqrt{n}} \sqrt{\dfrac{(N - n)}{(N - 1)}}$
Standard Error of Proportion $\sigma_p = \dfrac{\sqrt{\pi(1 - \pi)}}{\sqrt{n}} \sqrt{\dfrac{(N - n)}{(N - 1)}}$
Standard Error of Difference of Means $\sigma_d = \sqrt{\dfrac{(\sigma_1)^2}{n_1} + \dfrac{(\sigma_2)^2}{n_2}} \sqrt{\dfrac{(N - n)}{(N - 1)}}$

As an illustration of the calculations involved in the use of these rules, as well as a case where intuition can incorrectly guide us, let us consider the following example. It has been established practice to produce a certain item in batches of 5,000 units each, and to select a random sample of 100 of these for quality control testing. A batch size of 25,000 units is now used and our immediate question is: If the underlying process which produces the characteristic which quality control tests does not change with increased batch size, then what should our new sample size be in order to maintain the previous standard error? As the batch size increases fivefold should the new sample be 500 items?

In this problem we have not specified whether quality control calculates a mean value from the sample or a proportion of the items in some category. Also the standard deviation of the population has not been given, we just know that it will remain the same for both batch sizes. It turns out that none of this information is actually needed to solve the problem, and so in the computation we will use the symbol S which may represent either σ or $\sqrt{\pi(1-\pi)}$ whichever the case may be.

The 5,000 items comprising the old batch size is a finite population, and with sample size 100 the (corrected) standard error associated with either the sampling distribution of means or of proportions is:

$$\sqrt{(5,000 - 100)/(5,000 - 1)} \cdot S/\sqrt{100} = \sqrt{0.00980} \cdot S$$

And for the population of 25,000 items, with sample size n (as yet undetermined) we associate a sampling distribution with (corrected) standard error of:

$$\sqrt{(25,000 - n)/(24,999)} \cdot S/\sqrt{n}$$

The problem requires that we find the value of n which makes these two standard errors equal. Since S is the same in both expressions, it may be cancelled out, and setting the two resulting expressions equal to each other produces this equation:

$$\sqrt{0.00980} = \sqrt{\frac{25,000 - n}{24,999}} \cdot \frac{1}{\sqrt{n}}$$

If two expressions are equal, then their squares will also be equal, thus, if we square both sides of this last equation (to rid ourselves of the square roots) we will not disturb the equality between the expressions. Doing this will produce the following equation:

$$0.00980 = \frac{25,000 - n}{(24,999)n}$$

If we multiply both sides of this last equation by the quantity $(24,999)n$, cancel like terms in the numerator and denominator, and collect all terms involving n to the left-hand side of the equation, and then solve the resulting expression for n, we would find: $n = 25,000/245.99 = 102$ (which has been rounded-up from 101.6). This is our new sample size.

This result is certainly unexpected, and it says that even though our population size has increased fivefold, we need but add two more items to our regular sample size to achieve the same standard error as before. Without going through the arithmetic as we did, a much larger sample might have been prescribed on just intuition alone—leading to unnecessary testing costs, time delays, etc.

Point Estimates of Population Parameters

Up to this point we have been assuming that we begin our analysis with the values of all population parameters required to solve the problem. Normally, such values are taken from some prior study or from a direct calculation involving a very large number of population values. Very often, however, we will not have this prior knowledge, and it is either impractical or impossible to calculate the parameters using the total population, or even a fairly large portion of it. What we do in these situations is to sample the population, calculate the statistic from the sample, and by some means use this value to *estimate* the value of the population parameter. So that we are able to distinguish between the actual value of a parameter and our estimated value we use as the symbol for the estimate the usual parameter symbol but with the mark "$\wedge$" (referred to as a "caret") over it. Thus, for example, the symbol for an estimate of the population mean value would have the symbol $\hat{\mu}$, and for the standard deviation parameter we would use $\hat{\sigma}$, and so on.

When we use a *single number,* such as a sample mean value, to serve as the estimate for the parameter we refer to this as a *point estimate.* There is another device we can use to formalize our estimates, so-called *interval estimates,* and these will be covered in the next section.

In general, when working with a large sample randomly selected from the population, the particular parameter we are estimating can be taken as being equal to the corresponding statistic we calculate from the sample. This would hold for mean values, correlation coefficients, slopes of regression lines, medians, quartiles, and so on. There are, however, certain statistics which if used directly will not produce the "best" estimate for the population parameter. For example, the variance, standard deviation, and range will all tend to be smaller than the corresponding population parameters. These are called *biased estimates.* To correct for this bias we multiply our calculated statistics by a correction factor which involves the sample size value. In those cases where we are working with a finite population, the variance and standard deviation statistic should also be multiplied by another correction factor to give the most refined estimate.

If we have drawn a single random sample, and calculated its sample mean value, $\bar{X}$, then this is our "best" estimate of the population mean μ. If instead, we have drawn, say, three independent random samples from the population, of sizes n_1, n_2, n_3 and found their respective samples means to be $\bar{X}_1$, $\bar{X}_2$, $\bar{X}_3$, then our "best" estimate of the population mean is the weighted average of these three sample means, using as weights the individual sample sizes. In symbols we have:

Estimates for Population Mean for Either Finite or Infinite Populations
Sample Mean, $\bar{X} = \dfrac{\sum X}{n}$
Estimated Population Mean, $\hat{\mu} = \bar{X}$ (for single sample)
Estimated Population Mean, (for three independent samples)* $\hat{\mu} = \dfrac{n_1\bar{X}_1 + n_2\bar{X}_2 + n_3\bar{X}_3}{n_1 + n_2 + n_3}$

* The natural extension for an arbitrary number of independent samples is evident.

If from our single sample, drawn from an infinite population, we calculate the sample variance, symbol s^2, then to correct for the bias our "best" estimate of the population variance should be $s^2 \cdot n/(n-1)$, with the estimated standard deviation being the positive square root of this. If we are working with a finite population, of size N, then we should also multiply the variance estimate by the factor $(N-1)/N$. If we have drawn, say, three independent random samples from the population, of sizes n_1, n_2, n_3 and found their respective variances to be s_1^2, s_2^2, s_3^2 then our "best" estimate for the population variance is the weighted average of these three values, where we use the sample sizes as the weights, but as the denominator in this calculation we use *three less* than the sum of the weights. In symbols we have:

Estimates of Population Variance and Standard Deviation	
Sample Variance, s^2	$= \dfrac{n\sum X^2 - (\sum X)^2}{n^2}$
Sample Standard Deviation, s	$= \sqrt{s^2}$
Estimated Population Standard Deviation, $\hat{\sigma}$ (single sample, infinite population)	$= s\sqrt{\dfrac{n}{n-1}}$
Estimated Population Standard Deviation, $\hat{\sigma}$ (single sample, finite population)	$= s\sqrt{\dfrac{n}{n-1}}\sqrt{\dfrac{N-1}{N}}$
Estimated Population Standard Deviation, $\hat{\sigma}$ (3 independent samples, infinite population)*	$= \sqrt{\dfrac{n_1 s_1^2 + n_2 s_2^2 + n_3 s_3^2}{n_1 + n_2 + n_3 - 3}}$
Estimated Population Standard Deviation, $\hat{\sigma}$ (3 independent samples, finite population)*	$= \sqrt{\dfrac{n_1 s_1^2 + n_2 s_2^2 + n_3 s_3^2}{n_1 + n_2 + n_3 - 3}}\sqrt{\dfrac{N-1}{N}}$

* For k independent samples we replace the "3" with "k," and make the obvious extension of the formula.

The last two rules involved the so-called *pooled variance*. This same rule should also be used when the samples come from populations with the same variance (parameter) but different mean values (also parameters). In this situation if we combined all data and then calculated the overall variance from this one data set, we would be overestimating the variance of the population since we would be including the variability due to the difference among the population means.

As far as the proportion population parameter is concerned, if in a random sample we find X out of the total n objects in the sample with the attribute we are looking for, then the sample proportion $p = X/n$ is our "best" estimate of the population proportion; that is, $\hat{\pi} = p$. If we draw three independent random samples from the population, of sizes n_1, n_2, n_3 and find respectively X_1, X_2, X_3 objects with the attribute, then our "best" estimate for the population proportion is the weighted average of these X's, using the sample sizes as the weights. In symbols we have:

Estimates of Population Proportion for Either Finite or Infinite Populations	
Sample proportion, p	$= \dfrac{X}{n}$
Estimated Population Proportion, $\hat{\pi}$ (for single sample)	$= p$
Estimated Population Proportion, $\hat{\pi}$ (for 3 independent samples)*	$= \dfrac{n_1 X_1 + n_2 X_2 + n_3 X_3}{n_1 + n_2 + n_3}$

* The extension for an arbitrary number of independent samples is evident.

So far in our treatment of sampling distributions, we have assumed that we would know the required population standard deviation, or proportion, and in such cases our previous rules would apply. Usually, however, we will not be given these population parameters and we must therefore estimate them from the sample. Of course, this means that we will not have the actual standard errors but instead only estimates for these. The necessary changes in our rules can be determined by substituting the rules for estimating in place of the parameter values and doing this, and also making the algebraic cancellations of terms, we would produce the rules shown in the following table:

Estimates of Standard Errors When Population Parameters Must Be Estimated		
Standard Error	Infinite Parent Population	Finite Parent Population
Estimated Standard Error of Mean	$\hat{\sigma}_{\bar{x}} = \dfrac{s}{\sqrt{n-1}}$	$\hat{\sigma}_{\bar{x}} = \dfrac{s}{\sqrt{n-1}}\sqrt{\dfrac{N-n}{N}}$
Estimated Standard Error of Proportion	$\hat{\sigma}_p = \dfrac{\sqrt{p(1-p)}}{\sqrt{n-1}}$	$\hat{\sigma}_p = \dfrac{\sqrt{p(1-p)}}{\sqrt{n-1}}\sqrt{\dfrac{N-n}{N-1}}$
Estimated Standard Error of Difference of Means	$\hat{\sigma}_d = \sqrt{\dfrac{s_1^2}{n_1-1} + \dfrac{s_2^2}{n_2-1}}$	$\hat{\sigma}_d = \sqrt{\dfrac{s_1^2}{n_1-1} + \dfrac{s_2^2}{n_2-1}}\sqrt{\dfrac{N-n}{N}}$
Where: s, s_1, s_2 are sample standard deviations n, n_1, n_2 are sample sizes N is the parent population size p is the sample proportion		

There has been sufficient discussion of sampling variations to make it clear that the true value of a population parameter may be quite different from the point estimate of it produced from a sample, or even multiple samples. It is practically certain that it will not *exactly* equal our estimate. However, this is precisely the way in which we act in subsequent decisions involving the parameter. This does not mean that we have to be content to say that the parameter is some value "close" to our estimate, for with the use of standard errors we can actually describe the margin of error associated with each of our estimates. Essentially what we do is to define an interval around our estimated value wherein we "expect" the true value of the estimated parameter will fall. Associated with each such interval we construct, we have a level of confidence which in a prescribed sense indicates the accuracy of our estimate by indicating the "confidence" we can have that we have enclosed the parameter within our interval.

Confidence Intervals: An Example

Suppose that we wish to estimate the average daily yield of a chemical manufactured in a chemical plant under a new process. From a very large amount of data accumulated on actual daily yields of the old process we find that the standard deviation of this data is 120 tons. Suppose further that it is reasonable to believe that the standard deviation of the population under the new process will be quite close to that under the old process. Therefore, we assume that the population's standard deviation under the new process is 120 tons.

Let us suppose that we have selected a random sample of size $n = 25$ from the daily outputs of the new process and calculated its mean yield to be $\bar{X} = 350$ tons.

Since we have $\sigma = 120$ tons, then the standard deviation of the population of mean values of samples of size 25 is the standard error $\sigma_{\bar{x}} = \sigma/\sqrt{n} = 120/5 = 24$ tons. Now, to construct the 95 percent confidence interval for μ we find the distance on each side of μ within which 95 percent of all sample means will fall. Since the sampling distribution mean $\mu_{\bar{x}}$ equals μ we can frame our discussion in terms of either interchangeably, but naturally we are interested in the latter.

The sampling distribution is approximately normal and from Table 3–1 we find that 2.5 percent of the z values will lie above the value 1.96, which means that 2.5 percent of the values will lie below the value -1.96. Together, these statements say that 95 percent of the z values will fall somewhere between -1.96 and $+1.96$. The value of $\bar{X}$ corresponding to $z = 1.96$ is given by solving the equation $1.96 = (X - \mu_{\bar{x}})/\sigma_{\bar{x}}$ for $\bar{X}$. This gives:

$$\bar{X} = \mu + 1.96 \ (\sigma_{\bar{x}})$$
$$= \mu + 1.96 \ (24)$$
$$= \mu + 47.0$$

where we have substituted μ for $\mu_{\bar{x}}$. Likewise, corresponding to $z = -1.96$ we have $\bar{X} = \mu - 1.96(\sigma_{\bar{x}}) = \mu - 47.0$. And so, 95 percent of the $\bar{X}$'s fall within a distance of 47 tons from the mean μ. The 95 percent confidence interval for μ is thus:

$$\bar{X} \pm 1.96 \ (\sigma_{\bar{x}})$$
$$350 \pm 47.0$$
$$\text{or from 303 to 397 tons}$$

These calculations are depicted in the figures shown in Figure 3–5, where the confidence interval is shown in the derived population's curve.

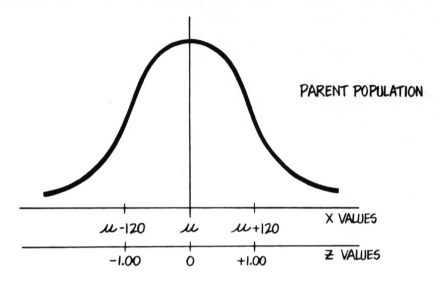

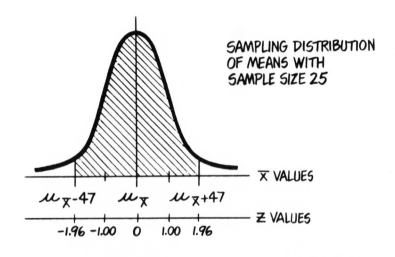

Figure 3–5

How do we interpret the confidence interval just produced? First our sample mean $\bar{X} = 350$ tons may or may not be "close" to the value of μ. If this mean falls within the shaded area in the lower diagram of Figure 3–5, then the interval 350 ± 47 includes the population mean μ. However, if the sample mean does not fall within this interval, then the interval will not contain μ. Although we do not know if $\bar{X}$ is close to μ or not, we do know that with repeated sampling 95 percent of the sample averages found will be close enough to μ so that the interval $\bar{X} \pm 47$ will contain μ.

A second sample would produce a mean which would probably be different from the 350-ton figure, and so the confidence interval constructed for it will also be different than the one above. However, the theory of our construction is such that in the long run about 95 percent of the intervals will contain μ.

Definition of Confidence Interval

A confidence interval on a population parameter is an interval obtained from a sample in such a way that, in repeated sampling, we can expect that the percent of the intervals thus obtained that will enclose the value of the parameter will be equal to the percent of confidence associated with the interval. The general rule for constructing a confidence interval is:

$$\boxed{\text{(Point Estimate)} \pm z \cdot \text{(Standard Error of the Statistic)}}$$

where z is a standardized normal z value selected in the same way as the 95 percent figure was in the previous section.

In the example of the previous section we have 95 percent as the *confidence level,* and we say we have 95 percent *confidence* that μ lies within the interval. In the interval from 303 to 397 tons, the 303-ton figure is *the lower confidence limit,* the 397-ton figure *the upper confidence limit,* and together we refer to them simply as *the confidence limits.*

A common misconception is to view the 95-percent figure as the *chances* or *probability* that the parameter falls within the confidence interval. Since the parameter is either inside or outside of the interval, we are dealing with a unique event and so we cannot legitimately bring probability into it. The 95-percent figure must always be interpreted as a *confidence* we have that our sample has been one of those whose interval contains the parameter.

Perhaps the most commonly used levels of confidence are 90, 95, and 99 percent, which correspond to the respective z values 1.645, 1.96, and 2.58. Of these the 95-percent level is probably seen the most, and, to simplify calculations, a value of 2.0 can be used instead of the 1.96—by so doing very little error will be introduced into our analysis. It will be our practice to use this simplification, except when refined results are required (as when calculating approximate t values).

The level of confidence associated with a confidence interval measures the *accuracy* of our estimate, while the distance between the two limits of the interval measures the *precision* of the estimate. To increase accuracy we must use larger z values which in turn means wider intervals, and so ultimately a decrease in precision. And, vice versa, to increase precision we must decrease accuracy, or else take a larger sample which will thereby decrease the standard error and so increase the precision. There is a "trade-off" between the two. To make the choice we normally look ahead at the decision to be made from our estimate and which will have an attendant level of risk we can tolerate in incorrectly estimating the parameter. This risk will determine the accuracy (and so the level of confidence) we require, and if the resulting precision is not sufficient then additional sampling will be our only recourse. Before we take additional samples we should look at the cost of collecting these and processing them and then compare this against the cost of working with lower precision. In this operation a systematic way for finding the desired sample size is most helpful and will be presented in a subsequent section.

A critical step in our example was our assuming that we knew the standard deviation of the parent population, that is we assumed $\sigma = 120$ tons. It is probably a natural question to ask: How can we ever know the value of a population standard deviation when we are in fact estimating its mean value? The hypothesis being applied here is that the relative variability of a process tends to remain fairly constant, or very nearly so, even in the presence of quite large changes in the population mean, which has a tendency to "drift," often with passing time. If our population supports this belief, then the value of the standard deviation as found from a previous study, from a large sample from the population, or from a parallel process can be used. If we do not believe this hypothesis, then we must estimate the parameter involved in our standard error term, and we do this from the sample as demonstrated in previous sections.

Confidence Limits on Estimates When Population Parameters Are Estimated	
Confidence Limits on Mean Estimate (infinite population)	$\bar{X} \pm z \cdot \dfrac{s}{\sqrt{n-1}}$
Confidence Limits on Mean Estimate (finite population)	$\bar{X} \pm z \cdot \dfrac{s}{\sqrt{n-1}} \sqrt{\dfrac{N-n}{N}}$
Confidence Limits on Proportion Estimate (infinite population)	$p \pm \left[\dfrac{1}{2n} + z \cdot \dfrac{\sqrt{p(1-p)}}{\sqrt{n-1}} \right]$
Confidence Limits on Proportion Estimate (finite population)	$p \pm \left[\dfrac{1}{2n} + z \cdot \dfrac{\sqrt{p(1-p)}}{\sqrt{n-1}} \sqrt{\dfrac{N-n}{N-1}} \right]$
Confidence Limits on Difference of Means Estimate (infinite population)	$\bar{X}_1 - \bar{X}_2 \pm z \cdot \sqrt{\dfrac{(s_1)^2}{n_1-1} + \dfrac{(s_2)^2}{n_2-1}}$
Confidence Limits on Difference of Means Estimate (finite population)	$\bar{X}_1 - \bar{X}_2 \pm z \cdot \sqrt{\dfrac{(s_1)^2}{n_1-1} + \dfrac{(s_2)^2}{n_2-1}} \cdot \sqrt{\dfrac{N-n}{N}}$
Where:	

Where:

$\bar{X}, \bar{X}_1, \bar{X}_2$ are sample means
s, s_1, s_2 are sample standard deviations
p is the sample proportion
n, n_1, n_2 are sample sizes
N is the population size

Table 3–3

The rules for any confidence interval, knowing the parameter value in our standard error term, is easily constructed by using the general rule and the appropriate standard error rule (correcting for a finite population when circumstances suggest this). However, when we must estimate the parameters in the standard error there is a certain amount of algebraic simplification which takes place, and so the actual rules have been collected for handy reference in Table 3–3 for the three types of estimates we have been considering.

A Technical Refinement

When we are working with *small samples,* that is, ones with *n* less than 30 observations, then the normal distribution of our sampling distribution breaks down. In these instances we should really be using a table of *Student's t values* rather than the normal *z* values to set our confidence intervals. For closer results when we are estimating the parameter in our standard error term, we should also use *t* values instead of *z* values. While in these cases the error is usually small, in the case of small samples the difference is usually of sufficient magnitude for us to make the change.

Rather than introduce another table, we can calculate adequate refinements in our *z* values to approximate the proper *t* value. The rule begins by selecting the value of *z* which will produce the desired confidence level. We then substitute this *z* value into the following formula with which we calculate the *t* value which is then used in our rules in place of the *z* value:

$$t = z \cdot \left[1 + \frac{z^2 + 1}{4f} \right]$$

where $f = n - 1$. In this formula we have elected to use f to represent one less than the sample size, rather than putting in $n - 1$, since we will subsequently need a *t* value calculated with this rule but where f will have a different value.

To illustrate the difference, and a case where this is important, let us suppose that we are working with a sample of size $n = 26$, so it is a small sample, and we seek a 95 percent confidence interval on our estimate. The value for *z* is 1.96, and the value of *t* we should use in place of this is found as:

$$t = 1.96 \left[1 + \frac{(1.96)^2 + 1}{4(26 - 1)} \right] = 2.05$$

Referring back to Table 3–1, we find that the *z* value 2.05 is associated with a 96 percent confidence level. This means that the *t* value we should use is equivalent to a *z* value giving a 96 percent confidence, and so if we had used the 1.96 value we would really have constructed a confidence interval which would be smaller than needed and so would indicate more accuracy than we actually have.

If our sample size was $n = 101$, the *t* value corresponding to $z = 1.96$ would be found to be 1.98 which corresponds to a 95.2 percent level and so for this size sample there is relatively little difference between the two.

Confidence Intervals on Estimates of a Total

Suppose that we have a total variable, T, which is equal to the sum of m other variables, X_1, X_2, . . . , X_m, that is:

$$T = X_1 + X_2 + \ldots + X_m$$

A population of totals may be defined, and will have mean value μ_T and standard deviation σ_T. If the X's are independent and the mean and standard deviation of the X_i population are μ_i and σ_i, then we have the following formulas give us the parameters for the total population:

$$\mu_T = \mu_1 + \mu_2 + \ldots + \mu_m$$

$$\sigma_T = \sqrt{(\sigma_1)^2 + (\sigma_2)^2 + \ldots + (\sigma_m)^2}$$

Furthermore, if we take a random sample of size n_i from the X_i population and calculate its mean $\bar{X}_i$ and standard deviation s_i, then we can estimate the total population parameters as follows:

$$\hat{\mu}_T = \bar{X}_1 + \bar{X}_2 + \ldots + \bar{X}_m$$

$$\hat{\sigma}_T = \sqrt{\frac{(s_1)^2}{n_1 - 1} + \frac{(s_2)^2}{n_2 - 1} + \ldots + \frac{(s_m)^2}{n_m - 1}}$$

taking the individual X populations as infinite.

Suppose that T is the sum of m variables each of which have the same population whose mean and standard deviation are μ and σ. If we select one sample of size n from this population and calculate the sample mean and standard deviation $\bar{X}$ and s, then the above rules reduce to the following:

$$\mu_T = m \cdot \mu$$
$$\sigma_T = \sqrt{\sigma^2 + \sigma^2 + \ldots + \sigma^2}$$
$$= \sqrt{m\,\sigma^2}$$
$$= \sqrt{m}\ \sigma$$
$$\hat{\mu}_T = m\bar{X}$$
$$\hat{\sigma}_T = s\sqrt{\frac{m \cdot n}{n - 1}}$$

Furthermore, for this latter situation the confidence interval on the total population's mean value estimate, point estimate $m \cdot \bar{X}$ would be:

$$m \cdot \bar{X} \pm z \cdot \frac{s\sqrt{m}}{\sqrt{n - 1}}$$

Total variables arise in a variety of practical situations. For example, T might be the total production over an extended period of days where the population covering each day's activity is the same. Other applications immediately suggest themselves, and being able to establish confidence limits on the total estimate offers us a useful control mechanism.

To illustrate, let us suppose that a highly mechanized production facility used to produce a certain item is being scheduled for the next M days and the production plan calls for G units of the item to be produced at the end of this period of time. A random sample of size $n = 101$ days is selected from the past daily production reports on this facility and we find the sample mean and standard deviation on daily output to be 250 units and 50 units respectively. Thus, we have $\bar{X} = 250$, $s = 50$, and $n = 101$.

We are interested in establishing a control which will enable us to determine at the end of each day whether of not we are "on schedule." To set up this problem in a general way let us suppose that at time "now" we are D days into the schedule, and as of this time we have S units produced. We therefore have $M-D$ days remaining in our production period during which time we must produce at least $G-S$ additional units.

If we assume that the daily output of each day is covered by a single population, then the total production over a given number of days will be a total variable and the last set of rules given above will apply. Thus, the 95 percent confidence interval (and we will use 2.0 in place of 1.96 here) on the total production in the next $M-D$ days is given by:

$$(M - D)\bar{X} \pm z \cdot \frac{s\sqrt{M - D}}{\sqrt{n - 1}}$$

or, with the numbers put into the rule:

$$(M - D)250 \pm 2 \frac{50\sqrt{M - D}}{\sqrt{101 - 1}}$$

or

$$(M - D)250 \pm 10\sqrt{M - D} \text{ units}$$

Thus, if 4 days remain in the production period, our interval will be $1{,}000 \pm 20$ or from 980 to 1,020 units.

To give us the most coverage we would probably look to the lower confidence limit, the 980 units, as the minimum amount of production we can expect to have in the next 4 days. And with this interpretation if our total plan calls for $G = 11{,}000$ units and at this time we have 10,000 units, then in the next 4 days we will have to produce 1,000 units to meet the plan on schedule. Since our minimum expected production is only 980 units, we can consider ouselves "behind schedule" by 20 units. As a control we could make these calculations at the end of each day to see where we stand.

Another way to evaluate our position is with the risk we face in not meeting the plan. These we develop with z values as we did in our discussion on sampling distributions. To begin, we need estimates for the mean and standard deviation of total production in 4 days (that is, for the parameters of this total population). These are calculated as:

$$\hat{\mu}_T = m \cdot \bar{X} = 4(250) = 1{,}000$$
$$\hat{\sigma}_T = s\sqrt{\frac{m \cdot n}{n - 1}} = 50\sqrt{\frac{4(101)}{100}} = 100.5$$

Continuing with the specifications given above we will need 1,000 units produced in the next 4 days, and the z value corresponding to this is: $(1{,}000 - 1{,}000)/100.5 = 0.00$. From

Table 3–1 we find the value 50.0 percent, which means that there is a 50 percent risk that we will produce more than 1,000 units in the next 4 days, and so 50 percent risk we will produce something less—this being our risk of missing the target of 11,000 units.

A fact which we have used in this analysis but which we did not explicitly state is that if each of m variables is normally distributed then the total of these is also normally distributed. This is why Table 3–1 was applicable to our total sampling distribution.

Confidence Intervals on Regression Line Estimates

In the previous chapter it was demonstrated how the least-squares method was used to fit a straight line, such as $Y = A + BX$, to a bivariate data set of observations on (X,Y). The line which we actually quantify from our sample data is then usually used to give estimates for Y values corresponding to specified X values which are most often values which were not present in the original data. The actual estimates are obtained by substituting directly into the equation for X the value corresponding to which the estimate of Y is desired.

For instance, if we found a line $Y = 100 + 5X$, then the value of Y estimated for the value $X = 6$ is $Y_{est} = 100 + 5(6) = 130$. It follows that all the estimates of Y are actual points on the line.

Just as with any estimate, there is a certain amount of estimation error associated with each Y_{est} we produce from the equation. This being the case, it is important for us to have a method for calculating confidence limits on each such estimate to serve as error bounds. The procedure is shown in Table 3–4. Here we suppose that a random sample of

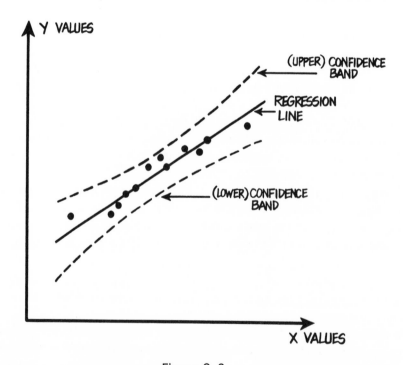

Figure 3–6

	Procedure for Fitting a Line to Data and Calculating Confidence Limits on an Estimated Y Value, Y_{est}
Sample Mean of X values, $\bar{X}$	$\dfrac{\sum X}{n}$
Sample Variance of X values, s_x^2	$\dfrac{n \cdot \sum(X^2) - (\sum X)^2}{n^2}$
Sample Mean of Y values, $\bar{Y}$	$\dfrac{\sum Y}{n}$
Sample Variance of Y values, s_y^2	$\dfrac{n \cdot \sum(Y^2) - (\sum Y)^2}{n^2}$
Sample Covariance, $s_{y,x}$	$\dfrac{n\sum(X \cdot Y) - (\sum X)(\sum Y)}{n^2}$
Regression Line Slope, B	$\left(\dfrac{s_{y,x}}{s_x^2}\right)$
Regression Line Intercept, A	$\bar{Y} - B(\bar{X})$
Sample Correlation Coefficient, r	$\left(\dfrac{s_x}{s_y}\right)B$
Value of X for which Y is being estimated	x_0
Point Estimate of Y for $X = x_0$, Y_{est}	$A + B \cdot x_0$
Confidence Limits On Y_{est}	$Y_{est} \pm t \cdot s_{y:x_0}$

Where: $s_{y:x_0} = \sqrt{s_y^2(1 - r^2)}\sqrt{\dfrac{n+1}{n} + \dfrac{(x_0 - \bar{X})^2}{n(s_x^2)}}$

and t is the t value computed with $f = n - 2$, and corresponding to the level of confidence desired in our confidence limits.

Table 3–4

size n is used (which means we have n pairs of observations on (X, Y)) and that we are estimating the value of Y corresponding to the value $X = x_0$.

In Figure 3–6 we have drawn a set of curves which represent the typical output of repeated use of the procedure in Table 3–4. The original data points are plotted as points and the least-squares regression line is shown with two dashed curves, one above and one below this. These dashed curves are *confidence bands on estimated values of Y,* which are located on the regression line, and to find these we simply connect upper and lower confidence limits calculated for strategically located Y estimates.

Since we do not normally calculate the confidence limits for each value of Y on the regression line, but a few selected points, it is important to recognize that these bands are curves not straight lines. The reason for this is that as we move away from the mean of the

X value, where the bands are the closest, the error in our estimate of the slope of the "true" line increases, thus the bands must widen in order to achieve a constant confidence level.

Confidence Intervals on Estimates of Intercept and Slope

Underlying a bivariate sample on (X,Y) are three populations: the population of X values, the population of Y values, and the so-called *joint population* of pairs of (X,Y) values. The regression line we quantify from a sample from this joint population is in essence an estimate of the line which we would quantify if all of the joint population members were processed through the procedure. This "true" line would have the form $Y = A + BX$, and if our sample line is $Y = A + BX$ then A is an estimate of a (which is the *intercept* of the line), and B an estimate of b (which is the *slope* of the line). Again, since we are dealing with estimates we will have estimation errors and so confidence intervals are necessary to quantify our margin of errors.

To calculate the confidence limits on the estimate of the population intercept, a, we use the same procedure as shown in Table 3–4, but we use for the value x_o the value *zero*. Our point estimate of a is then A, and the confidence interval on this estimate is $A \pm t \cdot s_{y:o}$ where:

$$s_{y:o} = \sqrt{s_y{}^2(1 - r^2)} \cdot \sqrt{\frac{n + 1}{n} + \frac{(\bar{X})^2}{n(s_x{}^2)}}$$

and where t is defined as in the table.

In most situations, the slope b is perhaps the more important parameter since this indicates the "growth" of the Y values, or the trend in the process giving rise to this variable's population. The importance of this parameter is clear if we recall our time series analysis section of the previous chapter where the slope played a most critical role in forecasting future weekly demands. To construct confidence limits on our estimate of this slope, where, of course, the point estimate is the value for B computed from the sample, we do the following:

**Confidence Limits on the
Estimate of the Slope of the
Population Line**

Confidence Limits on Estimate	$B \pm t \cdot s_B$

Where:

$$s_B = \sqrt{\frac{(1 - r^2)(r^2)}{n \cdot (B^2)}}$$

n is the sample size

and t is the t value computed with $f = n - 2$ and corresponding to the level of confidence desired in our confidence interval.

In chapter 2 a regression line was fit to a time series and the fitted line was found to be $D = 55 + 4t$, where the unrounded value of B was 3.71. The sample size was $n = 20$ and the correlation coefficient was $r = 0.81$. With this sample size the appropriate t value would be calculated for a 95 percent level of confidence to be equal to 2.09. The value of s_B, using $B = 3.71$, would be found to be equal to 0.03 (rounded from 0.0285). Thus, our confidence limits, at the 95 percent level, would be $3.71 \pm (2.09)(0.03)$ or 3.65 and 3.77. The range between these two limits is 0.12, which is approximately 3.2 percent of our estimate. This indicates very good precision.

Determining Sample Sizes

Another use we have for the confidence interval on an estimate is in determining the sample size we should select. In this application we will need certain initial information, some of which is specified by the investigator to achieve the precision he desires in his final estimate.

To illustrate the general procedure let us suppose that we are estimating the mean number of hours it takes to process a standard batch of yarn through a braiding operation. For the moment suppose that the standard deviation of the population of these processing times is 1.5 hours. We could be in the planning stages of our investigation and we wish to know what sample size we should use to estimate the mean processing time of a standard batch.

Considering our population as infinite, then the 95 percent confidence limits on our mean estimate are $\bar{X} \pm 2 \cdot \sigma / \sqrt{n}$, which means that the total length of this interval will be $[(\bar{X} + 2 \cdot \sigma / \sqrt{n}) - (\bar{X} - 2 \cdot \sigma / \sqrt{n})] = 4 \cdot \sigma / \sqrt{n}$. If we wish that this length be only 1.0 hour, we can solve the equation:

$$1.0 = \frac{4(\sigma)}{\sqrt{n}}$$

$$\sqrt{n} = \frac{4(1.5)}{1.0} = 6.0$$

$$n = 36$$

To meet our requirements we thus need a sample of size 36—our accuracy will be 95 percent, and our precision 1.0 hours.

Suppose now that we have no idea of what the population standard deviation is, then we will have to estimate this from an initial sample drawn from the population. Thus, in these situations we must sample before we can determine our full sample size, however, this initial sample accounts for part of the final sample.

Let us assume that we drew a random sample of size 10 and found the sample standard deviation to be 1.5 hours. Then the estimate for the population standard deviation is $s\sqrt{n/(n-1)} = 1.5\sqrt{10/9} = 1.6$ hours (rounded from 1.5810 hours). Our calculations are thus,

$$1.0 = \frac{4(\hat{\sigma})}{\sqrt{n'}}$$

$$\sqrt{n'} = \frac{4(1.6)}{1.0} = 6.4$$

$$n' = 40.96, \text{ or } 41$$

Thus, we need a larger sample to account for the estimation error introduced by our having to estimate the population standard deviation—of course, of these 41 observations we already have selected 10 in our initial sample.

Often, instead of specifying the length of the confidence interval we will specify the maximum amount of error we will tolerate in our final estimate. Thus, continuing with the above example, we might say that we wish to select a sample size which will allow us to be 95 percent confident that the estimation error will be no larger than 0.5 hours. With this level of error it turns out that we are simply restating our first requirements in a different way. To see this let us recall that our confidence interval will be centered on the value of $\bar{X}$, and we are 95 percent confident that the μ will fall somewhere in this interval. The largest error we can have would occur when μ was actually equal to either one of our confidence limits. If it was equal to the lower limit our error would be $\bar{X} - (\bar{X} - z \cdot \sigma/\sqrt{n}) = z \cdot \sigma/\sqrt{n}$, and if it equalled the upper limit our error would be $(\bar{X} + z \cdot \sigma/\sqrt{n}) - \bar{X} = z \cdot \sigma/\sqrt{n}$. Therefore, our maximum error is the same regardless of which side of $\bar{X}$ the value of μ is found. As we require that this error be equal to 0.5 hours, then we solve

$$0.5 = \frac{z \cdot (\sigma)}{\sqrt{n}}$$

$$\sqrt{n} = \frac{2(1.5)}{0.5} = 6.0$$

$$n = 36$$

as found before when σ was known.

In many situations we will be taking rather large samples. An area where this is usually true is in *work sampling,* where we sample an operation to determine what proportion of time is spent in the various work activities associated with the operation. Thus, in studying a particular machine we might consider the work activities: Running for Production, Running for Test, Running for Training, Down Due to Lack of Work, Down Due to Failure, and Down Due to Lack of Operator.

Again, we select the sample size to achieve some stated precision and accuracy levels, but it may not be necessary to select the full sample to effect these. What we do is to periodically (usually at the end of each day of sampling) recalculate our confidence interval on the estimate with all the sample collected so far, and when we find an interval which achieves the desired precision and accuracy we can stop sampling.

To illustrate, let us suppose that we are designing a work sampling study on maintenance craftsmen and the three categories of time we want to use are: Craft Work, Travel, and Personal Time. We want to estimate the proportion of a day which is used in each category and we want to have a maximum estimation error on the Craft Work category of no more than 0.05 with a confidence level of 95 percent. To establish sample size for estimates of proportions we can use the following confidence interval rule which simplifies the calculations and does not introduce any significant error:

$$p \pm z \cdot \frac{\sqrt{p(1 - p)}}{\sqrt{n}}$$

Let us also suppose that an initial sample of 25 observations are made (at random instances of time during a day) and the proportion of time devoted to Craft Work was found to be 0.60. Thus, to have a 95 percent level of confidence in having a maximum error of no more than 0.05 on this proportion we solve

$$0.05 = 2 \cdot \frac{\sqrt{0.60(1.00 - 0.60)}}{\sqrt{n}}$$

$$\sqrt{n} = \frac{2 \sqrt{0.60 (0.40)}}{0.05} = 19.6$$

$$n = 384.16, \text{ or } 384$$

In our first 25 observations the maximum error we could make in our estimate, 0.60 Craft Work, is simply $z\sqrt{p(1-p)}/\sqrt{n} = 2\sqrt{0.60(0.40)}/\sqrt{25} = 0.196$, or approximately 0.20. As this exceeds our desired 0.05 we cannot stop sampling yet.

Suppose that we select another 200 observations and when these are combined with our first 25 observations we calculate a Craft Work proportion of 0.70. Now our maximum error is $z\sqrt{p(1-p)}/\sqrt{n} = 2\sqrt{0.70(0.30)}/\sqrt{225} = 0.061$, so again we have not attained the desired level and sampling is continued.

Next 125 observations are made, making the total sample so far 350, and the Craft Work proportion is calculated to be 0.75 using all observations to date. Our maximum error is $z\sqrt{p(1-p)}/\sqrt{n} = 2\sqrt{0.75(0.25)}/\sqrt{350} = 0.046$, and since this is smaller than our prescribed maximum error of 0.05, we can stop sampling here. We have thus saved ourselves 34 observations.

One final comment is in order on prescribing maximum errors in proportion estimates. This has to do with the two ways we can state these. The way we have done this above is to state the error in *absolute* terms. The other way this can be stated is in *relative* terms. In our case we would say that we want the maximum error to be no larger than 0.05 *of* the estimate. Our formula for calculating the sample size would now be the following:

$$0.05p = z \cdot \frac{\sqrt{p(1-p)}}{\sqrt{n}}$$

$$\sqrt{n} = \frac{z\sqrt{(1-p)}}{0.05\sqrt{p}}$$

$$n = \frac{z^2(1-p)}{0.0025p}$$

In this formula, our initial proportion estimate of 0.60 would indicate a sample size of:

$$n = \frac{4(0.40)}{0.0025(0.60)}$$

$$= \frac{2.67}{0.0025} = 1,068$$

To achieve this error limit we will need almost threefold the number of observations as before. It is therefore extremely important to specify the error in the way we actually intend it and in the way we actually need it. This is particularly important when an outside agency is designing and conducting the study.

Even if our initial estimates are rather rough, perhaps simply judgments, or ones calculated from less-than-best procedures (as estimating the population standard deviation with its range), the calculated sample size serves as an important guideline. Aside from the fact that it is critical in planning the number of observations to make, the prescribed sample size provides us with information from which we can estimate the cost involved in collecting our data as well as the length of time we will have to wait until the data is collected. This type of information is naturally of vital importance to our decision to sample or find the needed information by some other means.

Hypothesis Testing with Confidence Intervals: An Example

Suppose that we are auditing a cost reduction program which led to our producing an item in a new way. In this new operation, as well as in the previous operation, a standard batch size is run and it is the equipment and routing of runs through this which has changed. The average direct cost per batch under the old operation was $3,500. The new operation has been functioning for a period of time sufficient to assume that it has stabilized itself as far as costs are concerned, and we must decide, on the basis of a sample, whether there has been a reduction in costs or whether these remain the same.

We formulate the so-called *null hypothesis* which is our theory concerning the costs and whose validity we propose to test. Our null hypothesis is: The mean of the population of batch costs under the new operation is still equal to that of the old operation, that is, $3,500. On the basis of the evidence we find in our sample we wish to either *reject the null hypothesis* or *accept it*. Thus, our null hypothesis is equivalent to saying that no cost reduction has been gained by the new operation. In symbols we write the null hypothesis as: H_o: $\mu = \$3,500$, where H_o denotes the null hypothesis and μ denotes the mean of the cost population under the new operation.

A random sample of twenty-six batches is selected from the new operation's output and these were costed-out to find their direct costs. The average of these costs were found to be $3,350 and their standard deviation $150. At this point we might conclude that since the average of this sample is less than the $3,500-figure, we have shown that the new operation does have a smaller per batch cost. However, due to sampling variations this particular sample mean may be quite far from the population mean; therefore, we must decide whether or not $\bar{X} = \$3,350$ is *significantly different* from $3,500, and for this we need the confidence interval on our estimate.

To start let us look at the sampling distribution on samples from the new cost population with sample size 26. From our sample we would estimate the mean of this distribution to be $3,350 and its standard deviation (our standard error of the mean) would be estimated as $s/\sqrt{n-1} = \$150/\sqrt{25} = \$30$. Our 95 percent confidence interval would thus be $\$3,350 \pm 2(\$30)$ or from $3,290 to $3,410 per batch. This distribution will be normal as long as the original cost population is not too far from normal.

We are 95 percent confident that we have enclosed the true population mean of the new cost population within these two confidence limits, and since *the hypothesized value of this mean,* the $3,500, *is not inside this interval,* we can therefore conclude (with 95 percent confidence that we are correct) that the mean is not equal to $3,500. On the basis of this evidence we therefore *reject our null hypothesis,* and we conclude that the cost per batch has *changed.* We should note that if the previous average cost had been any value from $3,290 to $3,410 (and so within our confidence interval) we would not have rejected the null hypothesis and as a result we could not have concluded there was any change in the per batch cost.

There exists the possibility that we have incorrectly rejected the hypothesis, again due to our sampling variations and estimating errors, and the new cost mean is $3,500. However, we have limited the risk of making this type of error to 5 percent. This level of risk of rejecting the null hypothesis when in fact it is true (and so should be accepted) is termed the *level of significance* associated with our test. In general, we denote this with the symbol a, the lower-case Greek letter "alpha."

Two-Sided Hypothesis Tests

Accompanying each null hypothesis is an *alternative hypothesis, H_a,* which indicates the alternative theory against which we are testing our null hypothesis, H_o. For our present example the alternative hypothesis would H_a: $\mu \neq \$3,500$, which says the mean is not equal to $3,500. Our complete statement would be:

$$H_o: \mu = \$3,500$$

$$H_a: \mu \neq \$3,500$$

$$a: 5 \text{ percent}$$

and in words our test is: Test, on the 5 percent level of significance, whether μ is *equal to* $3,500 or *not equal to* $3,500.

This is a *two-sided test*—the alternative hypothesis specifies values of μ on both sides of the null hypothesis value. By H_a: $\mu \neq \$3,500$ we mean either μ is smaller than $3,500 ($\mu < \$3,500$), or else it is larger than $3,500 ($\mu > \$3,500$); one or the other must occur if $\mu \neq \$3,500$. For the two-sided test we determine the confidence level to be used in building our confidence intervals from the calculation: $(100 - a)$ percent, where a is the specified level of significance in the test. Thus, for a 10-percent level of significance we would calculate a confidence level of $(100 - 10) = 90$ percent, and so in calculating our confidence interval on our mean a z value of 1.645 would be used. Also, for this type of test we *reject the null hypothesis* if the hypothesized value in the statement of the null hypothesis *does not lie in the constructed confidence interval.*

A two-sided test is appropriate when we are in a situation where our only interest is whether or not two values are *different,* and where we do not particularly care "how" they are different. Thus, in our example, we have stated that we simply want to know whether or not the mean equals $3,500, not caring whether (if not equal) it is smaller or larger than this value.

One-Sided Hypothesis Tests

Often it is appropriate to make a so-called *one-sided test,* and this is probably true in our present example. Here our alternative hypothesis specifies values on just one side of the hypothesized value in the null hypothesis. Thus, suppose, for example, that we are convinced that the new operation has a lower per batch cost (with our previous hypothesis test we were taking the position that we didn't know whether it had a lower or higher cost than the old operation). Then the question which should be asked is: Is the mean cost $3,500 or is it *lower than* $3,500? We therefore have to change the alternative hypothesis, and our full test statement would be:

$$H_o: \mu = \$3,500$$
$$H_a: \mu < \$3,500$$
$$a: \quad 5 \text{ percent}$$

To perform the statistical test indicated we again construct the confidence interval on the mean (in general, we construct these for whatever parameter is involved in the H_o statement), but we calculate the confidence level of this with a new rule. For a level of significance a we use the confidence level calculated by $(100 - 2a)$ percent. Thus, for $a = 5$ percent we need the $(100 - 2(5)) = 90$ percent confidence level, and so use $z = 1.645$ in finding the confidence interval. Another difference in this type of test (the one-sided test) is that we only look at one of the confidence limits to make the reject-or-accept decision on H_o. In our present setup, with H_a specifying values *less than* the null hypothesized value, we look at the *upper confidence limit.* If the value specified in the null hypothesis is *larger than this limit,* we *reject* H_o in favor of H_a. If it is smaller than this limit we can accept H_o.

The other one-sided test arises when H_a specifies values *greater than* the null hypothesized value. Thus, if we were convinced that the new operation had a higher cost than the old operation, our question would be: Is the mean cost $3,500 or is it *higher* than $3,500? The full statement of this test would be:

$$H_o: \mu = \$3,500$$
$$H_a: \mu > \$3,500$$
$$a: \quad 5 \text{ percent}$$

For this type of test we again calculate the confidence level from the rule $(100 - 2a)$ percent, but now we only look at the *lower confidence limit* of the confidence interval we construct. If the value specified in the null hypothesis is *smaller than this lower limit, we reject H_o* in favor of H_a. If it is larger than this limit we can accept H_o.

Hypothesis testing is usually used as a sequential procedure for uncovering information. Thus, we might start with a two-sided test and if we reject H_o we might then perform the two one-sided tests to try to answer how the difference arose. Hypothesis testing is also used to produce estimates of population parameters and here we might have to increment the hypothesized value in H_o until we reach a point where a rejection turns over to an acceptance of H_o, or vice versa. The use of confidence intervals for conducting the test is a definite advantage here, for once we set up the confidence interval, we immediately see the full range of hypothesized values which would be accepted and those which would be rejected. In other words, we see all those estimates which are consistent with our sample and all those which are inconsistent with it.

Everything which has been presented in terms of the mean value parameter is carried over directly for proportions. Here we would calculate the confidence intervals for the tests with the rules in Table 3–3 and from this point on our procedure is exactly the same. This is also true for those situations where t values are needed in place of z values, and in fact all we need to know to be able to run these tests is how to construct the confidence interval on a parameter. For certain parameters, such as correlation coefficients, we need special rules (which will be provided in subsequent sections), however, for those whose confidence intervals have already been discussed we have the necessary mechanism at this point.

Hypothesis Tests on Differences of Means

Testing hypotheses on differences of means has a certain condition associated with it which warrants separate treatment. This is that we must distinguish in these tests whether our data is *matched* or *unmatched data;* two examples will illustrate.

Suppose that we have two vendors who supply us with the same raw material. We are interested in the difference in the mean delivery time from each vendor in their deliveries of this material. To set up the test, we collect 50 actual delivery times from each vendor from a vendor file and we find the respective sample means to be $\bar{X}_1 = 18$ days, and $\bar{X}_2 = 15$ days, with sample standard deviations being $s_1 = 8$ days and $s_2 = 5$ days. On the 5 percent level of significance our full test statement is:

$$H_o: \mu_1 - \mu_2 = 0$$
$$H_a: \mu_1 - \mu_2 \neq 0$$
$$a: \quad 5 \text{ percent}$$

We are thus asking the question: On the 5 percent level of significance is the difference between the two vendors' average delivery time *zero* or is there a significant difference between them? Naturally, we could use any value in place of the "0" depending upon what we wish to test.

To construct the 95 percent confidence interval we do the following:

$$\bar{X}_1 - \bar{X}_2 \pm z \cdot \sqrt{\frac{(s_1)^2}{n_1 - 1} + \frac{(s_2)^2}{n_2 - 1}}$$

or

$$18 - 15 \pm 2 \cdot \sqrt{\frac{(64)}{49} + \frac{(25)}{49}}$$

$$= 3 \pm 2 \cdot \frac{\sqrt{89}}{7} = 3 \pm 2.69$$

or from 0.31 days to 5.69 days

Since the hypothesized value, *zero*, does not fall into this interval, we therefore would reject the null hypothesis and conclude from this that there is a significant difference between the two vendors on the basis of their mean delivery times. If we went ahead and tested this H_o against H_a: $\mu_1 - \mu_2 > 0$, thus testing to see if the two means are equal or if Vendor 1 has a larger lead time than Vendor 2, and again on the 5 percent significance level, we would again reject the null hypothesis and thereby conclude that it is likely that Vendor 1 does have the longer delivery time mean.

Matched data arises in situations where we are testing on the same process, but "before" some system change against "after" this change has been installed. Here our samples consist of the same objects, only one data set is taken from the objects "before" and the second data set "after" the change. In general, our two samples are developed by taking two different sets of observations on the same object set, rather than two different object sets. In such situations we must recognize that we actually have only one sample and our hypothesis must be tested as such.

An illustration will best present our procedure. For this let us suppose that as part of the finishing stages in the manufacture of a product each unit is subjected to three separate drying operations. The need for the last operation is under question. Does it really drive off additional moisture? If it does then there should be a change in the weight of a unit before and after this third drying. Suppose that we select 101 units and weigh each before the third drying and then again after this operation. Here is where the change in procedure is instituted, for we don't calculate means for the before and after data, but instead we subtract each unit's after-drying weight from its before-drying weight and these 101 weight differences are the data for which we calculate the mean value and standard deviation.

To follow this example through let us suppose that the average of these weight differences is $\bar{D} = 0.5$ grams, and the standard deviation of them is $s_D = 1.0$ gram. Then our hypothesis statement is:

$$H_o: \mu_D = 0$$

$$H_a: \mu_D \neq 0$$

$$a: \quad 5 \text{ percent}$$

Our 95 percent confidence interval is $0.5 \pm 2(1.0/\sqrt{101-1}) = 0.5 \pm 0.2$, or from 0.3 grams to 0.7 grams. As the *hypothesized value, zero, does not fall in this interval, we reject the null hypothesis* and conclude that there is a significant difference between the before and after drying weights of the objects. We may also conclude that the *difference* between these weights is between 0.3 grams and 0.7 grams (with 95 percent confidence), which is perhaps more pertinent to our decision of whether or not this drying operation should be continued. This again illustrates how we get as much information from our data as possible by framing our hypothesis testing in terms of confidence intervals.

Types of Errors

The decision procedures described above are subject to two types of errors which are prevalent in any two-choice decision problem. We may reject the null hypothesis when, in fact, it is true. This is referred to as a *Type I* error. The other type of error, *Type II,* is committed when we accept the null hypothesis when it is actually false and some alternative hypothesis is true. Thus we have the following possibilities:

If Our Decision Is to:	But in Fact the Null Hypothesis Is:	
	False	True
Reject H_o	Correct Decision	Type I Error
Accept H_o	Type II Error	Correct Decision

As we have already said, the value of the level of significance we choose for a test measures the risk associated with making a Type I error, so with $a = 5$ percent, we are running this level of risk in rejecting H_o when in fact it is true. As we increase the value of a we will decrease the risk of making a Type II error, while decreasing a decreases the chances for a Type I error but also increases the chances for making a Type II error. The risk associated with both types of error normally is used to indicate the "goodness" of the test. To decrease the risk of making both types of error we will have to increase our sample size thereby increasing the amount of information available upon which to base the decision.

We only get positive information from a test when we are able to reject the null hypothesis. Accepting H_o is a negative type of acceptance which means that we have simply failed to disprove the null hypothesis. This may appear to weaken the procedure, but this need not be the case, for by judicious use of the test, the investigator should be able to generate sufficient evidence for him to draw *his own* conclusions even though in the strictest sense of statistical theory he may not. What we have in mind here is the strategic selection of successive values in our null hypothesis so as to eventually lead us to the point where we can reject H_o. Isolating the value at which our previous acceptance of H_o changes to a rejection of it will provide us with a basis for drawing our conclusion.

Testing Hypotheses on Correlation Coefficients

For almost any bivariate data set we will calculate a nonzero linear or rank correlation coefficient, and just because the value is "small" this does not necessarily mean that there is not a *significant* association between the two variables. It is a question of the sample size and the relative variability found in the sample which determines the significance of r or r_{rank}.

The existence of a significant association in the underlying joint population is translated into the significance of the difference between the population correlation coefficient, ρ, and the value zero. Casting this into a two-sided hypothesis test would produce the following statement:

$$H_o: \rho = 0$$

$$H_a: \rho \neq 0$$

$$a: \quad 5 \text{ percent}$$

If the sample correlation coefficient is fairly large, then a one-sided test may be more appropriate where the alternative hypothesis is set up to be consistent with the plus or minus sign of the coefficient.

To be able to apply the same testing procedure as previously shown, we need something analogous to a confidence inteval, and for both r and r_{rank} we use the following:

$$\frac{r}{\sqrt{1 - r^2}} \pm \frac{t}{\sqrt{n - 2}}$$

where r is the sample linear or rank correlation coefficient, n the size of the sample and t the t value calculated with the rule previously given but with $f = n-2$. We select the t value for the level of confidence calculated from $(100-a)$ for the two-sided tests and from the rule $(100-2a)$ for one-sided tests—again, a is our level of significance. We again use the specified value in the null hypothesis to make our decision, thus in H_o: $\rho = 0$ we use the location of "0" with respect to the calculated interval to decide.

To illustrate, let us suppose that from a sample of size 18 we find a linear correlation coefficient of $r = 0.40$. Intuition might immediately suggest that we have a nonsignificant association indicated, but let us test this hypothesis. Since our coefficient is fairly large, and positive, a one-sided test is appropriate and the statement of this would be:

$$H_o: \rho = 0$$
$$H_a: \rho > 0$$
$$a: \quad 5 \text{ percent}$$

The appropriate z value is 1.645 and the calculated t value for this is 1.70. Our confidence limits are thus:

$$\frac{0.40}{\sqrt{(1 - (0.40)^2}} \pm \frac{1.70}{\sqrt{16}} = 0.436 \pm 0.425$$

or separately from 0.011 to 0.861. Invoking the rule for this type of test, we look at the lower confidence limit, 0.011, and since *zero* is smaller than this value, we may reject H_o, on the 5 percent level of significance. The conclusion is that, on this particular level of significance, there does exist a significant association (or correlation) between the two variables. In other words, the correlation coefficient of the joint population is *significantly different from zero.*

In the previous chapter, a rank correlation coefficient was calculated to be $r_{rank} = -0.774$ from a sample of size 8. To test this value for significance we would set up the following test:

$$H_o: \rho_{rank} = 0$$
$$H_a: \rho_{rank} < 0$$
$$a: 5 \text{ percent}$$

Again, our t value would be calculated using $z = 1.645$, but now with $f = 6$. The value we would compute is $t = 1.898$ and our interval would be 0.436 ± 0.774, or from -0.338 to

1.210. Since *zero* is not larger than the upper limit 1.210, we cannot reject H_o. Here is a situation where we would probably postpone the decision until additional sampling is performed, and the acceptance of H_o in the face of this apparently "large" coefficient is brought about due to the very small sample used.

Often it is necessary to test the hypothesis that the population correlation coefficient is equal to a specific value, not just against *zero*. For this test we do not use r nor ρ in our hypotheses, but instead a transformed quantity. Let us let ρ_o denote the hypothesized value for ρ we are testing, then we calculate a value for R and R_o using these rules:

$$R = 1.1513 \log_{10} [(1 + r)/(1 - r)] \text{ and } R_o = 1.1513 \log_{10} [(1 + \rho_o)/(1 - \rho_o)]$$

and we state our hypotheses in terms of the quantity R^*, where $R^* = 1.1513 \log [(1 + \rho)/(1 - \rho)]$. All this is a lot of work but is the only way we can effect the test. Our null hypothesis is $H_o: R^* = R_o$ and this is equivalent to $H_o: \rho = \rho_o$. Accompanying this we have a two-sided or one-sided alternative, whichever is appropriate.

With a sample size of n we calculate confidence limits from: $R \pm z/\sqrt{n - 3}$ with z being the standardized normal value associated with our confidence level and our testing procedure is the same as before only now using the location of the value of R_o relative to these limits to make our decision.

A sample of size 28 produced a correlation coefficient $r = 0.60$. We wish to test on the 5 percent level of significance the hypothesis that the population coefficient is equal or not equal to 0.80. The values of R and R_o are calculated as follows:

$$R = 1.1513 \log \frac{1 + 0.60}{1 - 0.60} = (1.1513) (0.6021) = 0.6932$$

$$R_o = 1.1513 \log \frac{1 + 0.80}{1 - 0.80} = (1.1513) (0.9542) = 1.0986$$

Our "transformed" test statement is:

$$H_o: R^* = 1.0986$$
$$H_a: R^* \neq 1.0986$$
$$a: \quad 5 \text{ percent}$$

The appropriate z value to use is 2.0 and the confidence limits are thus: $0.6932 \pm 2.0/\sqrt{25} = 0.6932 \pm 0.4000$, or 0.2932 and 1.0932. Since *the value in the hypothesis,* 1.0986, *does not fall between these two limits, we may reject the hypothesis* and conclude that there is a *significant difference between ρ and 0.80* on the 5 percent level. A one-sided test now would indicate on which side of 0.80 we can expect to find ρ, which is probably apparent from our sample r, that is, on the low side of 0.80.

Testing Hypothesis of Randomness

In our analysis of a time series we are particularly interested in knowing whether or not a significant trend movement is present. If we actually find a trend, quantify this with a trend line or curve, and then subtract the trend part out of each observation, we would then be interested in knowing whether this "detrended" data has a seasonal or periodic movement. In each situation we could make use of a test on the hypothesis that the data is random, which, if accepted would indicate no trend or no seasonal movement in the exemplified cases.

The so-called *run test* is a simple one to use to test any set of serial data for randomness. A *run* is defined as a succession of identical elements which are followed and preceded by different elements or by no elements at all. An "element" may be a number or a symbol such as a"+"or"−". In each case we work with only two different types of elements.

To test for randomness, we arrange the observations in the same order as they were recorded, observed, or as they occurred in time. It is this "order" which is being tested for randomness, perhaps to see if the sample can be taken as random. We compute the median of these observations and then: (1) place a "+" next to each observation which is larger than the median: (2) place a "−" next to each observation smaller than the median; and (3) place no symbol next to each observation equal to the median. We then count the number or runs, N, of these two elements.

Suppose we have the following sample, whose median is 10, where the + and − signs have been appropriately located:

12	14	12	7	13	9	11	6	10	7	12	10	9	11	14	13	9	10	10	13	12	8	9	10	8	7
+	+	+	−	+	−	+	−		−	+		−	+	+	+	−			+	+	−	−		−	−

The first run consists of the first three + signs, +++. The second run is the single minus sign, −, under the 7. The third run is the single + under the 13, and so on with the last run being the two minus signs, −−, under the 8 and 7. In all there are fourteen runs, so N = 14.

The three quantities we need are: the number of runs; the number of + signs used, N_1; and, the number of − signs used, N_2. From the above we find $N_1 = 11$, and $N_2 = 10$.

The confidence limits we calculate for this test are the following:

$$N \pm z \cdot \sigma_u$$

Where:

$$\sigma_u = \sqrt{\frac{2N_1N_2\,(2N_1N_2 - N_1 - N_2)}{(N_1 + N_2)^2\,(N_1 + N_2 - 1)}}$$

The z is the standard normal z value corresponding to the level of confidence we want in our test.

The value we use to make our decision is U, where:

$$U = \frac{2N_1N_2}{N_1 + N_2} + 1$$

In this test we reject the null hypothesis of randomness if U falls outside the confidence limits, accepting if U lies between them; that is, we perform a two-sided test.

For our given sample we would compute the values:

$$U = \frac{2(11)(10)}{11 + 10} + 1 = 11.476$$

$$\sigma_u = \sqrt{\frac{2\,(11)\,(10)\,(2 \cdot 11 \cdot 10 - 11 - 10)}{(11 + 10)^2\,(11 + 10 - 1)}} = \sqrt{4.964} = 2.228$$

And for a 5 percent level of significance the confidence level is 95 percent, so the z value to use is 2.0. The confidence limits are thus: $14 \pm 2.0\,(2.228) = 14 \pm 4.456$, or 9.544 and 18.456. As 11.476, *the value of U, lies between these limits, we cannot reject the hypothesis of randomness* on the 5 percent level of significance, concluding that the sample is indeed random.

With this conclusion in hand we could use this sample to calculate an estimate of, say, the population mean value with the conviction that we do in fact meet the randomness requirements. If the sample represented a time series, then we could say that no movement, trend or seasonal, is present; and, if it is some detrended data, our conclusion would be that no seasonal or periodic movement is present, just the trend movement which we have already quantified.

This same run test may also be used to test the null hypothesis that two random samples were drawn from populations with the same distribution, and without actually knowing what the distribution is. To illustrate, suppose that we have two samples, one of X values and the other of Y values, of sizes N_1 and N_2 respectively. We arrange *all* observations, from both samples, in ascending order of magnitude placing an "x" or a "y" next to each depending upon which sample it came from. Next, we determine the number of runs of these two elements, this being the value of N. For a level of significance of a we compute the $(100 - 2a)$ confidence limits $N \pm z \cdot \sigma_u$ and reject the hypothesis of consistency if the value of U is larger than the upper limit; otherwise accept H_o, and so conclude that the two populations have the same distribution.

Testing Hypothesis of Contingency

In chapter 2 the contingency coefficient, C, was introduced as a measure of the association or dependency between two possible classifications of observations. At that time an example was given where defective units were classified according to the machine producing them and by defect type. Also the rules for computing expected frequencies and then the value of the Chi-square χ^2 were given. In this section there will be provided a procedure for testing the null hypothesis that there is no dependency; rejection thus means that we may conclude there is a dependency between the two classifications.

Suppose that we have organized our data into a $n \times m$ contingency table (n rows and m columns), and that we have already computed the value of χ^2. We then evaluate T with the rule:

$$\boxed{T = \sqrt{2(\chi^2)} - \sqrt{(2k) - 1}}$$

where $k = (n - 1)\,(m - 1)$. For a level of significance attached to our test, we determine the standardized normal z value corresponding to the $(100 - a)$ level of confidence, and call this value z_a. *If the calculated value of T is greater than the value of z_a then we reject the null hypothesis* (concluding dependency); *otherwise we accept H_o.* In this application, the unrounded z values should be used for better results.

To illustrate, the example on page 49 produced a value of $\chi^2 = 2.38$, where we worked with a 2×2 contingency table: thus, $k = 1$. On the 5 percent level of significance, the value of z_a would be 1.96. The value of T is found as:

$$T = \sqrt{2\,(2.38)} - \sqrt{2 - 1} = 1.182$$

Since this T is not greater than 1.96, we cannot reject H_o on the 5 percent level. From this we could conclude that there is not a significant difference between machine types with respect to defect type produced.

If we have a situation where k is less than 4 we should really use the following rule to compute a more precise value for T; it involves a cube root.

$$T = \frac{h + g - 1}{\sqrt{g}}$$

Where:

$$h = \sqrt[3]{\frac{\chi^2}{k}} \text{ and } g = \frac{2}{9k}$$

For the example above there is no difference between the two values of T, which is an exception to the rule.

This test is usually termed the *Chi-square test* and is most useful when testing the fit of a sample distribution to a theoretical one. In this context it is called the *goodness-of-fit test.* We do not propose to go into this general area except to provide an illustration of how it works in a special situation.

Suppose that from a sample we have determined the (regular) frequency with which M different *categories* occurred (which may be attributes we assign to objects in the sample, or ranges of values of numbers). These are the observed frequencies O_i. We also suppose that we have a hypothesis on the expected frequencies with which these M categories "should have" occurred. Our null hypothesis is that there is no (significant) difference between observed and expected results. To test this hypothesis we use the same procedure as given above, but with $k = M - 1$.

As an illustration, we suppose that we are looking at the returns of six different products: A, B, C, D, E, and F. From a random sample of 120 returns we find the number for these products being respectively: 18, 25, 15, 16, 30, and 16. We had expected that there would be the same number of returns for each product, that is, the expected frequency is 20 for each product; and, we question whether or not the variation we see in the sample is due to sampling variations. Here $k = 5$, and the chi-square is computed as follows:

$$\chi^2 = \sum \frac{(O_i - E_i)^2}{E_i} = \frac{(18 - 20)^2}{20} + \frac{(25 - 20)^2}{20} + \ldots + \frac{(16 - 20)^2}{20} = 9.30$$

To illustrate its use we compute the value of T with the more precise rule and obtain:

$$h = \sqrt[3]{\frac{9.30}{5}} = 1.230$$

$$g = 2/45 = 0.044$$

$$T = \frac{1.230 + 0.044 - 1}{\sqrt{0.044}} = 1.31$$

Thus, on the 5 percent level of significance, where $z_a = 1.96$, we *cannot reject the hypothesis,* concluding no significant difference between observed and our expected results. On the 20 percent level we could make the rejection, as in this case $z_a = 1.28$, but of course, here our risk of Type I error is greater.

As one would expect, the difference between this type of test and that involved in testing goodness of fit is that in the former situation we hypothesized expected frequencies from judgment, whereas in the latter these come from tables of theoretical distributions.

CONCLUSION

In this chapter our interest has been in providing procedures by which statistical inferences may be made concerning a population based on calculations made on sampled data randomly selected from it. The concept of a sampling distribution of a statistic was looked at in more detail than actually needed as it was felt that with this knowledge the reader would be in a better position to apply the tools, appreciate additional topics not covered here, and play a more active role in any investigation drawing from this theory. In addition, a certain "tie-in" with previous materials was made through the use of hypothesis testing to test for significance in numerical descriptions of sampled data sets, but where now our hypotheses pertain to the population.

REFERENCES

Crow, E.L., et. al. *Statistics Manual.* New York, N.Y.: Dover Publications, Inc., 1960.

Dunn, O.J. *Basic Statistics: A Primer for the Biomedical Sciences.* New York, N.Y.: John Wiley & Sons, Inc., 1964.

Mendenhall, W. *Introduction to Statistics.* Belmont, California: Wadsworth Publishing Co., Inc., 1964.

Spiegel, M.R. *Theory and Problems of Statistics.* New York, N.Y.: McGraw-Hill, Inc. (Schaum's Outline Series), 1961.

Springer, C.H., et. al. *Mathematics for Management Series.* Homewood, Illinois: Richard D. Irwin, Inc., 1965.

Wallis, W.A., and H.V. Roberts. *Statistics: A New Approach.* The Free Press (Macmillian Co.), 1965.

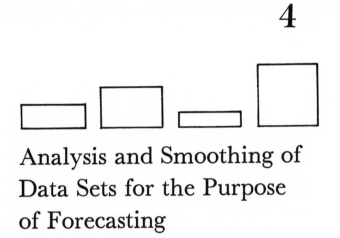

4

Analysis and Smoothing of Data Sets for the Purpose of Forecasting

Plans, decisions, and actions are almost always guided by some form of forecast we have as to what we can expect to happen at a future time, or under a certain set of conditions. The actual forecast may be for the workload we can expect on a certain workcenter in the next week, the in-plant usage of a particular material in the next month, or the number of stockouts which will occur in a particular inventory before receipt of the next stock replenishment order.

In some situations we know that the future will be greatly influenced, perhaps even directly, by one or more prior variables whose values we will know (or can reasonably estimate) before the event we are forecasting takes place. In such instances some form of regression analysis is appropriate to provide us with the needed basis for our forecast. A great deal of long-range forecasting for sales and needed plant capacity is performed in this way.

Estimation and hypothesis testing may be thought of as a form of "forecasting," where present knowledge, in the form of samples, serves as the input data to our estimates and conclusions.

Perhaps the more common circumstance we find ourselves in is where we have no meaningful prior variable and all we have is just the past record of the performance of the process we are forecasting. It is for these situations that the methods to be demonstrated in this chapter are most useful. Their purpose is to analyze past demand histories to uncover their basic components which are then projected out into the future as the forecast.

Although we restrict our information to knowledge of the past, this is not to say that this is *all* we put into the final forecast. It is just all that we put into the mathematical machinery, and what we get in return is not the ultimate forecast, but just an objective guideline on what a logical extension of the past would lead us to expect in the future. The final job of forecasting will always fall in the hands of the individual using the technique, for it is through him that judgments, nonquantifiable information, and experiences are applied. It is also through him that knowledge of influencing factors and conditions which were either not present in the past, or which have changed significantly, or will do so in the future are brought into the forecast.

Smoothing with Moving Averages

When we calculate an average value we are doing so to be able to look through the variability at the central tendency of the numbers. In the analysis of a demand history, or, in general, any time series, we would also like to accomplish this same "smoothing" of variability, but not to the same extent. What we mean by this is that our primary interest is to uncover any significant pattern of movement or variability in our data as this relates to evolving time, and the mean value of the complete data set would not provide us with this type of information—giving us instead just a single number. For example, the mean value of twelve consecutive monthly demand figures would simply show us the average demand per month as experienced over this year. We would not be able to see how the average monthly demands varied from month to month, which is precisely what we are trying to find out. To expose this variability we serially organize our data into overlapping groups of values, each group containing the same number of data values, and then we calculate the mean value for each of these groups. As the result we get a "chain" of averages, which are termed *moving averages*. The number of distinct values used in each group is termed the *order of the moving averages*.

Moving averages need not be reserved for the analysis of a time series, but instead may be used in any situation where we are working with a sequence of numbers where our objective is the same, which is to smooth out the extraneous variability so as to better see the significant variability which the former masks.

To illustrate the procedure, the following seven consecutive data values will be smoothed. Each figure has a symbol for reference purposes.

X_1	X_2	X_3	X_4	X_5	X_6	X_7
2	10	3	17	25	18	32

The line graph for this data is plotted in Figure 4–1. Also plotted in this figure are the moving averages of order 3. The first of these is calculated by finding the mean value of the first 3 numbers: $(X_1 + X_2 + X_3)/3 = 5$. The second moving average is found by dropping off the X_1 and adding on the X_4 giving: $(X_2 + X_3 + X_4)/3 = 10$. The other moving averages are calculated in the same way: dropping off the first value in the previous average and adding on the next value in the data set. If we had selected an order 5 we would start with the first five numbers, and follow the same procedure of dropping and adding numbers, always keeping five numbers in each average.

As shown in Figure 4–1 we associate the value of a moving average with the "middle" position of the sequence of values used to calculate it. Thus, the first moving average of

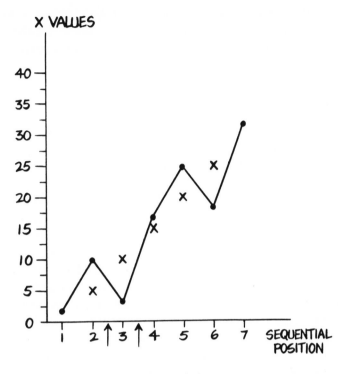

Figure 4–1

order 3 is associated with the second position, that is, with X_2. The second moving average, 10, is associated with X_3, and so on. By these associations we are saying that the value of X_2, for example, is really 5 instead of 10 once the extraneous variability has been taken away. The smoothed value of X_3 is thus estimated as 10, rather than its original value of 3. Thus, in logic, moving averages are used to "replace" our original data with their smoothed equivalents. Unfortunately, in the process of calculating moving averages, we will produce some variables for which smoothed values cannot be found directly. Thus, in the chain of moving averages of order 3, we will have no average associated with either X_1 or X_7. This is an inherent weakness of the procedure and usually means that we must start with sufficient data so that the general trend may be established. Once we have this pattern we can use it to estimate values for the missing positions. Thus, from Figure 4–1, we could estimate the smoothed values for X_1 and X_7 to be respectively 0 and 30. The larger the order used, the more missing terms we will have, and these will fall on both sides of the chain.

In many situations we will have to use orders which are even numbers, and in such cases there will not be a unique position to which we can assign our moving averages; there being in these cases two "middle" positions. Thus, if we computed moving averages of order 4 for our previous example, we will have the first and second moving averages as: $(X_1 + X_2 + X_3 + X_4)/4 = 8$, and $(X_2 + X_3 + X_4 + X_5)/4 = 13.75$. The middle position for the first of these is between X_2 and X_3, while that for the last average is between X_3 and X_4. These two locations are indicated in Figure 4–1 by the arrows drawn to the horizontal scale. To effect an association with a unique position, the process of *centering* is applied to the original chain. All we do in this is to go back through the chain and calculate moving averages of order 2, in other words, we calculate the mean value of successive pairs of our original moving averages. These centered moving averages may be associated with unique positions. For the two averages of order 4 shown above, we would calculate the centered average $(8 + 13.75)$ $/2 = 10.875$ and associate this with X_3.

Smoothing Out Specific Patterns

Smoothing with moving averages is useful in analyzing a demand history for the purpose of uncovering its basic components. In the process by making the proper choice of the order of the averages, we can smooth out specific patterns from the data, and thereby see what the data looks like without the influence of these.

To smooth away a random movement, which we have referred to as the extraneous variability, we use moving averages of odd orders, such as 3, 5, 7, and so on.

Suppose we suspect that our data has a periodic movement in it, and let's suppose that our data are monthly demand figures (for definiteness) and that this periodic movement is suspected to have a period of 12 months. In other words, we feel our demands are seasonal. By taking moving averages of order 12 we will smooth out this seasonal pattern from the data; centering would also be needed in this case. If our data are quarterly demands, and we again suspect a yearly seasonal pattern, then since 4 quarters constitute a year, we would take moving averages of order 4 to smooth out this seasonal movement. In general, if we have a periodic movement we put the moving averages in "sync" with it by taking the order used in the moving averages equal to the suspected period of the movement.

To illustrate this let's consider the time series of quarterly demands, in pieces per quarter, as shown in the third column of Table 4–1. In this table we have also listed the results of certain calculations which will presently be explained. Figure 4–2 has been drawn for these figures.

The original demand data is plotted in the figure as the solid line graph. A large amount of variability is indicated by this graph and so a smoothing analysis of this history appears appropriate. Noting that the second quarter of each year is a demand high-point, and the fourth quarters are consistently low-points we have reasonable grounds to suspect a seasonal pattern in our data with period of four quarters. A chain of moving averages of order 4 would thus smooth out this particular pattern, and these averages after centering are those shown in Table 4–1 under the heading "Centered 4–Quarter Moving Averages." This chain is plotted in Figure 4–2 as the dashed line graph.

At this point we might be somewhat disappointed since we had expected to smooth out the seasonal movement, whereas the dashed graph appears to be just such a pattern. We did in fact smooth out the four-quarter periodic movement and the periodic movement we see in the figure is another movement, with apparently a period of sixteen quarters (that is, four years). Such movements are termed *cyclical movements,* owing to their large periods; they play an important role in long-term economic forecasts where they represent business cycles.

Having identified the period of this cyclical movement we can smooth it away by taking moving averages of period 16 of our centered four-quarter moving averages. Again, we would have to center the results. These centered averages are shown in Table 4–1 under the heading of "Centered 16–Quarter Moving Averages," and they are plotted in Figure 4–1 as the solid line graph in the center of the figure. This line graph is approximately a straight line, which we can take as an estimate of the underlying trend in quarterly demands.

At this point we see that the smoothing analysis of the demand history has been quite profitable, uncovering basic movements which we could not have clearly seen from the

Years	Quarter of the Years	Original Demands psc/qt.	Centered 4–Quarter Moving Averages	Centered 16–Quarter Moving Averages
1st	1	46	–	–
	2	89	–	–
	3	57	67	–
	4	51	75	–
2nd	5	90	79	–
	6	115	77	–
	7	61	70	–
	8	31	61	–
3rd	9	57	52	52
	10	73	43	53
	11	26	34	54
	12	1	28	56
4th	13	17	27	57
	14	59	29	57
	15	30	37	58
	16	17	49	59
5th	17	66	60	60
	18	105	73	61
	19	78	84	62
	20	66	90	62
6th	21	102	93	64
	22	122	91	65
	23	83	85	66
	24	49	77	67
7th	25	71	69	–
	26	89	60	–
	27	45	51	–
	28	14	45	–
8th	29	36	43	–
	30	77	46	–
	31	42	–	–
	32	40	–	–

Table 4–1

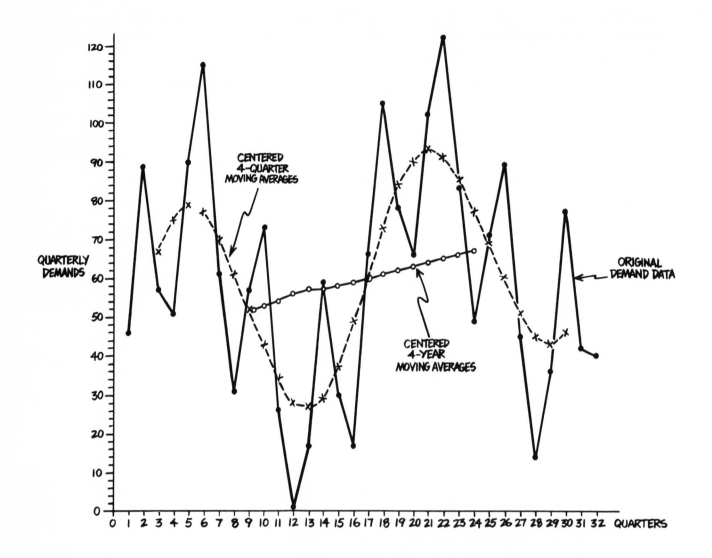

Figure 4–2

original figures. Knowing the details on our periodic movements is particularly important to us if we are planning production and inventory levels for the manufacture of this product. Of course, in using this information we are inherently assuming that the conditions which prevailed when this past demand history developed will continue into the future. Under this assumption we can prepare the actual demand forecast systematically by first characterizing and then extrapolating the patterns our analysis has uncovered.

In those cases where we find a trend we normally start with this movement as the basis for our forecast. We could graphically extend this trend, but in the case of a linear trend a better procedure would be to find the trend line equation by the least-squares method (introduced in chapter 2). This line, fitted to the centered 16–quarter moving averages of Table 4–1, would be $T = 44 + N$, where T stands for the "quarterly trend component," and N for the "quarter number." The estimates for trend components as calculated from this equation are listed in the second column of Table 4–2.

Quarter Number	T	$\dfrac{T \times C}{T}$	$\dfrac{D}{T \times C}$	Cyclical Indices	Seasonal Indices
1	45	–	–	0.98	1.13
2	46	–	–	1.18	1.52
3	47	1.42	0.85	1.37	0.90
4	48	1.56	0.68	1.47	0.45
5	49	1.61	1.14	1.51	1.13
6	50	1.54	1.49	1.45	1.52
7	51	1.37	0.87	1.32	0.90
8	52	1.17	0.51	1.15	0.45
9	53	0.98	1.10	0.98	1.13
10	54	0.80	1.70	0.82	1.52
11	55	0.62	0.76	0.67	0.90
12	56	0.50	0.36	0.56	0.45
13	57	0.47	0.63	0.53	1.13
14	58	0.50	2.03	0.56	1.52
15	59	0.63	0.81	0.63	0.90
16	60	0.82	0.35	0.82	0.45
17	61	0.98	1.10	0.98	1.13
18	62	1.18	1.44	1.18	1.52
19	63	1.33	0.93	1.37	0.90
20	64	1.41	0.73	1.47	0.45
21	65	1.43	1.10	1.51	1.13
22	66	1.38	1.34	1.45	1.52
23	67	1.27	0.98	1.32	0.90
24	68	1.13	0.64	1.15	0.45
25	69	1.00	1.03	0.98	1.13
26	70	0.86	1.48	0.82	1.52
27	71	0.72	0.88	0.67	0.90
28	72	0.62	0.31	0.56	0.45
29	73	0.59	0.84	0.53	1.13
30	74	0.62	1.67	0.56	1.52
31	75	–	–	0.63	0.90
32	76	–	–	0.82	0.45

Table 4–2

In those cases where no discernible trend movement is found the final chain of moving averages will appear to "bounce" around on either side of a horizontal line. Calculating the mean value of these averages will provide us with an estimate of the underlying average demand rate—which is the height at which this horizontal line would appear to be located. This average demand rate is then projected into the future as the base forecast for all future time periods.

Both cyclical and seasonal movements are measured by indices, and these will be relative to the trend or average demand rate depending upon which type of base forecast we have. If we use D to stand for the variable *quarterly demand, T* for *quarterly trend, S* for the *seasonal indices,* and C for the *cyclical indices,* then as a model for our time series we could use: $D = T \times S \times C$. If we have no trend movement then the calculated average demand rate would replace the T in this model. What this model says is that if we multiply the trend component of a particular quarter by the seasonal index for this quarter and then multiply this by the cyclical index for this quarter, what we will have is an estimate for the actual demand for this quarter. First we use the model to effect a characterization of the individual movements as uncovered in our analysis, and then as the model for forecasting into the future.

First let's find estimates for the cyclical indices. First we have the trend values, values of T, for each quarter in our historical period (in the second column of Table 4–2). Also, since the four-quarter moving averages have smoothed away the seasonal movement, these must be the values of $T \times C$; that is, the combination of trend and cyclical movements. Thus, if we divide these averages by the trend values, quarter by quarter, we will produce estimates for the quarterly values of the C's. These results are shown in the third column of Table 4–2. Since there are sixteen quarters in the period of the cyclical movement, we only want this many cyclical indices. We obtain these by averaging (when we have more than one value) the C values just obtained, averaging these for corresponding quarters in successive sixteen-quarter periods. These final cyclical indices are shown in the fifth column of Table 4–2. Actually, we have adjusted these so that their sum is 16.0. This is a necessary operation and in general we adjust any set of periodic indices so that their sum is equal to the total number of them—we have sixteen indices so their total must equal 16.0.

Next we find estimates for the seasonal indices. First we note that if our original demand figures are used for the values of D in our model, then as D equals the product $T \times S \times C$, dividing the values of D by $T \times C$ (the values of the four–quarter moving averages) we will thereby produce estimates for the values of S. These are initial estimates of the seasonal indices and by averaging these for corresponding quarters of successive years we will produce four final seasonal indices, which we must adjust, if needed, so that their sum equals 4.0. The results of these divisions are shown in the fourth column of Table 4–2 with the final seasonal indices in the last column. In this particular case there were extreme values in the initial estimates, and so we "averaged" these through the use of their median to produce the final indices.

At this point we could multiply the trend component of a quarter by first its seasonal index and then its cyclical index thereby producing an estimate for the actual demand in this quarter. Normally, these will not be the same as the original quarterly demands owing to a random movement which is always present. By subtracting the estimates from the actual demands, we would produce the series of estimation errors attributed to our model and the manner in which it fits our demand history. We could then analyze this series of errors as we would any univariate data set and thus develop information which would serve to indicate the error distribution we are likely to have in our forecasts with the model.

Once we have the model quantified, it is a simple matter to extrapolate it into the future. The trend part for each quarter we are forecasting is estimated from our trend line, either graphically, or more preferably, from the trend line equation. For any quarter we multiply its trend component estimate by the seasonal and cyclical indices and the result is the final forecast for this quarter. If we don't have a trend, we use the average demand rate as the base forecast. The forecast for any quarter is this average value times the two indices of this quarter.

To illustrate how these calculations would go, the forecast for the next four quarters in our example are presented in the following display.

Quarter Number	Trend T	Seasonal Index S	$T \times S$	Cyclical Index C	Forecast $T \times S \times C$
33	77	1.13	87	0.98	85
34	78	1.52	119	1.18	140
35	79	0.90	71	1.38	98
36	80	0.45	36	1.48	53

Forecasting by Exponential Smoothing

The forecasting procedure of the previous section can be very useful, but it would be impractical to apply it to short-term forecasting as needed in production and inventory control of hundreds of different products. In this situation we need a more efficient forecasting procedure which will produce forecasts of the customer demand for the upcoming period quickly so that this may be compared to available stock to determine production requirements. We also need a method which does not require our keeping large quantities of historical data on each product and one whose calculations may be performed by non-technical personnel.

The use of *exponential smoothing* in preparing demand forecasts is extremely popular in the production-inventory control context, and it meets all the cited requirements. It is a special kind of moving average and has the capability of responding to change, where in fact the rate of response can be adjusted as we see fit. Unlike moving averages, exponential smoothing can be extended to specifically handle trend movements, and seasonal patterns.

To illustrate the use of this technique, let us assume that last month we prepared a forecast for the *average rate of demand* for a product in this current month. The forecast was for 100 units. The actual demand for this month turned out to be for 150 units, meaning we were off by 50 units, or suffered a forecast error of 50 percent. Should we continue with the same 100 units forecast for the next month? We would probably be willing to do this if the actual demand had been closer to our forecast in this month, but with a 50 percent error we might suspect that a fundamental change has taken place in the demand pattern making our 100 unit forecast no longer applicable. Should we then forecast next month to have a demand of 150 units? We would probably not be comfortable with this extreme either. We might have experienced a "fluke" of some kind to which we would not like to overreact. More likely we would add on a portion of the forecast error to our previous forecast, and, if we decide to include 20 percent of this error, then our forecast for the demand in the next month would be: $100 + 0.20 (150 - 100) = 110$ units.

We have written out the operations in this way since it represents a particular case of our general procedure. The 0.20 value is an adjusting factor, or control knob, and is called the *smoothing constant*. We denote this by θ, the lower-case Greek letter "theta" (normally alpha, a, is used, but because we have used this in the previous chapter we have elected this substitute). The 100 units is referred to as the OLD AVERAGE, the 150 units as the ACTUAL DEMAND, and the 110 units as the NEW AVERAGE. If, in addition, we denote the difference between actual and forecasted demand, the $150 - 100$, as the FORECAST ERROR, then our general rules for preparing an exponentially smoothed forecast of *average demand rate* are:

---

1. (FORECAST ERROR) = (ACTUAL DEMAND − OLD AVERAGE)
2. (NEW AVERAGE) = (OLD AVERAGE) + θ (FORECAST ERROR)
3. (DEMAND FORECAST) = (NEW AVERAGE)

---

where the smoothing constant, θ, can have any value between *zero* and *one*.

The technique is illustrated in Table 4–3, where a smoothing constant of $\theta = 0.20$ is used and where our initial estimate for the average demand is 100 units, this being the demand we forecast for January.

Once the January demand becomes known, which is 150 units in our example, we go to Rule 1 and put this demand in for ACTUAL DEMAND. Our initial estimate of average demand, the 100 units, we put in as OLD AVERAGE. With these two values we thus find from Rule 1, FORECAST ERROR = 50 units. This value is used in Rule 2, again with our 100 units as OLD AVERAGE. We find NEW AVERAGE = 110 units, which by Rule 3 is our DEMAND FORECAST, this being the demand we forecast for the "next" month, February.

When the demand in February, 130 units, becomes known, we again return to Rule 1 with this value as our ACTUAL DEMAND, and with the NEW AVERAGE, 110 units, which we calculated "last" month being "this" month's OLD AVERAGE. We therefore calculate FORECAST ERROR = 20 units. Again, the 110–figure is the OLD AVERAGE, now in Rule 2, along with the 20 units of error just calculated. The NEW AVERAGE we thus calculate is 114 units, which is the demand we forecast for the "next" month, March.

Each month we recycle "last" month's NEW AVERAGE as "this" month's OLD AVERAGE, and introduce "this" month's demand as the ACTUAL DEMAND. Thus, the only input we need, once we get started, is the current month's demand figure. This recycling of "NEW" for "OLD" is basic to all exponential smoothing and is the feature which allows us to forecast with almost no data files.

Of main importance in using this dynamic forecasting technique is the choice of the smoothing constant. The larger we make this, the more responsive will be our forecasts to the most recent demands. A value of $\theta = 1.0$ will cause the forecasts to exactly reproduce "this" month's actual demand as "next" month's forecasted demand. The smaller the value of θ, the less reactive will be our forecasts to recent demands. Setting $\theta = 0$ will force the procedure to completely ignore the most current demand in our forecasts.

To illustrate this point, in Table 4–4 we show the forecasts which would be calculated for the same data as in Table 4–3 but with a smoothing constant of 0.8. The actual demands and both forecasts are shown in Figure 4–3, where we see that the forecasts with the larger θ react more dramatically to swings in demand than do those with the smaller value for θ.

Initial Estimate of Average	Month	Actual Demand	Old Average	Forecast Error	New Average*
100	Jan.	150	100	+50	110
	Feb.	130	110	+20	114
	Mar.	104	114	−10	112
	Apr.	107	112	− 5	111
	May	111	111	0	111
	Jun.	121	111	+10	113
	Jul.	108	113	− 5	112

*Smoothing constant $\theta = 0.20$

Table 4–3

Initial Estimate of Average	Month	Actual Demand	Old Average	Forecast Error	New Average*
100	Jan.	150	100	+50	140
	Feb.	130	140	−10	132
	Mar.	104	132	−28	110
	Apr.	107	110	− 3	108
	May	111	108	+ 3	110
	Jun.	121	110	+11	119
	Jul.	108	119	−11	110

*Smoothing constant $\theta = 0.80$

Table 4–4

Is a smaller value of θ therefore preferable? To answer this question we must have prior knowledge on the demand pattern for the particular item we are forecasting. If, for instance, we judge that the demand is entering a period of rapid and dramatic change in average level, perhaps growing or decaying to a new level as a new product might or as might be due to a heavy promotion of the item, then in these instances we would like to "keep up" with these changes and so large values of θ are appropriate. Once our demand pattern has stabilized, or if it is already well-established, then the smaller values of θ should be used since in this situation we don't want to chase after random movement. In most situations some value between 0.01 and 0.3 is used for θ, but, of course, the final decision should be made based on some simulation with past data or else in the course of normal use of the method.

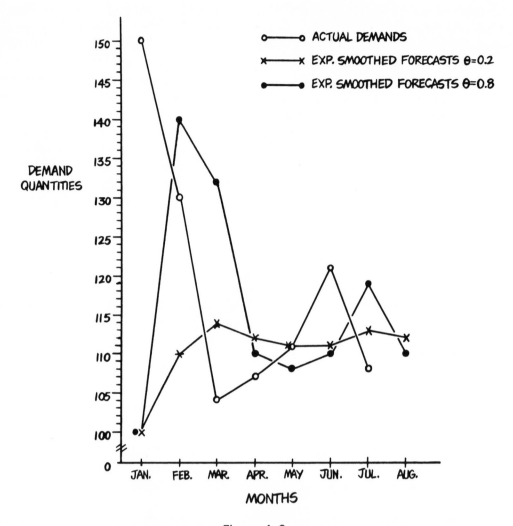

Figure 4–3

Another question concerning the initial start-up of the method is: Where do we get the initial forecast (the first value of OLD AVERAGE)? This should be obtained in a manner consistent with the smoothing constant we use and as a rule if we have the value for θ then our initial forcast for average demand rate can be the mean value of the most recent n actual demands, where n is calculated from the formula:

$$n = \frac{2}{\theta} - 1$$

Thus, for example, if a smoothing constant of 0.4 is chosen, then the average of the previous $(2/0.4) - 1 = 4$ demands is an appropriate initial forecast for the average demand rate.

Recalling that the NEW AVERAGE for the current month is the smoothed estimate of the *average* demand rate, we see that if we also knew the standard deviation of the demand rate we could set up confidence limits. These we could set up as control limits which if exceeded by an ACTUAL DEMAND would indicate a significant change in average demand rate. We may also use them to perform hypothesis testing procedures. An approximation to this standard deviation can be developed (and updated each month) from the so-called *Mean Absolute Deviation,* or as commonly known the *MAD.* It has been shown that under the assumption that demands are approximately normally distributed, an estimate for the standard deviation of demand is $1.25 \times$ MAD. As MAD can change each month, so also can our estimated standard deviation.

The exact method for computing the MAD requires that we keep track of the FORECAST ERROR from the very start of our program, as well as a running total of the number of forecasts made. We accumulate the absolute values of FORECAST ERROR, where by "absolute value" we mean that we ignore the plus or minus sign attached to these error terms, and dividing this sum for the current month by the number of forecasts whose errors comprise it we will have the value of MAD for this month. The MAD values we would calculate for the errors of Table 4–3 are shown in the fourth column of Table 4–5, where our running sum of absolute values of our errors is shown in the third column of the table.

A more efficient way to find MAD values, one which does not require our maintaining and updating summations, is by smoothing. In this smoothing process there is no argument against using the smoothing constant θ, and the procedure of smoothing is given as follows:

NEW MAD = OLD MAD + (θ | FORECAST ERROR | − OLD MAD)

---

where the vertical bars on the FORECAST ERROR term indicate we mean the absolute value of this figure. We will need an initial estimate of MAD (which is our first OLD MAD value), and this can be obtained from the exact method applied to the first few periods of our program. After this point the NEW MAD will be recycled as the next month's OLD MAD as in our previous smoothing procedure.

In Table 4–5 we also show the results of the smoothing procedure for calculating MAD values, where an initial estimate for MAD of 50 is given. A value of 0.3 for θ would have caused the MAD values to home in to the exact values better.

Initial Estimate of MAD	FORECAST ERROR	Total of Absolute Errors	MAD (Exact)	MAD (Smoothed)*
50	+50	50	50.0	50.0
	+20	70	35.0	44.0
	−10	80	26.7	37.2
	− 5	85	21.2	30.8
	0	85	17.0	24.6
	+10	95	15.8	21.7
	− 5	100	14.2	18.4

*Smoothing constant $\theta = 0.20$

Table 4–5

Thus, as of the last month of our data, that is, July, our average demand rate would be 112 units and the standard deviation of demand rate would be estimated by (using the smoothed MAD value for July), $1.25 \times 18.4 = 23.0$ units. With this information we can establish the 95 percent confidence limits on demand rate as $112 \pm 1.96\,(23) = 112 \pm 45$, or 67 units to 157 units. As a routine procedure, management may wish to be alerted whenever demand falls outside of these limits at which time it may choose to alter the smoothing constant or take some other action. In any case, with such warning management will be able to review the stock status on critical materials, look for possible spots in production plans where capacity can be increased or decreased depending upon where the demand falls with respect to the limits, and it will be able to do this in advance of the demand level change.

Another procedure used in flagging significant changes in demand rate would involve two sets of confidence limits. For instance, the 80 percent confidence limits would be 112 $\pm 1.28\,(23)$ or from 83 units to 141 units. Now, if a demand falls between 67 and 83, or between 141 and 157 this might be flagged as a "minor" change; whereas, if demand goes beyond 157 or below 67 it would be a "major" change. Management may then have two alternative courses of action planned for minor and major changes. Naturally, the confidence levels used in these limits should reflect management's risk levels which it associates with not reacting to a demand rate change.

A procedure which can be instituted to control the forecasting system itself is based on the so-called *tracking signal*. This is the ratio of the smoothed error and the smoothed absolute error and cannot go outside the range ± 1. We thus have:

$$\text{Tracking Signal} = \frac{\text{(NEW SMOOTHED ERROR)}}{\text{(NEW SMOOTHED ABSOLUTE ERROR)}}$$

$$\begin{pmatrix}\text{NEW SMOOTHED}\\ \text{ERROR}\end{pmatrix} = \begin{pmatrix}\text{OLD SMOOTHED}\\ \text{ERROR}\end{pmatrix} + \theta(\text{FORECAST ERROR} - \text{OLD SMOOTHED ERROR})$$

$$\begin{pmatrix}\text{NEW SMOOTHED}\\ \text{ABSOLUTE ERROR}\end{pmatrix} = \begin{pmatrix}\text{OLD SMOOTHED}\\ \text{ABSOLUTE ERROR}\end{pmatrix} + \theta\left[\,|\text{FORECAST ERROR}| - \begin{pmatrix}\text{OLD SMOOTHED}\\ \text{ABSOLUTE ERROR}\end{pmatrix}\right]$$

To start we will need initial values for OLD SMOOTHED ERROR and OLD SMOOTHED ABSOLUTE ERROR, and as usual, from the first period on we recycle the "NEW" for the "OLD."

The tracking signal is used to detect a bias in the forecast errors. If such bias occurs in the system, the signal will move toward $+1$ or -1; it will go toward the former if the system is consistently *understating* demands, and toward the latter value if the system is consistently *overstating* demands. Some texts may make the reverse statement, but this is due to their reversing ACTUAL DEMAND and OLD AVERAGE in the FORECAST ERROR formula as we have given it.

The ideal situation is where forecast errors are truly random and have *zero* mean value. If the variance of forecast error is s^2 then the variance of the smoothed errors will be $\theta \cdot s^2/(2-\theta)$, and the variance of the tracking signal (which also has zero mean value in the ideal case) is approximately $1.5\theta/(2-\theta)$.

With these we can set up confidence limits on the smoothed error and the tracking signal which are used to raise exception flags in the program. But, of course, if we wish to use confidence limits, we will have to make provision for the accumulation of the forecast errors, their squares, as well as a running total of the number of forecasts made so that we will be able to estimate the current value of s^2 (chapter 1 has the rule we have in mind here).

When we are simply forecasting the average demand rate, it makes good sense to use the tracking signal for it will indicate when we should introduce the mechanism for adjusting our forecasts for trend. How we would go about doing this in our next topic.

Accommodating Trend

To handle a trend movement we introduce another smoothing constant, β, which is the lower-case Greek letter "beta," and the following set of smoothing rules:

---

1. FORECAST ERROR = (ACTUAL DEMAND − OLD AVERAGE)
2. NEW AVERAGE = OLD AVERAGE + θ (FORECAST ERROR)
3. CURRENT TREND = (NEW AVERAGE − OLD AVERAGE)
4. TREND FORECAST ERROR = (CURRENT TREND − OLD TREND)
5. NEW TREND = OLD TREND + β·(TREND FORECAST ERROR)
6. DEMAND FORECAST = NEW AVERAGE + $\dfrac{\text{NEW TREND}}{\theta}$

---

which are presented in the order of their execution.

Rules 1 and 2 are those of the previous section which are used to prepare smoothed forecasts for the average demand rate. Rule 3 estimates a current (or intermediate) value for trend using the difference of the old and new average forecasts. Rule 4 uses this current value for trend to estimate the error in our trend forecasts; here we see that an initial estimate for trend (the first value for OLD TREND) will be needed at the start. Rule 5 produces the updated forecast for the trend in our demand rate and this will become the OLD TREND for the "next" month. Rule 6 produces the actual forecast for "next" month's demand.

Rule 6 perhaps needs some explanation. In some texts this rule would be written as "DEMAND FORECAST = NEW AVERAGE + NEW TREND," however, in this form our calculated forecasts would lag behind actual demands. In our Rule 6 a lag correction term has been incorporated into the rule to compensate for this lag.

What we have said about the values of θ also applies to those of β. The larger we set β, the more reactive will be our trend forecast to demand trend, and the smaller we set it, the less reactive will be our forecasts. Again, some form of testing is recommended in selecting the value to use for β, but in most instances some value between 0.01 and 0.3 will be adequate.

A word of caution is in order at this point, and this is that the trend smoothing mechanism is best used only when it is known that there is definite trend present in our demand pattern. Otherwise, the forecast may interpret a random movement in demands as trend and "chase" after it—in fact both the average and trend will attempt to "home" on these movements. If we do not follow this advice, we may produce poorer forecasts than the average method.

To illustrate the rules, let us suppose that our initial forecast for the average demand rate and trend are respectively 70 and 2.0, and we have selected $\theta = 0.20$, and $\beta = 0.30$. Our example is depicted in Table 4–6. As indicated in this table the demand in January turned out to be for 80 units and the forecast for the demand in February is calculated to be 82 units. The following steps show how this was calculated:

FORECAST ERROR	$= 80 - 70$	$= 10$
NEW AVERAGE	$= 70 + 0.2(10)$	$= 72$
CURRENT TREND	$= 72 - 70$	$= 2.0$
TREND FORECAST ERROR	$= 2.0 - 2.0$	$= 0.0$
NEW TREND	$= 2.0 + 0.3(0.0)$	$= 2.0$
DEMAND FORECAST	$= 72 + (2.0/0.2)$	$= 82$

The rest of the table is filled in by recycling through these steps with the appropriate use of the updated figures. The DEMAND FORECAST values are plotted in Figure 4–4 along

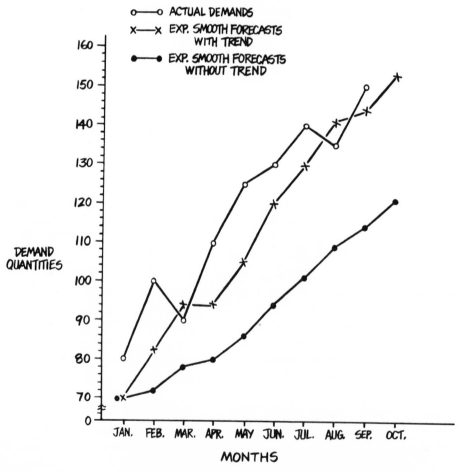

Figure 4–4

Initial Estimate of Average	Initial Estimate of Trend	Month	Actual Demand	Forecast Error	New Average	Current Trend	Trend Forecast Error	New Trend	Demand Forecast (next month)
70	2.0	Jan.	80	10	72	2.0	0.0	2.0	82
		Feb.	100	28	78	6.0	4.0	3.2	94
		Mar.	90	12	80	2.0	-1.2	2.8	94
		Apr.	110	30	86	6.0	3.2	3.8	105
		May	125	39	94	8.0	4.2	5.1	120
		Jun.	130	36	101	7.0	1.9	5.7	130
		Jul.	140	39	109	8.0	2.3	6.4	141
		Aug.	135	26	114	5.0	-1.4	6.0	144
		Sep.	150	36	121	7.0	1.0	6.3	153

Table 4–6

with the values of the ACTUAL DEMAND. These forecasts are labeled as "Exponentially Smoothed Forecasts with Trend." If we had not introduced the trend smoothing portion of the procedure, and instead just used the average portion, then our forecasts would be our calculated values for NEW AVERAGE. These are also plotted in Figure 4–4, labeled "Exponentially Smoothed Forecasts Without Trend." We can see from this figure that with trend included our forecasts are much better.

To illustrate the use of the tracking signal, let us suppose that we did in fact use the NEW AVERAGE forecasts in the above example. Then assuming that we had initial estimates for smoothed error and smoothed absolute error of respectively 5 and 20 units, the calculations of tracking signals would produce the results shown in Table 4–7. According to our rules for interpreting the tracking signal, we can conclude from the tabled signals that our NEW AVERAGE forecasts are consistently understating actual demands, and trend should be introduced into our system.

Initial Smoothed Error	Initial Smoothed Absolute Error	Forecast Error	New Smoothed Error*	New Smoothed Absolute Error*	Tracking Signal
5	20	+10	6.0	18.0	0.33
		+28	10.4	20.0	0.52
		+12	10.7	18.4	0.58
		+30	14.6	20.7	0.70
		+39	19.5	24.4	0.80
		+36	22.8	26.7	0.85
		+39	26.0	29.2	0.89
		+26	26.0	28.5	0.91
		+36	28.0	30.0	0.93

*Smoothing constant $\theta = 0.20$

Table 4–7

As we have said, exponential smoothing is best used for the short-term forecast, however, if we must have an extended forecast we can develop this from our most current smoothed data. A linear model, $D = A + Bt$, is usually assumed for this purpose, where the most current values of DEMAND FORECAST and NEW TREND are used as A and B respectively. In this model D is the forecasted demand for month number t, and we start in the "next" month with $t = 0$, and for each month thereafter we increment t by 1. Thus, from Table 4–6, as of the end of September we could construct the model $D = 153 + 6.3t$, and use this to produce the forecast $153 + 6.3\,(2) = 165.6$ (or rounded, 166) units for the month of December.

Accommodating Seasonals

The smoothing procedures up to this point will not correct for any seasonal pattern in our demands. A modification of the computational procedures, however, handles this type of pattern effectively. We need another smoothing constant, γ, which is the lower-case Greek letter "gamma," and an appropriate smoothing procedure for producing smoothed estimates of seasonal indices. At the start we will need initial estimates for these indices, and these we can determine from a previous year of demand history using the appropriate procedure as discussed in chapter 2.

To cover the most general situation we will introduce the mechanism in the context of the previous section's rules. The first thing we change is the rule used to determine FORE-CAST ERROR; in place of Rule 1 of the previous section we use:

$$1.'\ \text{FORECAST ERROR} = \left(\frac{\text{ACTUAL DEMAND}}{\substack{\text{SEASONAL INDEX FOR} \\ \text{THIS MONTH}}} - \text{OLD AVERAGE} \right)$$

Thus, the actual demand for a month is divided by the seasonal index for this same month and this result (which is the deseasonalized actual demand) is used in calculating the forecast error term.

The value of DEMAND FORECAST we calculate with Rule 6 will be a deseasonalized forecast for "next" month. To bring the seasonality into our final forecast we must multiply this deseasonalized forecast by the seasonal index for the "next" month. Therefore, we need the additional rule:

$$7.\ \left(\substack{\text{SEASONALIZED} \\ \text{DEMAND FORECAST}} \right) = (\text{DEMAND FORECAST}) \times \left(\substack{\text{SEASONAL INDEX FOR} \\ \text{NEXT MONTH}} \right)$$

Along with producing a forecast for the demand in "next" month we also calculate an updated (smoothed) estimate of the seasonal index for "this" current month. Having the previous value for this seasonal index, and the assigned value of the smoothing constant, γ, we calculate this updated index as follows:

$$8.\ \left(\substack{\text{NEW SEASONAL} \\ \text{INDEX FOR} \\ \text{THIS MONTH}} \right) = \left(\substack{\text{OLD SEASONAL} \\ \text{INDEX FOR} \\ \text{THIS MONTH}} \right) + \gamma \left(\frac{\text{ACTUAL DEMAND}}{\text{NEW AVERAGE}} - \substack{\text{OLD SEASONAL} \\ \text{INDEX FOR} \\ \text{THIS MONTH}} \right)$$

Every time we calculate a new seasonal index we must review all indices to make sure that their sum equals 12.0. Suppose that with the addition of our new index the twelve indices sum to S rather than to 12.0. The adjustment we make is to multiply each of the indices by the factor $(12.0/S)$, which should produce indices which sum to 12.0. This is a vital step since it keeps the seasonal pattern from "creeping" into our average and trend forecasts.

For those instances where we have no trend but a definite seasonal movement we would still use this same procedure just illustrated. Here we would have Rule 1', Rule 2 and Rule 6 of the previous section, and also Rule 7; however, in Rule 6 the value of NEW TREND would always be set equal to *zero*. This would cover the case where we were forecasting average demand rate along with seasonal adjustments.

There is also a theory of exponential smoothing which works from a trend curve rather than the trend line as we have used. In most situations the procedures we have described and illustrated will suffice.

CONCLUSION

In this chapter we have demonstrated the use of moving averages in the analysis of demand histories where our purpose is to uncover basic patterns underlying the demands. Along with characterizing these, we have also shown how this may be used to produce forecasts into the future. The main assumption is that the conditions which existed when our historical demands occurred will continue into the future period for which we are forecasting. In addition, the techniques by which short-term smoothed forecasts can be prepared were demonstrated, along with procedures for controlling the forecasts as well as the system producing these.

REFERENCES

Brown, R.G. *Smoothing, Forecasting, and Prediction of Discrete Time Series.* Englewood Cliffs, N.J.: Prentice-Hall, Inc., 1963.

_____. *Statistical Forecasting for Inventory Control.* New York, N.Y.: McGraw-Hill Book Co., 1959.

Geoffrion, A.M. "A Summary of Exponential Smoothing," *Journal of Industrial Engineering,* July-August, 1962.

Montgomery, D.C. "An Introduction to Short-Term Forecasting," *Journal of Industrial Engineering,* October, 1968.

Trigg, D.W., and A.G. Leach. "Exponential Smoothing with an Adaptive Response Rate," *Operations Research Quarterly,* Vol. 18, No. 53, 1967.

Winters, P.R. "Forecasting Sales by Exponentially Weighted Moving Averages," *Management Science,* Vol. 6, No. 3, April, 1960.

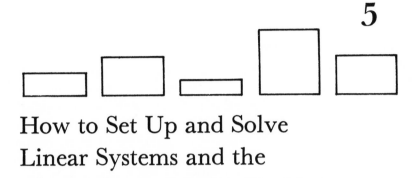

How to Set Up and Solve
Linear Systems and the
Linear Programming Problem

An equation in the variables X, Y, and Z is said to be *linear* if it has the following form:

$$aX + bY + cZ = d$$

where a, b, c, and d are numbers, and at least one of the a, b, or c is different from *zero*. Such an equation is simply an abstract statement of a relationship existing between the three variables. If such an equation arose in the context of our previous chapters, we would probably be hypothesizing it as the relationship between the variables. Most likely, our next step would be to collect and analyze a sample of observations (X, Y, Z), from which we would calculate estimates for the values a, b, c, and d, along with an appropriate measurement of the "goodness of fit" of the resulting equation to the actual data.

In this chapter we will be using linear equations in a completely different way: we start with a known relationship between the variables, one which allows us to immediately write down the equation with actual numerical values for a, b, c, and d. What we won't know are those particular values for the variables which when substituted will make the equation a true statement. These values are termed the *solution to the equation*. Thus, the equation:

$$2X + Y + 3Z = 50$$

has a solution $X = 4$, $Y = 12$, $Z = 10$, since $2(4) + 1(12) + 3(10) = 50$.

It is convenient to write a solution as a triple of values (X, Y, Z), thus, for this illustration, the solution would be written in the shorthand: (4, 12, 10).

In any practical situation we will have our variables standing in more than one relationship to each other simultaneously, and so more than one equation will be needed to properly describe the situation. These equations, as a group, are termed *the system of equations* for the problem, and *linear systems* when all the equations are linear. The solution to a system of equations consists of a value for each variable which will simultaneously make each of the system equations a true statement. This is why one often refers to the process of finding the solution as "solving a system of simultaneous equations."

The system of equations need not have a solution, and if it does, this need not be the only solution; having two solutions will in fact mean we have an infinite number of solutions. A system with a unique solution is said to be a *consistent system,* while one with no solution is *inconsistent.* If we have an infinite number of distinct solutions to the system, we say that the system is *dependent,* and in this situation at least one of the equations is a combination of some of the other equations—the equations are not independent of one another. How we can analyze a general linear system will be demonstrated in this chapter.

For many problems we will not have the variables related in a statement of "equality," but rather in one of "inequality." Such inequations arise when we must place restrictions on the combined effect of our variables. For instance, if X, Y, and Z represent the production quantities of three products, in units, which require respectively 2, 3, and 5 hours per unit of processing on a certain machine which has only 100 hours of available capacity. Then the amounts we produce of each product (the values of the variables) must, in total, call for no more than 100 hours of processing time. This restriction would be written as the following inequation:

$$2X + 3Y + 5Z \leq 100.$$

The symbol "$\leq$" signifies that the expression on the left-hand side of it must be "less than or equal to" the quantity on the right-hand side.

As with equations, it is more the normal situation to have a system of inequations which must be simultaneously satisfied by a set of values before we would consider this set as a feasible solution to the system.

Quite naturally, such systems of inequations arise from our need to allocate some scarce resource to various uses, such as in our illustration where we are allocating machine capacity to three products. In such problems we will usually find many solutions to the system of inequations, that is, we will have many feasible solutions. However, according to some objective, we will view one of these as "better" than the others, this we term the *optimum solution.* We may, for example, want that feasible solution (or allocation of resources) which will in turn produce the largest possible profit. In another situation we might want that solution representing the minimum production costs.

These objectives are also expressed in the form of equations. For the above illustration we might have profits, P, related to the variables by the *objective equation:*

$$P = 0.25X + 1.35Y + 2.01Z$$

where the coefficients in this equation are the per unit profits for the three different products. Here we desire that feasible solution which maximizes the value of P according to this equation. The optimum solution to this trivial problem is (0, 33, 0), with profit of 44.55 profit units.

Solving such restricted problems will also be a topic of this chapter. Here we will deal only with the case where all inequations and the objective equation are linear in form. Our solution techniques will be procedures which start with an initial feasible solution from which the optimum solution (if one exists) will be developed by iterating through a sequence of calculations and tests. Basically, these procedures are taken from the general topic of *linear programming theory*.

Analyzing a System of Linear Equations

Our first general statement is: *If our system of equations has more variables than individual equations, there will be an infinite number of distinct solutions to the system.* With m variables and n equations, with $m > n$, our solution procedure is to assign arbitrary values to any $m - n$ of the variables, giving us a system of n variables and n equations which we then solve. This solution to the reduced system along with the assigned values to the selected $m - n$ variables will constitute *a solution* to the original system.

To illustrate, let's consider the following system of three variables in two equations ($m = 3, n = 2$):

$$2X + Y + 3Z = 50$$
$$X + Y + 4Z = 40$$

We are told that we may assign an arbitrary value of $3 - 2 = 1$ variable thereby eliminating it from the system. Let's select Z and assign it a value of 0. The resulting reduced system is:

$$2X + Y = 50$$
$$X + Y = 40$$

which has the unique solution $X = 10$, $Y = 30$. A solution to the original system is therefore (10, 30, 0).

If we had assigned the value 10 to Z we would have obtained this reduced system:

$$2X + Y = 20$$
$$X + Y = 0$$

whose unique solution is $X = 20$, $Y = -20$. Thus, another solution to the original system is (20, −20, 10).

We can continue assigning values to Z and solving the resulting reduced systems which will provide us with additional solutions to the original system. This is our only recourse without a third equation in the system. Of course, in the practical situation, we do not want an infinite number of solutions and so we would make just one assignment to Z. Which variable is selected, and what its value will be, should be decided from the circumstances surrounding the problem.

Even when we have the same number of variables as equations, we may still have an infinite number of solutions; here, however, this condition will be due to the relationship among the equations and not a direct conclusion as above. The following system has an infinite number of solutions, as we will subsequently show:

$$X + Y + 4Z = 40$$
$$2X + Y + 3Z = 50$$
$$4X + 3Y + 11Z = 130$$

By writing the equations of a system so that the variable terms appear in the same sequential order in each equation we are able to delete the variable symbols and work directly with the coefficients. This is termed *detaching the coefficients* and is done to ease our computations by not having to carry along the variable symbols.

To illustrate, we consider the following system with unique solution $(25, -45, 15)$:

$$2X + Y + 3Z = 50$$
$$X + Y + 4Z = 40$$
$$2X + Y + Z = 20$$

We may detach the coefficients and write these in the following rectangular array:

$$\begin{pmatrix} 2 & 1 & 3 \\ 1 & 1 & 4 \\ 2 & 1 & 1 \end{pmatrix}$$

An array of numbers such as this is termed a *matrix,* and when it arises from a system of equations we further distinguish it as the *coefficients matrix.* In general, a matrix with n rows and m columns is said to be of *size* "$n \times m$" (to be read "n by m"). Our coefficients matrix is thus of size 3×3. It is also an example of a *square matrix* since the number of rows in it is the same as its number of columns.

The three constants on the right-hand sides of our equations may also be displayed as a matrix, this being the following:

$$\begin{pmatrix} 50 \\ 40 \\ 20 \end{pmatrix}$$

This is appropriately called a *column matrix,* being of size 3×1. A matrix with elements written in a row is a *row matrix* which will be of size $1 \times n$ where n is the number of columns (elements) in it.

Our first step in the analysis of a system is to form the *augmented matrix* for the system. To do this we simply juxtapose the coefficients matrix and the constants column matrix, writing the result as a single matrix. For our example we would have this augmented matrix:

$$\begin{pmatrix} 2 & 1 & 3 & 50 \\ 1 & 1 & 4 & 40 \\ 2 & 1 & 1 & 20 \end{pmatrix}$$

where we have widened the space between the two matrices to keep them distinct in our subsequent operations.

The augmented matrix completely specifies the system (assuming we know the order of the variables), and vice versa; the two are *equivalent*. Thus, with the same order of variables as above, the following augmented matrix

$$\begin{pmatrix} 1 & 0 & 0 & 10 \\ 0 & 1 & 0 & 30 \\ 0 & 0 & 1 & 25 \end{pmatrix}$$

is equivalent to the system:

$$X + 0 \cdot Y + 0 \cdot Z = 10$$
$$0 \cdot X + Y + 0 \cdot Z = 30$$
$$0 \cdot X + 0 \cdot Y + Z = 25$$

that is:

$$X = 10$$
$$Y = 30$$
$$Z = 25$$

which explicitly gives us the solution to the system. This particular augmented matrix is termed the *canonical form*. The coefficients matrix portion of it has all 0's except along the *main diagonal* going diagonally from the upper left-hand corner of the matrix to the lower right-hand corner, where we have all 1's. It is this characteristic which gives us the solution directly.

In the analysis of a system with the same number of equations as variables, we start with the original augmented matrix and perform arithmetical operations on its rows, applying whatever combination of operations is necessary to lead us to the canonical form. The solution we read off this canonical form will be the solution to the original system with which we started.

How do we perform an operation on a row? Simply by performing the exact same arithmetic on each and every element in the row. Thus, we may say "multiply the row by —1," by which we mean "multiply each element in this row by —1 and substitute these results for the original elements of the row."

What operations are we allowed to perform on the rows? Any of the following, or any combination of these:

1. Multiply a row by a nonzero number.
2. Interchange any two rows in the matrix.
3. Add a nonzero multiple of one row to another row, adding element by element.

First, we transform the first column of the augmented matrix into the canonical form, then the second column, and so on across the matrix. If in the process we develop a row of 0's, then the original system is dependent, whereas, it is an inconsistent system if we develop a row with 0's in the coefficients matrix portion of the augmented matrix, with a nonzero number in the constants matrix portion.

To illustrate the procedure, let's apply the process to our example above. In the following, the augmented matrix is shown with Roman numerals identifying the rows so that our individual operations may be explicitly shown.

$$
\begin{array}{c}
\text{I} \\
\text{II} \\
\text{III}
\end{array}
\qquad
\begin{pmatrix}
2 & 1 & 3 & 50 \\
1 & 1 & 4 & 40 \\
2 & 1 & 1 & 20
\end{pmatrix}
$$

The "2" in the upper left corner is to be replaced with a "1," and we can accomplish this by: interchanging II and I; multiplying I by $\frac{1}{2}$; multiplying II by -1 and adding the result to I; or, multiplying III by $-\frac{1}{2}$ and adding the result to I. As a practical matter we should not introduce fractions until they are absolutely necessary, so let's follow the first suggestion. We would thus have the following transformed matrix:

$$
\begin{array}{c}
\text{I}' = \text{II} \\
\text{II}' = \text{I} \\
\text{III}' = \text{III}
\end{array}
\qquad
\begin{pmatrix}
1 & 1 & 4 & 40 \\
2 & 1 & 3 & 50 \\
2 & 1 & 1 & 20
\end{pmatrix}
$$

Both the "2's" in the first column must be replaced with "0's" and this we can do by multiplying the first row by -2 and adding the result in turn to the second and third rows. We would have:

$$
\begin{array}{c}
\text{I}'' = \text{I}' \\
\text{II}'' = \text{II}' - 2\text{I}' \\
\text{III}'' = \text{III}' - 2\text{I}'
\end{array}
\qquad
\begin{pmatrix}
1 & 1 & 4 & 40 \\
0 & -1 & -5 & -30 \\
0 & -1 & -7 & -60
\end{pmatrix}
$$

The first column is in the correct form, so we turn next to the second column. Here we need a "0" in the first and third rows. To get the former we simply have to add the second row to the first, and to achieve the latter we subtract the second row from the third. The result will be:

$$
\begin{array}{c}
\text{I}''' = \text{I}'' + \text{II}'' \\
\text{II}''' = \text{II}'' \\
\text{III}''' = \text{III}'' - \text{II}''
\end{array}
\qquad
\begin{pmatrix}
1 & 0 & -1 & 10 \\
0 & -1 & -5 & -30 \\
0 & 0 & -2 & -30
\end{pmatrix}
$$

If we now multiply II''' by -1, and III''' by $-\frac{1}{2}$ we will have the following matrix, which shows that only the third column needs further transformation:

$$
\begin{array}{c}
\text{I}^{\text{iv}} = \text{I}''' \\
\text{II}^{\text{iv}} = -\text{II}''' \\
\text{III}^{\text{iv}} = -\frac{1}{2}\text{III}'''
\end{array}
\qquad
\begin{pmatrix}
1 & 0 & -1 & 10 \\
0 & 1 & 5 & 30 \\
0 & 0 & 1 & 15
\end{pmatrix}
$$

If we multiply III^{iv} by 5 and subtract this from II^{iv}, and then just add III^{iv} to I^{iv} we will have the canonical form:

$$\begin{array}{l} \text{I}^{\text{v}} = \text{I}^{\text{iv}} + \text{III}^{\text{iv}} \\ \text{II}^{\text{v}} = \text{II}^{\text{iv}} - 5\text{III}^{\text{iv}} \\ \text{III}^{\text{v}} = \text{III}^{\text{iv}} \end{array} \begin{pmatrix} 1 & 0 & 0 & 25 \\ 0 & 1 & 0 & -45 \\ 0 & 0 & 1 & 15 \end{pmatrix}$$

from which we read off the final solution $X = 25$, $Y = -45$, $Z = 15$ as previously cited.

As we have said, if in the process we develop a row with only zero elements then the system is dependent, and for as many zero rows we uncover we may assign arbitrary values to this same number of variables. To illustrate we consider the previously cited dependent system, starting with its augmented matrix.

$$\begin{array}{l} \text{I} \\ \text{II} \\ \text{III} \end{array} \begin{pmatrix} 1 & 1 & 4 & 40 \\ 2 & 1 & 3 & 50 \\ 4 & 3 & 11 & 130 \end{pmatrix}$$

$$\begin{array}{l} \text{I}' = \text{I} \\ \text{II}' = \text{II} - 2\text{I} \\ \text{III}' = \text{III} - 4\text{I} \end{array} \begin{pmatrix} 1 & 1 & 4 & 40 \\ 0 & -1 & -5 & -30 \\ 0 & -1 & -5 & -30 \end{pmatrix}$$

$$\begin{array}{l} \text{I}'' = \text{I}' + \text{II}' \\ \text{II}'' = -\text{II}' \\ \text{III}'' = \text{III}' + \text{II}'' \end{array} \begin{pmatrix} 1 & 0 & -1 & 10 \\ 0 & 1 & 5 & 30 \\ 0 & 0 & 0 & 0 \end{pmatrix}$$

The last row of this matrix is equivalent to the equation $0 \cdot Z = 0$, and since this holds for any value we may give to Z, we have an infinite number of distinct solutions to the system, each with a different value for Z. To develop the general solution we let a be the symbol for the arbitrary value we assign to Z. The system equivalent to the last augmented matrix with this a used in place of Z is as follows:

$$\begin{array}{l} X - a = 10 \\ Y + 5a = 30 \end{array}$$

or:

$$\begin{array}{l} X = 10 + a \\ Y = 30 - 5a \end{array}$$

Thus, the general solution to the original system is $(10 + a, 30 - 5a, a)$ where a may be any value we choose.

In general, as we find a zero row we can substitute a symbol in place of the variable associated with this row, carry over the column associated with this variable to the constants matrix portion of the augmented matrix, and continue, performing the row arithmetic on the symbol just as if it were a number. Doing this will provide us with the general solution directly.

To illustrate an inconsistent system, let's consider the following development, starting with the system and then its augmented matrix:

$$X + Y + 4Z = 40$$
$$2X + Y + 3Z = 50$$
$$2X + 2Y + 8Z = 100$$

$$
\begin{array}{cc}
\text{I} \\
\text{II} \\
\text{III}
\end{array}
\begin{pmatrix}
1 & 1 & 4 & 40 \\
2 & 1 & 3 & 50 \\
2 & 2 & 8 & 100
\end{pmatrix}
$$

$$
\begin{array}{cc}
\text{I}' = \text{I} \\
\text{II}' = \text{II} - 2\text{I} \\
\text{III}' = \text{III} - 2\text{I}
\end{array}
\begin{pmatrix}
1 & 1 & 4 & 40 \\
0 & -1 & -5 & -30 \\
0 & 0 & 0 & 20
\end{pmatrix}
$$

The last row of this matrix is equivalent to the equation $0 \cdot Z = 20$, and since there is no number which when multiplied by 0 will give the value 20, we cannot have this last equation satisfied by any number, and so there is no solution to this system. The system is inconsistent.

In general, if we have m variables and n equations in the system, and these are not equal, then we will not have a unique solution to the system. As already stated, if we have more variables than equations, that is $m > n$, then we will have to assign values to some $m - n$ of the variables and solve the resulting reduced system. This solution, along with the assigned values, will constitute a solution to the original system. If, on the other hand, we have more equations than variables, that is $n > m$, then any $n - m$ of the n equations will be deleted from the system, and a solution attempted for the remaining m equations in m variables. Depending upon which equations we are left with, we may or may not have a solution to the reduced system, thus, we may have to try various combinations of equations before we find a system which is solvable.

The analysis scheme just presented is usually referred to as the *Gauss Elimination Process,* and while it is not the only method of attack, it is perhaps the easiest to apply by hand.

Simplex Solution of Linear Programming Problems

The rest of this chapter will be devoted to solution methods for the linear programming (or linear allocation) problem. The characteristic of such problems is that we must allocate available resources to a collection of activities whose total needs exceed the amount of resource available. Our objective is to allocate the resources in some "best" way, while not violating any of the resource limitations. Once an objective has been selected, we could list all the possible allocations which are feasible in the sense that they do not violate any limitations and then choose that one which comes the closest to the objective we have set. The drawback of this total enumeration procedure is that it is often impossible to list all the allocation schemes which are feasible, and when possible it is impractical. For this reason, certain mathematical procedures are used which seek the optimum solution without looking at all the possible solutions.

The most general solution procedure for solving the linear problem is the *simplex method.* The word "simplex" refers to the geometrical shape defined by the system of linear inequations and does not imply that this is the simplest method to apply. The basic method will be demonstrated with the following problem.

A manufacturer has two products, Products I and II, both of which require processing on three machines, Machines A, B, and C. The required processing times per unit of each product on these machines are as follows:

Product	Machine A	Machine B	Machine C
I	2 min.	4 min.	3 min.
II	5 min.	2 min.	4 min.

In the next production period there will be 10,000 minutes of processing time available on Machine A, 15,000 minutes on Machine B, and 30,000 minutes on Machine C. The product profit margins are $2 per unit of Product I and $3 per unit of Product II. Assuming that sales potential for the products exceeds the maximum production in the available time, we wish to determine the amounts of both products to make in the next period so as to maximize the total profits without violating any of the machine capacities.

We let X_I denote the number of units of Product I we will make in the next period and X_{II} the number of units of Product II. Since we cannot make negative quantities, these two variables are required to be either greater than or equal to zero. The capacity restrictions put limitations on the values we may assign to X_I and X_{II}, and these may be expressed as the following inequations:

$$\text{On Machine A:} \quad 2X_I + 5X_{II} \leq 10,000$$
$$\text{On Machine B:} \quad 4X_I + 2X_{II} \leq 15,000$$
$$\text{On Machine C:} \quad 3X_I + 4X_{II} \leq 30,000$$

A *feasible solution* is a pair of values (X_I, X_{II}) which satisfy all three of these inequations simultaneously.

Letting P denote the total profit from our production of these two products in the next period, we can formulate our objective equation in terms of X_I and X_{II} and the individual profit margins. We would have the following:

$$P = 2X_I + 3X_{II}$$

where P is in units of dollars profit. A feasible solution which gives the largest possible value of P, according to this equation, will be *an optimum solution* to the problem, and if it is unique it will be *the* optimum solution.

The simplex method works with a system of equations rather than inequations, and so our first step must be to reformulate our system of inequations into one of equations. To do this we introduce a *slack variable* into each inequation which makes it an equation. The system of equations in our problem would be the following, where W_A, W_B, and W_C are the slack variables:

On Machine A: $2X_I + 5X_{II} + W_A = 10,000$

On Machine B: $4X_I + 2X_{II} + W_B = 15,000$

On Machine C: $3X_I + 4X_{II} + W_C = 30,000$

We restrict the values of the slack variables to be either zero or a positive quantity.

To see the logic of what we have done, let's look at the original inequation for Machine A. This said that the quantity $2X_I + 5X_{II}$ must be less than or equal to 10,000 minutes, which means that the difference between these two quantities must be a quantity greater than or equal to zero; this difference we have symbolized as W_A. The actual value of $2X_I + 5X_{II}$ plus the value of this difference, W_A, must then *equal* 10,000 minutes, and so the resulting equation. And likewise for the other inequations.

From a practical point of view we may interpret, say, W_A as the "slack," or idle time planned for Machine A in the next period. Or, instead, we could view it as corresponding to a fictitious product which requires 1 minute per unit of processing on Machine A, and only on this machine. We can interpret W_B and W_C in a similar fashion. In any case, our first step in the simplex method is to change all inequations into equations by the introduction of slack variables; of course, if our restrictions are originally given as equations then slack variables are not needed.

Since idle time does not contribute to profit, we associate a profit margin of 0 with each of the W's, making the complete objective equation:

$$P = 2X_I + 3X_{II} + 0 \cdot W_A + 0 \cdot W_B + 0 \cdot W_C$$

With our system of equations we associate the following augmented matrix, where variable symbols have been placed over the coefficients columns corresponding to them:

$$
\begin{array}{ccccc}
X_I & X_{II} & W_A & W_B & W_C \\
\end{array}
$$
$$
\begin{pmatrix}
2 & 5 & 1 & 0 & 0 & & 10,000 \\
4 & 2 & 0 & 1 & 0 & & 15,000 \\
3 & 4 & 0 & 0 & 1 & & 30,000
\end{pmatrix}
$$

As we have cited, to start the simplex method we must have an initial feasible solution. Recalling the discussion of the previous section, we would look for a solution to this system by assigning arbitrary values to two of the variables and then transform the reduced system into the canonical form. The most expedient thing to do is to assign the value 0 to both X_I and X_{II}, which would produce a reduced system with the following augmented matrix:

$$
\begin{array}{ccc}
W_A & W_B & W_C \\
\end{array}
$$
$$
\begin{pmatrix}
1 & 0 & 0 & 10,000 \\
0 & 1 & 0 & 15,000 \\
0 & 0 & 1 & 30,000
\end{pmatrix}
$$

This is already in canonical form, and gives us the solution $W_A = 10,000$, $W_B = 15,000$, $W_C = 30,000$ to the reduced system. Therefore, the initial feasible solution to the original system is: $X_I = 0$, $X_{II} = 0$, $W_A = 10,000$, $W_B = 15,000$, $W_C = 30,000$.

This is admittedly a poor solution since it says to plan all available machine time as idle time, with a resulting profit of zero. It does, however, give us the needed starting solution. In general, when each of our resource limitations takes the form of a "less than or equal to" inequation, then by assigning the value 0 to all nonslack variables, we will have this same type of initial feasible solution available to us. Additional variables will have to be introduced to get the starting solution when we have "greater than or equal to" inequations, or equality restrictions in the problem.

The simplex procedure looks at the variables not in the solution and determines whether or not anything can be gained by introducing one of these into the solution in place of a variable already in the solution. If an improvement can be made, it determines which variable should come in and which should go out of the present solution. While the steps could be applied directly to the system of equations, it is more efficient to work with a tabular format. For our present initial feasible solution this table would be as follows:

p:	2	3	0	0	0			
	X_I	X_{II}	W_A	W_B	W_C	Q	V	p
	2	5	1	0	0	10,000	W_A	0
	4	2	0	1	0	15,000	W_B	0
	3	4	0	0	1	30,000	W_C	0

The main body of this table is just the augmented matrix of the system of equations, where we have titled the constants with Q. Above each of the variable symbols we have shown their profit margins to ease a computation we make in the procedure. In the V column we show the variables in the present solution, these appear in the rows in which the "1" appears in their coefficients column, and the value in the Q column alongside of them is the value they have in the present solution. In the p column we show the profit margins for the variables in the present solution, again as this will ease a subsequent calculation. As we enter a new variable into the solution, we will substitute it for one of those in the V column, and the procedure itself will produce its solution value in the correct position in the Q column.

By computing a column index for each variable column we can determine whether or not an improvement can be gained (if not, the present solution is the optimum one we seek), and if so which variable should be introduced. To calculate these indices we do the following:

Step 1.   For each variable column multiply each of its entries by the p value in the same row (found in the p column). Add all these products, and subtract this sum from the p value for this column (found in the p row). The result is the index number of this column, which is placed underneath the column.

Step 2.   If all column indices are 0's or negative numbers, then the present solution is the optimum. However, if there are positive indices, then the variable associated with the column having the *largest* index number is the one to be brought into the next solution. We refer to this column as the *key column*.

To find which variable should be taken out of the present solution, when an improving variable has been found, we calculate an index for each row of the present table. To calculate these we do the following:

Step 3. Knowing the key column from Step 2, divide the Q value of each row by the entry in the key column in this same row. We can make this division only with positive numbers; if 0 or a negative number is in the key column we do not compute an index for this row. These ratios are the row indices placed alongside the rows.

The variable (found in the V column) associated with the row with the *smallest* row index is the one to be replaced. We refer to this row as the *key row*.

Working with the table above we would calculate both sets of indices, and the results are shown in the following:

p:	2	3	0	0	0				
	X_I	X_{II}	W_A	W_B	W_C	Q	V	p	
	2	5	1	0	0	10,000	W_A	0	$10,000/5 = 2,000$ ✓
	4	2	0	1	0	15,000	W_B	0	$15,000/2 = 7,500$
	3	4	0	0	1	30,000	W_C	0	$30,000/4 = 7,500$

$2-$	$3-$	$0-$	$0-$	$0-$
$(2\times 0$	$(5\times 0$	$(1\times 0$	$(0\times 0$	$(0\times 0$
$+4\times 0$	$+2\times 0$	$+0\times 0$	$+1\times 0$	$+0\times 0$
$+3\times 0)$	$+4\times 0)$	$+0\times 0)$	$+0\times 0$	$+1\times 0)$
$=2$	$=3$	$=0$	$=0$	$=0$
	✓			

According to Step 2 we do not have the optimum solution, and X_{II} is the variable whose introduction would give us the most gain. From Step 3 we conclude that W_A is the variable to be replaced by X_{II}.

Next we make the indicated substitution of variables, and for this we identify a *pivot element* which is that entry common to the key column and the key row. The pivot element for the above table is the "5," common to the X_{II} column and W_A row. We next do the following:

Step 4. Perform row operations on the augmented matrix portion of the table which will transform the pivot element into a "1" with all other elements in the key column being transformed into 0's.

We see that Step 4 is just the usual procedure of getting our new system (involving the variables X_{II}, W_B, and W_C) into canonical form. For our particular situation, we would multiply the first row by 1/5 which would put a "1" in the pivot position. Next, we would multiply this transformed row by -2 and add this to the second row, and then multiply it by -4 and add this to the third row. Zeros would thus be properly positioned in the key column. As a result of these operations, the new values for our solution variables will be developed in the Q column, given that we make the substitution of the symbol X_{II} for W_A in the V column. The variable leaving the solution, W_A, is set equal to *zero*.

The resulting table would be that shown below, where we have also indicated the calculations associated with this solution for testing its optimality and for going on to the next solution.

$p:$ 2	3	0	0	0				
X_I	X_{II}	W_A	W_B	W_C	Q	V	p	
$\frac{2}{5}$	1	$\frac{1}{5}$	0	0	2,000	X_{II}	3	$2{,}000/(2/5) = 5{,}000$
$\frac{16}{5}$	0	$-\frac{2}{5}$	1	0	11,000	W_B	0	$11{,}000/(16/5)=3{,}437$ ✓
$\frac{7}{5}$	0	$-\frac{4}{5}$	0	1	22,000	W_C	0	$22{,}000/(7/5) = 15{,}714$

$$2-\qquad 3-\qquad 0-\qquad 0-\qquad 0-$$
$$(\tfrac{2}{5}\times 3\quad (1\times 3\quad (\tfrac{1}{5}\times 3\quad (0\times 3\quad (0\times 3$$
$$+\tfrac{16}{5}\times 0\quad +0\times 0\quad -\tfrac{2}{5}\times 0\quad +1\times 0\quad +0\times 0$$
$$+\tfrac{7}{5}\times 0)\quad +0\times 0)\quad -\tfrac{4}{5}\times 0)\quad +0\times 0)\quad +1\times 0)$$
$$=\tfrac{4}{5}\qquad =0\qquad =-\tfrac{3}{5}\qquad =0\qquad =0$$
$$\checkmark$$

First, the solution associated with the above table is $X_I = 0$, $X_{II} = 2{,}000$, $W_A = 0$, $W_B = 11{,}000$, $W_C = 22{,}000$, which means a profit of:

$$P = 2 \times 0 + 3 \times 2{,}000 + 0 \times 0 + 0 \times 11{,}000 + 0 \times 22{,}000 = \$6{,}000.$$

Looking at the column indices we see that this solution is not the optimum, since the X_I column has a positive index, $4/5$. Again applying Step 3 we conclude that W_B is the variable to be replaced by X_I. The pivot element is the $(16/5)$ figure in the X_I column (we note that the pivot element is just that element in the coefficients column of the variable coming in which is located in the same row as the "1" in the coefficients column of the variable going out). Transforming this key column into the canonical form required, and calculating the column indices to test the solution, would develop the following table:

$p:$ 2	3	0	0	0			
X_I	X_{II}	W_A	W_B	W_C	Q	V	p
0	1	$\frac{1}{4}$	$-\frac{1}{8}$	0	625	X_{II}	3
1	0	$-\frac{1}{8}$	$\frac{5}{16}$	0	3,437	X_I	2
0	0	$-\frac{5}{8}$	$-\frac{7}{16}$	0	17,189	W_C	0
0	0	$-\frac{1}{2}$	$-\frac{1}{4}$	0			

Since all column indices are nonpositive numbers, the solution associated with this table is the optimum one. Explicitly it is: $X_I = 3,437$, $X_{II} = 625$, $W_A = 0$, $W_B = 0$, $W_C = 17,189$, with a profit of:

$$P = 2 \times 3,437 + 3 \times 625 + 0 \times 0 + 0 \times 0 + 0 \times 17,189 = \$8,749$$

The presence of W_C in the optimum solution means that we cannot make use of all of the available time on Machine C, owing to the interaction with the other constraints. Thus, 17,189 minutes will still be available on this machine in the next period.

Additional facts can be obtained from an interpretation of the column indices for the optimum solution's table. From the above table we see that the index for the W_A variable column (slack time on Machine A) is $-\frac{1}{2}$, read as $-\frac{1}{2}$ dollar, or -50¢. This is interpreted to mean that the introduction of an additional minute of slack time on Machine A would reduce the total profit P by 50¢. And so, the other way around, if we had one more minute of available processing time on Machine A (having 10,001 minutes instead of 10,000), we would have been able to increase P by 50¢. Similarly, the profit worth of a minute of Machine B time is 25¢. These implied values for our resources are termed *implicit values,* or *shadow prices,* and provide managment with vital information.

We can carry this interpretation further by calculating a total value of the machine capacities. The 10,000 minutes of Machine A time are given the implied worth of $\$\frac{1}{2} \times 10,000 = \$5,000$, and the 15,000 minutes of Machine B time the worth of $\$\frac{1}{4} \times 15,000 = \$3,750$. The total of these two values equals \$8,750, which differs from the optimum solution's profit of \$8,749 only due to rounding-off errors in the simplex procedure.

If in Step 2 of the simplex procedure we find that two or more columns have the largest index number, then any of the tied variables may be selected as the next entering variable. However, if in Step 3 we find that two or more rows are tied with the smallest row index, then we cannot be arbitrary in our choice between them for the variable to leave the solution. This latter situation is called the *degenerate situation* and if we do not make the proper choice between the tied variables we may get into a "cycling" routine where two variables are alternately interchanged leading us nowhere. There is a rule to apply in making the proper choice, and to illustrate it let's suppose that in our example we had 4,000 minutes of available time on Machine B instead of the 15,000 minutes originally given.

In determining the key row we would compute the following row indices (in this example we would be working with the second table shown above):

> First Row, for W_A: $10,000/5 = 2,000$
> Second Row, for W_B: $4,000/2 = 2,000$
> Third Row, for W_C: $30,000/4 = 7,500$

A tie exists between W_A and W_B as the variable to be replaced by X_{II}. To break this tie we perform the following computations:

1. Knowing the key column, divide each element in a tied row by the element in the key column located in this row. Do this for all tied rows.
2. Starting with the ratios thus produced in the Q column and continuing to the left,

compare the resulting ratios column by column for the tied rows. The first comparison that yields unequal ratios breaks the tie.

3. The tied row which had the algebraically smaller ratio in (2) above is taken as the key row, and its associated variable is the one to be taken out of the solution. We recall here that a "small" negative number is *larger* than a "large" negative number (for example $-3 > -10$).

For our illustration we would divide the elements in the first row by 5, and those of the second row by 2. The resulting ratios would be:

X_I	X_{II}	W_A	W_B	W_C	Q
$\frac{2}{5}$	1	$\frac{1}{5}$	0	0	2,000
2	1	0	$\frac{1}{2}$	0	2,000

The ratios in the W_B column break the tie, and in favor of taking the first row as the key row, as 0 is smaller than $\frac{1}{2}$.

Modifications in the Simplex Method

The allocation problem we may be faced with will often differ from the standard type presented in the previous section: maximizing the objective equation with all inequations of the "less than or equal to" type. Certain modifications would then be needed, but once these are made the same procedure as presented above would be applied to find the optimum solution. Here we will present the complication and the modification needed to resolve this.

1. Instead of seeking the maximum of the objective equation, we may instead want the allocation which will minimize it. This is most appropriate when we are working with costs or times, rather than profit margins. All we need to do in these situations is to attach minus signs to the coefficients in the objective equation to be minimized. These are introduced into our tables as the "p values" and then the simplex method is performed as before. The values assigned to the variables in the optimum solution will also be those for the minimization problem, but the objective equation value we obtain will be the negative of the minimized objective equation. Thus, if in our previous illustration we had a production cost of $2.5 per unit of *I* and $3.2 per unit of *II*, we would have the objective equation $C = 2.5X_I + 3.2 X_{II}$ to be minimized. The p values used in the solution procedure would be -2.5 for X_I and -3.2 for X_{II}. If the optimum solution, under these conditions, was -50, then the minimum cost would be 50.

2. Often we will be working with variables which are allowed to take on negative as well as positive values, such as production rates or values which are measured from a fixed reference point. Since the simplex method requires that all variables be restricted to non-negative values, we must make a modification to accommodate such variables. Suppose that X_1 is such a variable, then we introduce two new variables U_1 and V_1, and everywhere we use X_1 in setting up the problem we substitute the expression $U_1 - V_1$. Both of these

variables are restricted to being nonnegative, and X_1 will be negative in the solution only if V_1 is larger than U_1. From the final assigned values to U_1 and V_1 we determine the value for X_1 according to this same expression. Thus, if in the optimum solution $U_1 = 10$, and $V_1 = 5$, then X_1 has the value $10 - 5 = 5$. Of course, this move adds another variable to the problem, and also another column to our table.

3. A similar problem arises when we have a lower bound on one or more of our variables, as might arise due to a minimum production level or allocation. Thus X_1 might have to "at least" be equal to d, that is, $X_1 \geq d$, in any solution. We substitute $U_1 + d$ everywhere for X_1 and then evaluate X_1 at the end as follows: $X_1 = U_1 - d$. A constant term will thus appear in the objective equation, and this is not introduced into our tables, but used only when we calculate the profit (or cost, etc.) associated with a particular solution.

4. When we must achieve a certain minimum level of equipment utilization, or must meet a specified minimum amount of production, we will have to use an inequation restriction of the "greater than or equal to" type to properly set up our allocation problem. We might have, for example, a restriction such as:

$$2X_1 + 3X_2 + 2X_3 \geq 100$$

To formulate this as an equation we again introduce a slack variable, but now we subtract this rather than add it. With a slack variable of W we would thus have the reformulated constraint in the following form:

$$2X_1 + 3X_2 + 2X_3 - W = 100$$

Again, in our profit (or cost) objective equation we assign a *zero* profit margin (or cost rate) to all these slack variables.

5. When our system of restrictions involves a "greater than or equal to" inequation or a restricting equation, then the system of equations we develop will not have an initial feasible solution consisting of slack variables; for the former type of restriction we will have negative slack variables, and for the latter we will have no slack variables. For example, we might have the following system of inequations associated with our problem:

$$2X_1 + 3X_2 + 2X_3 \geq 100$$
$$3X_1 + 2X_2 \qquad \leq 50$$
$$4X_1 + 5X_2 + 3X_3 = 200$$

Introducing the slack variables W_1 and W_2 we would reformulate this system as the following system of equations:

$$2X_1 + 3X_2 + 2X_3 - W_1 = 100$$
$$3X_1 + 2X_2 + W_2 \qquad = 50$$
$$4X_1 + 5X_2 + 3X_3 \qquad = 200$$

Setting the nonslack variables equal to zero will not achieve a feasible solution to this system. We could, of course, include one of the nonslack variables in our initial solution, but this would require some trial and error to find a feasible solution. A more efficient way to develop the initial feasible solution is to introduce so-called *artificial variables* into the system of equations, and these are only introduced to give us a simple initial solution which is feasible. For the second of our equations above, $3X_1 + 2X_2 + W_2 = 50$, we do not need an artificial variable since we can use W_2 in the same way as in the previous section. For the first and third equations we would introduce the artificial variables Y_1 and Y_2 giving us the system:

$$2X_1 + 3X_2 + 2X_3 - W_1 + Y_1 = 100$$
$$3X_1 + 2X_2 + W_2 \qquad\qquad = 50$$
$$4X_1 + 5X_2 + 3X_3 + Y_2 \qquad = 200$$

Now, for the initial feasible solution we would set equal to zero the following variables: X_1, X_2, X_3, W_1, giving us the initial solution:

$$Y_1 = 100$$
$$W_2 = 50$$
$$Y_2 = 200$$

and this is feasible.

Artificial variables are simply a device and should not appear in the final optimum solution (with other than a zero value), in fact, if they do we may conclude that the system is in reality infeasible and the problem has no solution. To ensure this we assign to each artificial variable an extremely large value if our objective equation is to be minimized, or an extremely large negative value if we are looking to maximize the objective equation. Knowing the actual profit margins or cost rates associated with real variables, we can always select an appropriate value here, and with such extreme values these artificial variables will be driven out of our solutions quite rapidly. Naturally, we usually assign the same extreme value to all artificial variables in the problem. A illustrative example will be developed below, but first two remaining points must be attended to.

6. At times we will have multiple solutions to our allocation problem, that is, solutions involving different sets of variables, but giving the same optimum value to the objective equation. By knowing of such alternatives management will have a greater flexibility in their ultimate choice, which may now be made on the basis of some other factor, and so we should know what to look for to identify this situation. Suppose that we have found an optimum solution, but we have a variable which is not in this solution which has a *zero* column index associated with it. Then we know that there is another optimum solution involving this variable in place of one of those already in the solution at this point. This alternate solution can be completely identified by resuming the simplex method with Step 3 of the simplex procedure, using this column with zero index as the key column.

7. In rare situations, and usually due to an error in formulating the problem, we may find that the objective function may be "optimized" without bound. For instance, we may find that we can achieve infinite profits. In certain situations such unbounded solutions may have physical meaning, but even when they don't we would like to know of their existence.

The way we will know is that we will have a key column identified by Step 2 of the procedure, but we will not be able to determine a key row from Step 3. In other words, we will have all negative elements in this key column. What this means is that we may increase this key column variable without bound without disturbing the present solution. And, again, uncovering such a situation usually means that we have not restricted this variable sufficiently in our system of inequations for the problem.

To complete our discussion of the simplex method, the following problem will be solved which will involve some of the complications, and their resolutions, as just discussed.

A manufacturer is faced with the problem of determining which input materials to use in the production of a material which is subsequently used in a fabrication operation. There are four input materials, I, II, III, and IV, and any combination of these, in any desired amounts, may be "blended" together to produce the final material. This final material must have a specified amount of each of three active ingredients, A, B, and C, and every gram of each input material contributes a different amount of each of these ingredients. These contribution rates, the minimum levels of active ingredients, and the cost per gram of each input material are shown in the following table:

Active Ingredients	Units of Active Ingredient per Gram of Input Materials				Minimum Level of the Active Ingredients
	I	II	III	IV	
A	1	5	10	4	250
B	50	100	200	20	1,200
C	.5	.5	0	2	50*
Cost per Gram of Input Materials	$1.50	$3.50	$2.50	$2.00	

*There must be exactly this level of C

As noted in the table we must have exactly 50 units of ingredient C in the final material, whereas we need "at least" 250 units of A and 1,200 units of B. Therefore, we will have the following system of inequations for this problem, where X_I, X_{II}, X_{III}, and X_{IV} are the grams of each of our input materials we will use in making the final material (our objective being to obtain the least costly blend):

$$\text{Of Ingredient A:} \quad X_I + 5X_{II} + 10X_{III} + 4X_{IV} \geq 250$$
$$\text{Of Ingredient B:} \quad 50X_I + 100X_{II} + 200X_{III} + 20X_{IV} \geq 1{,}200$$
$$\text{Of Ingredient C:} \quad .5X_I + .5X_{II} + 2X_{IV} = 50$$

Our objective equation, using C for total cost, is given by the following:

$$C = 1.5X_I + 3.5X_{II} + 2.5X_{III} + 2.0X_{IV}$$

with C in units of dollars of cost.

Our first step is to reformulate our system of restrictions as a system of equations.

To do this we will need two slack variables, W_A and W_B, for the first two inequations. The resulting system would be:

$$X_I + 5X_{II} + 10X_{III} + 4X_{IV} - W_A = 250$$
$$50X_I + 100X_{II} + 200X_{III} + 20X_{IV} - W_B = 1,200$$
$$.5X_I + .5X_{II} + 2X_{IV} = 50$$

where we associate a zero cost with these two slack variables.

To obtain our initial feasible solution we introduce three artificial variables Y_1, Y_2, and Y_3 as follows:

$$X_I + 5X_{II} + 10X_{III} + 4X_{IV} - W_A + Y_1 = 250$$
$$50X_I + 100X_{II} + 200X_{III} + 20X_{IV} - W_B + Y_2 = 1,200$$
$$.5X_I + .5X_{II} + 2X_{IV} + Y_3 = 50$$

Associated with each of these artificial variables we have a (selected) cost of $10 per "gram." Any other extreme value could be used here, but this will suffice.

The development of the solution to this problem is shown in Table 5–1, where the four subtables required in the procedure are listed one under another. This is the typical display of our procedure.

In the first table we start with the initial feasible solution consisting of just the artificial variables, with cost $15,000. We note here that the cost rates are listed as negative quantities. We do not have the optimum solution, and our indices indicate that X_{III} should come in next in place of Y_2. The results of this substitution are shown in the second subtable. Here we see that X_{IV} should come in next, in place of Y_3, leading us to the third subtable, where W_B is indicated as the next variable to come in as substitute for Y_1. The fourth subtable shows that we have found the optimum solution, and that this is unique. Explicitly, the solution is: $X_I = 0$, $X_{II} = 0$, $X_{III} = 15$, $X_{IV} = 25$, $W_A = 0$, $W_B = 2,300$, and no artificial variables. The total cost is $C = \$87.50$.

The fact that $W_B = 2,300$ means that this many units of ingredient B will be included in excess to minimum 1,200 required. Looking at the shadow prices on X_I and X_{II} in the bottom section of Table 5–1 indicates that it would cost respectively $1.00 and $1.70 per gram of these two materials if used in making the final material, these costs being over the optimum cost of $87.50.

A flowchart of the simplex method, as we have presented it, is given in Figure 5–1. This starts with the initial formulation of the problem as a linear programming problem, which, as one would expect, is the most critical phase in using the procedure.

Distribution Solution of Linear Programming Problems

The simplex method is the most general solution procedure for solving linear programming problems. There are, however, certain problems which due to their special characteristics can be solved with a more efficient method known as the *distribution* (or

Table 5–1

p: -1.5	-3.2	-2.5	-2.0	0	0	-10.0	-10.0	-10.0				
X_I	X_{II}	X_{III}	X_{IV}	W_A	W_B	Y_1	Y_2	Y_3	Q	V	p	
1	5	10	4	-1	0	1	0	0	250	Y_1	-10.0	25
50	100	200	20	0	-1	0	1	0	1200	Y_2	-10.0	6✓
0.5	0.5	0	2	0	0	0	0	1	50	Y_3	-10.0	—
513.5	1051.8	2097.5✓	258	-10	-10	0	0	0	Cost:	$15,000.00		
-1.5	0	0	3	-1	0.05	1	-0.05	0	190	Y_1	-10.0	63.3
0.25	0.5	1	0.1	0	-0.005	0	0.005	0	6	X_{III}	-2.5	60
0.5	0.5	0	2	0	0	0	0	1	50	Y_3	-10.0	25✓
-10.875	3.05	0	48.25✓	-10	4.9875	0	-10.4875	0	Cost:	$2,415.00		
-2.25	-0.75	0	0	-1	0.05	1	-0.05	-1.5	115	Y_1	-10.0	2300✓
0.225	0.475	1	0	0	-0.005	0	0.005	-0.05	3.5	X_{III}	-2.5	—
0.25	0.25	0	1	0	0	0	0	0.5	25	X_{IV}	-2.0	—
-22.9375	-9.0125	0	0	-10	0.4875 ✓	0	-10.4875	-24.125	Cost:	$1,208.75		
-45	-15	0	0	-20	1	20	-1	-30	2300	W_B	0	
0	0.4	1	0	-0.1	0	0.1	0	-0.2	15	X_{III}	-2.5	
0.25	0.25	0	1	0	0	0	0	0.5	25	X_{IV}	-2.0	
-1.00	-1.70	0	0	-0.25	0	-9.75	-10	-9.5	Cost:	$87.50		

160

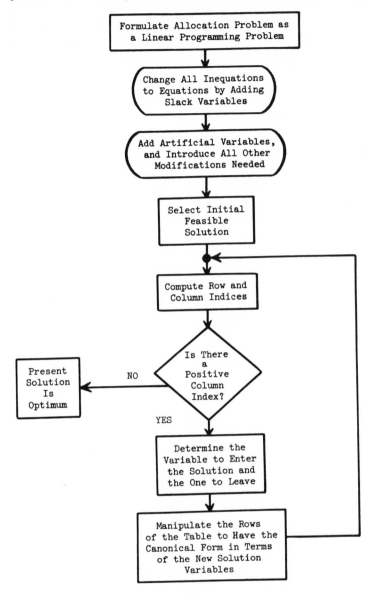

Figure 5–1

transportation) *method.* Most linear problems of the source-to-destination type, such as the transportation of goods from various origins to various markets, can be resolved with this technique.

The distinguishing characteristic of an allocation problem suitable for solution by the distribution method is that of homogeneity. By this we mean that both the requirements and the resources used to fill these are expressed in the same kinds of units. Looking at the constraining inequations of the problem, this means that all the coefficients in these will be 1's, which is unlike the situation we met in the previous section for the simplex method where the coefficients were included to "convert" one type of unit to another.

The distribution method, like the simplex method, is an iterative procedure which starts with an initial feasible solution and then develops improved solutions until some test condition is met which indicates that we have found the optimum solution (or else shows that no solution exists). Again we may wish to maximize or minimize the objective equation. The coefficients in this equation will not normally be 1's since these are used to convert allocated units into profits, costs, etc. The nature of the basic steps of the method will be demonstrated with the following problem.

A company has four warehouses, A, B, C, and D, located in different cities across the country. At each warehouse is a specified amount of a finished product and there are five customers, a, b, c, d, and e, to whom this stock must be distributed. Thus the warehouses are "sources" and the customers are "destinations." The total number of units in all four warehouses is 1,000 and this is also the total amount demanded by the five customers. The specifics are as follows:

Warehouse	Units of Supply	Customers	Units of Demand
A	300	a	100
B	350	b	200
C	200	c	400
D	150	d	250
		e	50
	1,000		1,000

Associated with each warehouse-customer combination is a unit cost of shipping from this warehouse to this customer. These are as follows:

From \ To	a	b	c	d	e
A	$10	$18	$22	$24	$30
B	$15	$17	$35	$32	$12
C	$20	$40	$16	$14	$34
D	$25	$11	$19	$13	$16

The objective is to distribute the stocks to the customers so that all demands are met, but in such a way as to minimize the total shipping cost.

This type of problem can be solved with the simplex method and it is illustrative to set up the problem for this procedure. This is all we will do in this regard. To start, we introduce a symbol for the quantity shipped from each warehouse to each customer. Thus, the symbol $X_{A,a}$ will be used to represent the number of units shipped from Warehouse A to Customer a; the other symbols follow this same logic.

Associated with each warehouse we have the imposed restriction that the sum of all the quantities shipped from this point to the customers will exactly equal the quantity on hand (subsequently we will see how we handle the situation where equality is not required). We thus have the following restricting equations:

$$\begin{array}{ll}
\text{Warehouse A:} & X_{A,a} + X_{A,b} + X_{A,c} + X_{A,d} + X_{A,e} = 300 \\
\text{Warehouse B:} & X_{B,a} + X_{B,b} + X_{B,c} + X_{B,d} + X_{B,e} = 350 \\
\text{Warehouse C:} & X_{C,a} + X_{C,b} + X_{C,c} + X_{C,d} + X_{C,e} = 200 \\
\text{Warehouse D:} & X_{D,a} + X_{D,b} + X_{D,c} + X_{D,d} + X_{D,e} = 150
\end{array}$$

Associated with each customer we have another equality restriction which states that the sum of the shipments to this customer, from all the warehouses, must exactly equal the demand of this customer. Our equations are as follows:

$$\begin{array}{ll}
\text{Customer a:} & X_{A,a} + X_{B,a} + X_{C,a} + X_{D,a} = 100 \\
\text{Customer b:} & X_{A,b} + X_{B,b} + X_{C,b} + X_{D,b} = 200 \\
\text{Customer c:} & X_{A,c} + X_{B,c} + X_{C,c} + X_{D,c} = 400 \\
\text{Customer d:} & X_{A,d} + X_{B,d} + X_{C,d} + X_{D,d} = 250 \\
\text{Customer e:} & X_{A,e} + X_{B,e} + X_{C,e} + X_{D,e} = 50
\end{array}$$

We thus have a system of nine equations in twenty variables, and our objective equation, specifying the total shipping cost C, is given by:

$$C = 10X_{A,a} + 18X_{A,b} + \ldots + 16X_{D,e}$$

involving twenty individual terms.

By introducing nine artificial variables, with an attendant unit shipping cost of say $100, we can set this problem up in the simplex table and apply the method to find the least cost distribution plan. One can easily appreciate what an arduous task this would be without the assistance of a mechanical device. The distribution method, on the other hand, gives us the solution very quickly and only involves arithmetic well within the range of hand computations.

To start the method we construct a table displaying all our information on supply, demand, and costs. This also serves as the worksheet for the method. In Table 5–2 we show

SOURCE \ DESTINATION	CUST. a	CUST. b	CUST. c	CUST. d	CUST. e	SUPPLY
WAREHOUSE A.	$X_{A,a}$ [10]	$X_{A,b}$ [18]	$X_{A,c}$ [22]	$X_{A,d}$ [24]	$X_{A,e}$ [30]	300
WAREHOUSE B.	$X_{B,a}$ [15]	$X_{B,b}$ [17]	$X_{B,c}$ [35]	$X_{B,d}$ [32]	$X_{B,e}$ [12]	350
WAREHOUSE C.	$X_{C,a}$ [20]	$X_{C,b}$ [40]	$X_{C,c}$ [16]	$X_{C,d}$ [14]	$X_{C,e}$ [34]	200
WAREHOUSE D.	$X_{D,a}$ [25]	$X_{D,b}$ [11]	$X_{D,c}$ [19]	$X_{D,d}$ [13]	$X_{D,e}$ [26]	150
DEMAND	100	200	400	250	50	1000

Table 5–2

SOURCE / DESTINATION	CUST. a	CUST. b	CUST. c	CUST. d	CUST. e	SUPPLY
WAREHOUSE A.	[10] 100 →	[18] 200 ↘	[22]	[24]	[30]	300
WAREHOUSE B.	[15]	[17]	[35] 350	[32]	[12]	350
WAREHOUSE C.	[20]	[40]	[16] 50 →	[14] 150	[34]	200
WAREHOUSE D.	[25]	[11]	[19]	[13] 100 →	[26] 50	150
DEMAND	100	200	400	250	50	1000

Table 5–3

the table format for our problem where the symbols have been placed in the appropriate boxes. In the procedure we will have actual values in place of the symbols, and we normally leave empty those boxes corresponding to variables not in the solution. Within each larger box is a smaller box and in these we place the cost rates (in general the coefficients of the objective equation are placed here). The units of supply and those of demand are also shown in the rows and columns to which they correspond; these are usually referred to as the *rim conditions* of the problem.

How do we find an initial feasible solution? There are actually several ways, of which we will consider just two. The first is the so-called *Northwest Corner Rule,* and for our problem this is illustrated in Table 5–3. We start at the northwest corner of the table (that is, at the (A,a) box) and simply fill in allocations of supply to demand as quickly as possible. Thus in the (A,a) box we have 300 units of supply and 100 units of demand so we assign 100 units to this box. We remain in a row until we completely allocate all the supply of the row at which point we drop down to the next row and continue in the same way. Thus, at this point, we have 200 units remaining at Warehouse A and we assign these to the "next" demand, that of Customer b, which is 200 units. This completely exhausts our supply so we drop down to the B row. We slant over to the c column since Customer b has been fully satisfied; if this had not been the case we would drop down to the B row but remain in the b column, and stay here (going down through the rows) until this customer demand was filled at which point we would move on to the next column. Table 5–3, from this point, illustrates the procedure well enough and at the end we finish with an allocation of the supply to the demand which satisfies the rim conditions, which means the restricting equations have been satisfied. The cost of this plan would be found to be $22,350.

At this point we could begin the procedure starting with the initial feasible solution just found. The shortcoming of the Northwest Corner Rule is that it pays no attention to the cost of the allocations it makes, and what this will mean is that we can expect to make many iterations of the method to correct for a bad initial solution. Another way we can develop an initial feasible solution is via the *Vogel Approximation Method.* This method does pay heed to the costs and in fact very often will develop the optimum solution; and even if this is not the case, it will in general be closer to the optimum than any other starting solution and so will reduce the number of iterations we must make. The method is quite simple to apply, and involves the following steps.

Step 1. For each row of the initial (empty) table find the two "smallest" cost values. Subtract the smaller of these from the larger one and post this difference alongside the row. After all rows have been treated, do the exact same thing for each column putting the differences above their respective columns.

For our example these differences are posted in Table 5–4, where, for example, for the Warehouse A row we find the difference 8 calculated from $18 - 10$.

Step 2. Select that row or column which have the *largest* difference value; circle this value. Looking down this column or across this row, find the square with the *smallest cost,* and assign as much as possible to this square. If a tie exists between rows and/or columns for the largest difference, we can break this by selecting that one which has the smaller "smallest cost."

In Table 5–4 we see that the Customer e column has the largest difference, 14, and so is our selected column. The smallest cost in this column is found to be 12 associated with $X_{B,e}$, that is, shipments from Warehouse B to Customer e. We have 350 units which we can assign, but this customer only needs 50 units, and so this is the maximum amount we can possibly assign and is what we post in the (B,e) box.

Step 3. Cross out the boxes of any row or column which have had all its supply exhausted or its demands met by the assignment just made (if there are any). We re-determine the differences as may be necessary due to the crossing out of boxes, since these boxes are omitted from further consideration. Next, we return to Step 2 and continue until all assignments have been made, at which point the initial feasible solution will have been developed.

In Table 5–4 we have crossed out the last column since our assignment of 50 units has satisfied the demand of Customer e. We also note that by no longer using the (B,e) box in finding differences we will have to recalculate the difference associated with the B row. This

		5	6	3	1	(14)	
	DESTINATION SOURCE	CUST. a	CUST. b	CUST. c	CUST. d	CUST. e	SUPPLY
8	WAREHOUSE A.	10	18	22	24	X 30	300
3	WAREHOUSE B.	15	17	35	32	50 12	350
2	WAREHOUSE C.	20	40	16	14	X 34	200
2	WAREHOUSE D.	25	11	19	13	X 26	150
	DEMAND	100	200	400	250	50	1000

Table 5–4

new value is shown in Table 5–5 which shows the results of our second pass through the method. Here we selected the *A* row, allocated 100 units to the (*A,a*) box and so crossed out the first column. The full development is shown in Tables 5–4 through 5–9 and in this last table we have our initial feasible solution. This differs from our Northwest Corner Rule solution, and when costed-out the total cost associated with this plan is $17,850. It will subsequently be seen that this solution differs from the optimum one by only $800.

As with the simplex method, our next step is to test our present solution to determine whether or not it is the optimum (in the sense that no cost reduction can be gained by finding a different solution; there may exist others with the same total cost). If it turns out that our solution is not the final one, then we find that variable which will make the greatest improvement if brought into the solution. Unlike the simplex method, when we bring in this selected variable we may replace more than just one present variable, and the procedure followed in bringing in a new variable will take care of this automatically.

There is a necessary step we must take with each solution we produce before we can start anything else. We must check, and then correct for the condition of *degeneracy*. How

		5	6	3	1		
SOURCE \ DESTINATION		CUST. a	CUST. b	CUST. c	CUST. d	CUST. e	SUPPLY
⑧	WAREHOUSE A.	[10] 100	[18]	[22]	[24]	X [30]	300
2	WAREHOUSE B.	X [15]	[17]	[35]	[32]	50 [12]	350
2	WAREHOUSE C.	X [20]	[40]	[16]	[14]	X [34]	200
2	WAREHOUSE D.	X [25]	[11]	[19]	[13]	X [26]	150
	DEMAND	100	200	400	250	50	1000

Table 5–5

			6	3	1		
SOURCE \ DESTINATION		CUST. a	CUST. b	CUST. c	CUST. d	CUST. e	SUPPLY
4	WAREHOUSE A.	[10] 100	X [18]	[22]	[24]	X [30]	300
⑮	WAREHOUSE B.	X [15]	200 [17]	[35]	[32]	50 [12]	350
2	WAREHOUSE C.	X [20]	X [40]	[16]	[14]	X [34]	200
2	WAREHOUSE D.	X [25]	X [11]	[19]	[13]	X [26]	150
	DEMAND	100	200	400	250	50	1000

Table 5–6

| | | 3 | 1 | | |
SOURCE \ DESTINATION	CUST. a	CUST. b	CUST. c	CUST. d	CUST. e	SUPPLY
2 WAREHOUSE A.	[10] 100	[18] X	[22]	[24]	[30] X	300
3 WAREHOUSE B.	[15] X	[17] 200	[35]	[32]	[12] 50	350
2 WAREHOUSE C.	[20] X	[40] X	[16]	[14]	[34] X	200
(6) WAREHOUSE D.	[25] X	[11] X	[19] X	[13] 150	[26] X	150
DEMAND	100	200	400	250	50	1000

Table 5–7

| | | | 6 | (10) | |
SOURCE \ DESTINATION	CUST. a	CUST. b	CUST. c	CUST. d	CUST. e	SUPPLY
2 WAREHOUSE A.	[10] 100	[18] X	[22]	[24] X	[30] X	300
3 WAREHOUSE B.	[15] X	[17] 200	[35]	[32] X	[12] 50	350
2 WAREHOUSE C.	[20] X	[40] X	[16]	[14] 100	[34] X	200
WAREHOUSE D.	[25] X	[11] X	[19] X	[13] 150	[26] X	150
DEMAND	100	200	400	250	50	1000

Table 5–8

SOURCE \ DESTINATION	CUST. a	CUST. b	CUST. c	CUST. d	CUST. e	SUPPLY
WAREHOUSE A.	[10] 100	[18] X	[22] 200	[24] X	[30] X	300
WAREHOUSE B.	[15] X	[17] 200	[35] 100	[32] X	[12] 50	350
WAREHOUSE C.	[20] X	[40] X	[16] 100	[14] 100	[34] X	200
WAREHOUSE D.	[25] X	[11] X	[19] X	[13] 150	[26] X	150
DEMAND	100	200	400	250	50	1000

Table 5–9

we check for this condition will be given here and the correction procedure postponed to that time where it arises in our subsequent development. What we do is to count the number of "used" boxes in our solution, and by a used box we mean one which has a quantity assigned to it. There are eight used boxes in our Vogel solution (Table 5–9), whereas there are only seven in our Northwest Corner Rule solution (Table 5–3). We then count the number of columns and rows in our table and one less than this total must be the number of used boxes in our solution for a *nondegenerate solution*. In our example we have 5 columns and 4 rows, so the number of used boxes must be $5 + 4 - 1 = 8$. The Vogel solution is thus nondegenerate while the Northwest Corner Rule solution is degenerate. As a rule we have:

> A *solution is nondegenerate* if it uses k boxes, and the table has m rows and n columns, and also $k = m + n - 1$.

A degenerate situation will arise when a new variable comes into the solution and causes two or more variables to be deleted from a previously nondegenerate solution, thus we can usually see when it is coming.

At this point in our development, we have a nondegenerate initial feasible solution and so we can continue. Our next step is to test for optimality and this procedure will also indicate which variable should come into the next solution if we do not have the optimum solution already in hand. The so-called *Modified Distribution Method,* or simply the *MODI Method,* is perhaps the most convenient procedure for our next step, but it is not the only one available.

The MODI Method has two phases. The first develops an index for each row and each column of the table with our present solution. Thus, in our example, we would be working with Table 5–9. These indices can be positive or negative numbers and to determine them we use the cost terms corresponding to *used boxes only*. The next phase of the method uses these row and column indices to calculate an index for each *unused box* in the present solution table, and these may also be negative or positive numbers. If none of these indices are negative, our present solution is optimum; but if there is at least one negative index, we can make an improvement in our present solution. That unused box with the "most negative" index corresponds to the variable which should be brought into the next solution for the greatest improvement.

To introduce the procedure, let us generically represent the row indices with the letter $R,$ and the column indices with the letter K. Subscripts are attached to these to identify the row or column we are dealing with, and so R_A is the row index for the Warehouse A row, and K_C the column index for the Customer c column. The unit cost associated with each box also needs a unique symbol, and we use $C,$ with subscripts, for this. Thus, the symbol $C_{A,d}$ represents the unit shipping cost associated with the (A,d) box, that is, for shipments from Warehouse A to Customer d (its value is 24).

To start the routine, we select one of the row indices and assign this an index of 0; normally, the first row is selected. In our example, this means that we start with $R_A = 0$. From this point on, using only the used boxes, we determine the other indices from the relation :

$$\boxed{R_i + K_j = C_{i,j}}$$

where i may be A, B, C, or D, and j may be a, b, c, d, or e (in our present example). In words, this means that every cost rate for each used box in our present solution is set equal to the row index corresponding to the row in which the cost is located *plus* the column index corresponding to the column in which this cost is located.

In performing this phase of the method the calculations are a lot easier than they might at first appear. To simplify these somewhat we will find that whenever we calculate a row or column index we will know two things: the cost rate involved in the relationship and one of the indices. We simply have to subtract the known index value from the cost rate to produce the value of the other unknown index, and most often this is performed mentally. In doing this, we must recall that an index may be a negative number, which means that if we *subtract* a negative number we simply have to *add* its numerical part to the cost.

Since this is a crucial step, let us illustrate each calculation for our present initial solution. Starting with $R_A = 0$, and knowing the value of $C_{A,a}$, which is 10 (see Table 5–9) then:

$$R_A + K_a = C_{A,a} \quad \text{implies} \quad K_a = C_{A,a} - R_A = 10 - 0 = 10$$

This value is posted at the top of the first column in Table 5–10. With what we now know we search the table for a used box whose row or column index we already know. The only one we can find is the $C_{A,c}$ cost, which is 22. Thus, we have:

$$R_A + K_c = C_{A,c} \quad \text{implies} \quad K_c = C_{A,c} - R_A = 22 - 0 = 22$$

	DESTINATION \\ SOURCE	CUST. a ($K_a=10$)	CUST. b ($K_b=4$)	CUST. c ($K_c=22$)	CUST. d ($K_d=20$)	CUST. e ($K_e=-1$)	SUPPLY
$R_A=0$	WAREHOUSE A.	[10] 100	[18]	[22] 200	[24]	[30]	300
$R_B=13$	WAREHOUSE B.	[15]	[17] 200	[35] 100	[32]	[12] 50	350
$R_C=-6$	WAREHOUSE C.	[20]	[40]	[16] 100	[14] 100	[34]	200
$R_D=-7$	WAREHOUSE D.	[25]	[11]	[19]	[13] 150	[26]	150
	DEMAND	100	200	400	250	50	1000

Table 5–10

This index is posted over the c column in Table 5–10. At this point we know the column index, K_c, for the cost terms $C_{B,c}$ and $C_{C,c}$ which means we can next calculate the values of R_B and R_C. These follow from:

$$R_B + K_c = C_{B,c} \quad \text{implies} \quad R_B = C_{B,c} - K_c = 35 - 22 = 13$$
$$R_C + K_c = C_{C,c} \quad \text{implies} \quad R_C = C_{C,c} - K_c = 16 - 22 = -6$$

Knowing R_C we can turn to the term $C_{C,d}$ to find K_d, and knowing R_B we can evaluate K_b through the term $C_{B,b}$ and K_e through $C_{B,e}$. Thrse calculations are as follows:

$$R_C + K_d = C_{C,d} \quad \text{implies} \quad K_d = C_{C,d} - R_C = 14 - (-6) = 20$$
$$R_B + K_b = C_{B,b} \quad \text{implies} \quad K_b = C_{B,b} - R_B = 17 - 13 = 4$$
$$R_B + K_e = C_{B,e} \quad \text{implies} \quad K_e = C_{B,e} - R_B = 12 - 13 = -1$$

Finally, since we now know the value of K_d, we can evaluate R_D through $C_{D,d}$ as follows:

$$R_D + K_d = C_{D,d} \quad \text{implies} \quad R_D = C_{D,d} - K_d = 13 - 20 = -7$$

and with this all row and column indices have been found —these are all posted in Table 5–10.

As we have said, our next phase is to use these indices to evaluate each unused box in our solution table. This is done in Table 5–11. The rule is simple in that all we need do is to locate an unused box, add the values of the row and column indices corresponding to this box, and then subtract this sum from the cost term for this box. Thus our formula is:

$$\boxed{\text{Index for the } (i,j) \text{ box} = C_{i,j} - (R_i + K_j)}$$

Thus, for example, and looking at Table 5–11, we see that for the (B,a) box we have the following: $C_{B,a} = 15$, $R_B = 13$, and $K_a = 10$; which means that the index for this box is: $15 - (13 + 10) = -8$. This value is posted in this box and enclosed in a circle to keep it distinct from quantity assignments in the table.

The other unused box indices are shown in the table and we see that the box with the "most negative" index is the (B,a) box with index -8. Thus, the $X_{B,a}$ variable should be brought into our next solution, which means we should now include assignments of units

		$K_a=10$	$K_b=4$	$K_c=22$	$K_d=20$	$K_e=-1$	
	DESTINATION / SOURCE	CUST. a	CUST. b	CUST. c	CUST. d	CUST. e	SUPPLY
$R_A=0$	WAREHOUSE A.	10 / 100	18 / (14)	22 / 200	24 / (4)	30 / (31)	300
$R_B=13$	WAREHOUSE B.	15 / (-8)	17 / 200	35 / 100	32 / (-1)	12 / 50	350
$R_C=-6$	WAREHOUSE C.	20 / (16)	40 / (42)	16 / 100	14 / 100	34 / (41)	200
$R_D=-7$	WAREHOUSE D.	25 / (22)	11 / (14)	19 / (4)	13 / 150	26 / (34)	150
	DEMAND	100	200	400	250	50	1000

Table 5–11

from Warehouse B to Customer a. This will in turn mean that (to continue to satisfy the rim conditions) we will have to take away units presently assigned to other customers from the supply at Warehouse B; these are customers b, c, and e.

DESTINATION \ SOURCE	CUST. a	CUST. b	CUST. c	CUST. d	CUST. e	SUPPLY
WAREHOUSE A.	(−) ⌐10⌐ 100 ←	⌐18⌐	(+) ⌐22⌐ ↑200	⌐24⌐	⌐30⌐	300
WAREHOUSE B.	↓⌐15⌐ (+) —	⌐17⌐ 200	(−)⌐35⌐ → 100	⌐32⌐	⌐12⌐ 50	350
WAREHOUSE C.	⌐20⌐	⌐40⌐	⌐16⌐ 100	⌐14⌐ 100	⌐34⌐	200
WAREHOUSE D.	⌐25⌐	⌐11⌐	⌐19⌐	⌐13⌐ 150	⌐26⌐	150
DEMAND	100	200	400	250	50	1000

Table 5–12

The shifting of units into the (*B,a*) box is accomplished by following these steps (Table 5–12 illustrates the path):

Step 1. Starting at the box we wish to include in our next solution (the (*B,a*) box in our example), move along this same row either left or right until a used box is reached which has another used box in the same column (the (*B,c*) box is the one to select since it has the used (*A,c*) box in its column). In this phase we can skip over used boxes in the row when necessary (as we do over the (*B,b*) box).

Step 2. Now at the box located in Step 1 (the (*B,c*) box), move up or down in this column until we reach a box which has another used box in its row (here the (*A,c*) box is the one since it has the (*A,a*) box in its row). We continue in this manner, moving first in a column and then in a row, until we reach the original box we started from; that is, in our case, until we reach the (*B,a*) box. In other words, we form a closed path taking us from the box we want in our next solution back to this same box passing through used boxes. The final four-step path is indicated in Table 5–12 with arrows.

Step 3. Assign alternative plus and minus signs to each used box in our closed path, starting with a plus sign for the starting box (see Table 5–12). This sets up the necessary mechanism to ensure that we again satisfy the rim conditions after the shifting of units.

Step 4. To determine how much we can shift, find the *smallest quantity* in those boxes in our path with *negative signs* in them. From Table 5–12 we see that this quantity is 100 units found in both the (*B,c*) box and the (*A,a*) box, This is the largest amount we can shift to our new box. Noting that we have found two boxes with our 100 units should prepare us for a degenerate solution.

Step 5. Assign the quantity determined in Step 4 to the new box and add this same amount to all boxes on the path with plus signs and also subtract this amount from all boxes with minus signs. Thus, in our example, we add 100 units to the (*B,a*) box and the (*A,c*) box, and subtract this from the (*A,a*) box and the (*B,c*) box: the resulting solution is shown in Table 5–13.

DESTINATION / SOURCE	CUST. a	CUST. b	CUST. c	CUST. d	CUST. e	SUPPLY
WAREHOUSE A.	10	18	22 / 300	24	30	300
WAREHOUSE B.	15 / 100	17 / 200	35	32	12 / 50	350
WAREHOUSE C.	20	40	16 / 100	14 / 100	34	200
WAREHOUSE D.	25	11	19	13 / 150	26	150
DEMAND	100	200	400	250	50	1000

Table 5–13

We were fortunate in our example to need a rather simple path, and while in general our paths take us through more boxes, the procedure is simply a matter of routine and is not as involved as it might first appear. The key thing to remember is that we can turn "corners" only at used boxes.

The solution shown in Table 5–13 has a total cost of $17,050 and since it only uses seven boxes, it is a degenerate solution. This means that before we can test to see if it is optimum we must correct for this degeneracy.

To handle the degenerate solution, we simply have to introduce an additional used box, but one which does not actually involve any real allocation. In other words, we introduce a symbol and treat this as if it were an actual allocation. The symbol we use is the lower-case Greek letter "epsilon," written as "ε." We should think of ε as some very small number of units and this is so small that it does not effect any addition or subtraction we may subsequently make. That is, $10 + \varepsilon = 10$, $0.34 - \varepsilon = 0.34$, and so on. It is merely a device which allows us to meet the nondegeneracy condition. If in our degeneracy test we find that we are two "short" in the number of used boxes, then we will introduce the epsilon in two different boxes to bring us to the correct number of used boxes. When we do this we usually assign one epsilon a minus sign and the other a plus sign. Normally, the procedure will automatically delete these epsilons, but if it hasn't and we again face a degenerate situation, then we introduce a second abstract symbol, say, ε_2, and so on.

In Table 5–14 we have shown the ε in the (*A,a*) box, and the particular box we choose is very important. Basically, we must place the epsilon in a box which will enable us to calculate the MODI row and column indices, and for this reason we can start the procedure for calculating these and when we reach a "dead end" put in the ε in that box which will allow us to continue. If we go ahead and calculate these indices, and then the indices for the unused boxes, we will develop the table shown in Table 5–15. Since no unused box has a

DESTINATION / SOURCE	CUST. a	CUST. b	CUST. c	CUST. d	CUST. e	SUPPLY
WAREHOUSE A.	[10] ϵ	[18]	[22] 300	[24]	[30]	300
WAREHOUSE B.	[15] 100	[17] 200	[35]	[32]	[12] 50	350
WAREHOUSE C.	[20]	[40]	[16] 100	[14] 100	[34]	200
WAREHOUSE D.	[25]	[11]	[19]	[13] 150	[26]	150
DEMAND	100	200	400	250	50	1000

Table 5–14

$$K_a=10 \quad K_b=12 \quad K_c=22 \quad K_d=20 \quad K_e=7$$

	DESTINATION / SOURCE	CUST. a	CUST. b	CUST. c	CUST. d	CUST. e	SUPPLY
$R_A=0$	WAREHOUSE A.	[10] ϵ	[18] ⑥	[22] 300	[24] ④	[30] ㉓	300
$R_B=5$	WAREHOUSE B.	[15] 100	[17] 200	[35] ⑧	[32] ⑦	[12] 50	350
$R_C=-6$	WAREHOUSE C.	[20] ⑯	[40] ㉞	[16] 100	[14] 100	[34] ㉝	200
$R_D=-7$	WAREHOUSE D.	[25] ㉒	[11] ⑥	[19] ④	[13] 150	[26] ㉖	150
	DEMAND	100	200	400	250	50	1000

Table 5–15

negative index, we have found the optimum solution (Table 5–14) and the $17,050 cost associated with this is the minimum cost possible for the problem.

An important point should be mentioned concerning the epsilon and the shifting operation to form our next solution. It may happen that the epsilon is in a minus sign box in our closed path. This means that our smallest quantity (in Step 4 of the procedure) is the ε. Adding this to the plus sign boxes in the path will not change any of them except the box we are bringing into the solution (also it will not change any of the minus sign boxes except the one with the ε). What we therefore accomplish is just a relocation of the ε and the procedure does this because our location for the epsilon was not the correct location. This situation is particularly frustrating when working with large tables because we do not develop a new solution, but it is one of the rules of the game. To reduce the procedure somewhat when we go to recalculate the row and column indices again (as part of the MODI method) most of these will be the same, and so those unused box indices which correspond to the previous indices will not change either and so need not be recalculated.

Modifications in the Distribution Method

The distribution method has been illustrated for a problem which had the following characteristics:

1. There were only equality constraints restricting our allocations.
2. The total quantity available at the sources was equal to the total quantity demanded by the destinations.
3. The minimum value of the objective equation was to be found.
4. All boxes in the table were potential candidates for the final solution.

In a particular problem we may have one or more of these characteristics lacking and to accommodate this situation certain modifications are required. These changes are made in the initial table we start with, rather than in the actual arithmetical calculations, and how we make these will be illustrated with examples. These illustrations are taken from a variety of situations so as to provide the reader with a "feeling" for when his problem can be solved with the distribution method.

First, let us consider the situation where we have more units available at the sources than is demanded by the destinations. To stay on familiar ground, let us work with the example of the previous section, but with a different interpretation. Let us suppose that instead of the four warehouses we have four production plants, A, B, C, and D, and in place of the five customers we now have five market areas a, b, c, d, and e. Furthermore, let us suppose that the cost rates in Table 5–14 are now the sum of the unit production cost at the indicated plant plus the unit shipping cost to the indicated market. These changes are shown in Table 5–16 where we are assuming that the capacity tapped at each source is straight time production. We have also included another row for overtime production at Plant C, which shows a $2 per unit increase in the production cost, the capacity from this source is 150 units. To add a little more reality to the problem, let us suppose that these supply figures are monthly figures from each source and the indicated demands are the same for each month of the

SOURCE \ DESTINATION	MKT. a	MKT. b	MKT. c	MKT. d	MKT. e	DUMMY	SUPPLY
PLANT A. STR. TIME	10	18	22	24	30	0	300
PLANT B. STR. TIME	15	17	35	32	12	0	350
PLANT C. STR. TIME	20	40	16	14	34	0	200
PLANT C. OVERTIME	22	42	18	16	36	0	150
PLANT D. STR. TIME	25	11	19	13	26	0	150
DEMAND	100	200	400	250	50	150	1150

Table 5–16

year and we are planning the production and distribution for a year. With this new source we have 150 units more supply than demanded, and since we must have total supply equal to total demand, we simply introduce a "dummy" market (which means an extra column) and attribute to this market the "extra" supply of 150 unit demand. For the dummy market, since we will not actually produce nor ship for it, is given all *zero* cost rates. At this point all the conditions which held for our previous example also hold for our new problem.

The Vogel method when applied to Table 5–16 will develop the initial solution shown in Table 5–17. The cost associated with this is $17,850, and is the same one we previously found in Table 5–9. Applying the distribution method, we would find the optimum solution shown in Table 5–18 and the cost of this plan is $15,950, or $191,400 per year. The cost of our optimum plan without the use of the overtime at Plant C was $17,050 per month or

DESTINATION / SOURCE	MKT. a	MKT. b	MKT. c	MKT. d	MKT. e	DUMMY	SUPPLY
PLANT A. STR. TIME	10 / 100	18	22 / 200	24	30	0	300
PLANT B. STR. TIME	15	17 / 200	35 / 100	32	12 / 50	0	350
PLANT C. STR. TIME	20	40	16 / 100	14 / 100	34	0	200
PLANT C. OVERTIME	22	42	18	16	36	0 / 150	150
PLANT D. STR. TIME	25	11	19	13 / 150	26	0	150
DEMAND	100	200	400	250	50	150	1150

Table 5–17

DESTINATION / SOURCE	MKT. a	MKT. b	MKT. c	MKT. d	MKT. e	DUMMY	SUPPLY
PLANT A. STR. TIME	10 / 100	18	22 / 150	24	30	0 / 50	300
PLANT B. STR. TIME	15	17 / 200	35	32	12 / 50	0 / 100	350
PLANT C. STR. TIME	20	40	16 / 200	14	34	0	200
PLANT C. OVERTIME	22	42	18 / 50	16 / 100	36	0	150
PLANT D. STR. TIME	25	11	19	13 / 150	26	0	150
DEMAND	100	200	400	250	50	150	1150

Table 5–18

$204,600 per year, which means that by tapping this overtime source we have reduced our monthly costs by $1,100 and so our annual costs by $13,200.

Let us suppose now that with an investment of $60,000 (including the fixed costs associated with the investment, which might be new equipment or the like) we can increase our capacity to supply at Plant D. This annex to this plant will provide us with an additional 300 units per month and will have a smaller cost per unit in production. Table 5–19 shows the new table where we note that we do not have to add a second dummy market but merely increase the demand at the previous one to equal the difference between supply and demand, that is, now the demand here is for 450 units per month. Table 5–20 shows the Vogel solu-

SOURCE \ DESTINATION	MKT. a	MKT. b	MKT. c	MKT. d	MKT. e	DUMMY	SUPPLY
PLANT A. STR. TIME	10	18	22	24	30	0	300
PLANT B. STR. TIME	15	17	35	32	12	0	350
PLANT C. STR. TIME	20	40	16	14	34	0	200
PLANT C. OVERTIME	22	42	18	16	36	0	150
PLANT D. STR. TIME	25	11	19	13	26	0	150
PLANT D. NEW ANNEX	16	36	12	10	30	0	300
DEMAND	100	200	400	250	50	450	1450

Table 5–19

SOURCE \ DESTINATION	MKT. a	MKT. b	MKT. c	MKT. d	MKT. e	DUMMY	SUPPLY
PLANT A. STR. TIME	10 / 100	18	22 / 100	24 / 100	30	0	300
PLANT B. STR. TIME	15	17 / 200	35	32	12 / 50	0 / 100	350
PLANT C. STR. TIME	20	40	16	14	34	0 / 200	200
PLANT C. OVERTIME	22	42	18	16	36	0 / 150	150
PLANT D. STR. TIME	25	11	19	13 / 150	26	0	150
PLANT D. NEW ANNEX	16	36	12 / 300	10	30	0	300
DEMAND	100	200	400	250	50	450	1450

Table 5–20

tion with monthly cost of $15,150. The final optimum solution is shown in Table 5–21 with monthly cost of $13,010, or $156,120 per year. In summary we have:

Sources Tapped	Annual Costs
Straight Time at all Plants	$204,600
Plus Overtime at Plant C	$191,400
Plus Annex at Plant D	$156,120

Thus, the savings we can attribute to the annex at Plant D are $191,400 — $156,120 or $35,280 per year. Whether or not this investment should be made depends on the way in which the company evaluates such investments, but at least through the analysis this information on annual savings can be included into the decision.

Looking at Table 5–21 we notice several things. First we see that the capacity at each source is tapped. If it had turned out that one of these was not included in the solution, then we could exclude it from the system altogether using its capacity somewhere else. Also we note that 200 units of Plant A capacity and 250 units of Plant B capacity are assigned to the dummy market, which means that these quantities will not be tapped by the plant and so also may be directed to some other use. In addition, we see that even though the annex production has a smaller per unit cost than the straight time production at Plant D, we call for both in the final solution.

There are times when for some reason some of the boxes in our table are to be prohibited from the final solution, but must be included in the table to meet the requirements of the method of solution. The way we handle these is the same as we did with artificial variables in the simplex method—we assign them an extremely high cost (or extremely negative profit) and then the procedure will exclude them automatically.

SOURCE \ DESTINATION	MKT. a	MKT. b	MKT. c	MKT. d	MKT. e	DUMMY	SUPPLY
PLANT A. STR. TIME	10 · 100	18	22	24	30	0 · 200	300
PLANT B. STR. TIME	15	17 · 50	35	32	12 · 50	0 · 250	350
PLANT C. STR. TIME	20	40	16 · 100	14 · 100	34	0	200
PLANT C. OVERTIME	22	42	18	16 · 150	36	0	150
PLANT D. STR. TIME	25	11 · 150	19	13	26	0	150
PLANT D. NEW ANNEX	16	36	12 · 300	10	30	0	300
DEMAND	100	200	400	250	50	450	1450

Table 5–21

To illustrate, let us consider a manufacturer who must produce a certain product to meet contracted sales for the next five months, where the actual sales vary considerably over this period (this same situation would arise when we are planning production for a highly seasonal item). The cycle time of this item is such that production in a month can be used to meet sales in this same month, but the product may also be produced in one month and then held for sale in a later month. The estimated inventory carrying cost is $2 per unit per month, and units sold in the same month as produced incur no storage cost.

The production facilities used to produce this item do not have the same capacity in each month and the unit production cost (labor, materials, and variable shop overhead) also varies according to the facilities and personnel available. In addition, we have two sources of production capacity in each month—straight time and overtime production, with varying amounts of each in the different months. The variable unit cost on overtime is $10 more than on the straight time production of the same month. The data we have is the following, where we assume that we are now planning the production starting with September:

| Month | Contracted Sales | Available Capacity & Costs | | | |
| | | Straight Time | | Overtime | |
		Capacity	Unit Cost	Capacity	Unit Cost
Sept.	50	120	$25	30	$35
Oct.	50	120	$25	30	$35
Nov.	100	100	$24	30	$34
Dec.	200	100	$24	10	$34
Jan.	200	100	$22	10	$32
Totals:	600	540		110	

The problem is to determine how many units should be manufactured in the early monihs of low sales and high capacity and held in inventory in anticipation of the later months of higher sales and lower capacities. In this type of problem we would probably have another source in the form of on-hand inventory, but here we assume that we do not have any and also that we do not want any at the end of the period. Thus, this might be a specialty item as under a job shop contract. Since we cannot produce units in one month for sales in the previous month (the problem could be modified to do this if a backorder cost was included), we therefore cannot have allocations appearing in our solution for these boxes. To ensure that this does not happen we have assigned a $100 per unit cost for all boxes to be excluded. Table 5-22 shows the resulting table. In this table we also have included a "dummy" month which is needed since our total supply is greater than the total demand. Actually this is a slack variable as used in the simplex method and is needed since we no longer have equality constraints, but rather inequality constraints. To appreciate this fact let us look at the September straight time production row. Here the restriction is not that *all* 120 units of capacity must be used, but rather that *no more than* this amount can be scheduled; thus, rather than equality we have inequality. This is also true for the other capacities and so the last column represents the ten slack variables needed to make the problem one with equality constraints only.

SOURCE / DESTINATION	SEPT. SALES	OCT. SALES	NOV. SALES	DEC. SALES	JAN. SALES	DUMMY	SUPPLY
SEPT. S.T. PRODUCTION	25	27	29	31	33	0	120
SEPT. O.T. PRODUCTION	35	37	39	41	43	0	30
OCT. S.T. PRODUCTION	100	25	27	29	31	0	120
OCT. O.T. PRODUCTION	100	35	37	39	41	0	30
NOV. S.T. PRODUCTION	100	100	24	26	28	0	100
NOV. O.T. PRODUCTION	100	100	34	36	38	0	30
DEC. S.T. PRODUCTION	100	100	100	24	26	0	100
DEC. O.T. PRODUCTION	100	100	100	34	36	0	10
JAN. S.T. PRODUCTION	100	100	100	100	22	0	100
JAN. O.T. PRODUCTION	100	100	100	100	32	0	10
DEMAND	50	50	100	200	200	50	650

Table 5–22

Table 5–23 shows the Vogel solution which is also the optimum solution for this problem. The cost of this plan is $16,010. We notice that all 120 units of capacity will be used in September straight time, 50 units of which will be used for meeting this month's sales, 30 units for the sales in December and 40 units for sales in January. This, of course, does not mean that we actually "tag" these units and dispense them only in the indicated months. What we would do is to phase these by tapping on-hand stocks to meet current sales and putting new production in inventory. Thus, 50 units of those produced in September would most likely go out in October with this month's production going into inventory. If we were dealing with an item which suffered physical deterioration, there may be a limit on how long we can keep it in stock. To handle this situation we could introduce other prohibitive boxes in the table which would limit the period over which stocks could be held as anticipation inventory.

If our objective equation is written in terms of profit, or some other quantity which we wish to maximize, then all we need do is to introduce the profit margins as negative numbers

SOURCE \ DESTINATION	SEPT. SALES	OCT. SALES	NOV. SALES	DEC. SALES	JAN. SALES	DUMMY	SUPPLY
SEPT. S.T. PRODUCTION	25 / 50	27	29	31 / 30	33 / 40	0	120
SEPT. O.T. PRODUCTION	35	37	39	41	43	0 / 30	30
OCT. S.T. PRODUCTION	100	25 / 50	27	29 / 70	31	0	120
OCT. O.T. PRODUCTION	100	35	37	39	41 / 10	0 / 20	30
NOV. S.T. PRODUCTION	100	100	24 / 100	26	28	0	100
NOV. O.T. PRODUCTION	100	100	34	36	38 / 30	0	30
DEC. S.T. PRODUCTION	100	100	100	24 / 100	26	0	100
DEC. O.T. PRODUCTION	100	100	100	34	36 / 10	0	10
JAN. S.T. PRODUCTION	100	100	100	100	22 / 100	0	100
JAN. O.T. PRODUCTION	100	100	100	100	32 / 10	0	10
DEMAND	50	50	100	200	200	50	650

Table 5–23

into the cost rate boxes of our table. The same procedure will develop the allocation which gives the maximum profit. In applying the procedures we must recall that when they ask for the "smallest" value this will be the "most negative" number. Thus, -34 is "smaller" than -12, or *zero*. Also, when we must find the "largest" value this will be the "least negative" number.

Also when working with profit, we may find that we have more "demand" than we do "supply." Here some of the demands will go unfilled in the quest of maximizing overall profits. Now, to handle this situation, we will introduce a "dummy" row, or source, and any allocation from this source will indicate the demand which will go unfilled.

To illustrate both of these modifications let us consider the following problem. A critical raw material is used in four different proposed products, and in each case the material is processed with direct labor to produce the end product. For example, the material might be used in making precision castings or some other item involving direct labor. The market prospects and engineering designs give the following information:

Product	a	b	c	d
Weekly Sales (finished units)	300	250	200	150
Selling Price (net $)	$8.00	$20.00	$11.20	$8.20
Raw Material per Unit (pounds)	5.2	16.3	10.25	7.1
Direct Labor Cost per Unit Plus Variable Overhead	$3.05	$ 6.00	$ 2.00	$2.15

From this information we calculate the following weekly demands for the raw material in pounds:

Product	a	b	c	d
Weekly Requirements of Material	1,560	4,075	2,050	1,065

for an overall total demand of 8,750 pounds per week.

There are only three vendors who can supply the needed raw material and their prices and quantities are as follows:

Vendor	Maximum Weekly Supply	Price: $ per Pound
I	1,250	0.50
II	2,000	0.60
III	3,500	0.85
Total:	6,750	

From this we see that weekly demand for the material exceeds the total supply, and so either some products will not be made or else weekly sales will not be fully met; the optimum solution will tell us which.

First we must find the unit profits for the four products working with material from each vendor. For Product c using material from Vendor I we would do the following:

Selling Price	$11.20
Material Cost 0.50 × 10.25	−$ 5.12
Direct Labor & Variable Overhead Cost	−$2.00
Net Profit per Unit	$4.08

This we have written as $4.1 in the ($I,c$) box of Table 5-24 , and also posted the other net profit rates. Again, we post these as negative numbers. In addition, we have included a dummy source with a supply of $8,750 - 6,750 = 2,000$ pounds per week.

The Vogel solution, which is also the optimum one, is shown is Table 5-25; in Table 5-26 we show the results of the MODI method which proves this fact. Looking at the final solution we see that the 2,000 pounds of dummy supply are allocated to Products b, c, and d. For the first two products this means that we will not be able to produce to meet the full demands of these products, but for the last product it means that for maximum profits we should not produce this product at all. Since we do have a profit margin for Product d, if we had actual extra supply we might then find this product profitable enough to produce.

SOURCE \ DESTINATION	PROD. a	PROD. b	PROD. c	PROD. d	SUPPLY
VENDOR I	-2.4	-5.9	-4.1	-2.5	1250
VENDOR II	-1.8	-4.2	-3.1	-1.8	2000
VENDOR III	-0.5	-0.1	-0.5	-0.0	3500
DUMMY	0	0	0	0	2000
DEMAND	1560	4075	2050	1065	8750

Table 5-24

SOURCE \ DESTINATION	PROD. a	PROD. b	PROD. c	PROD. d	SUPPLY
VENDOR I	-2.4	-5.9 / 1250	-4.1	-2.5	1250
VENDOR II	-1.8	-4.2 / 2000	-3.1	-1.8	2000
VENDOR III	-0.5 / 1560	-0.1	-0.5 / 1940	-0.0	3500
DUMMY	0	0 / 825	0 / 110	0 / 1065	2000
DEMAND	1560	4075	2050	1065	8750

Table 5-25

At this point we have discussed the modifications needed to adapt most problems so that they have the necessary "standard" format for the distribution method. There is, however, another type of problem which can arise and which may or may not be resolved.

$$K_a=-5.9 \quad K_b=-5.9 \quad K_c=-5.9 \quad K_d=-5.9$$

SOURCE \ DESTINATION	PROD. a	PROD. b	PROD. c	PROD. d	SUPPLY
$R_I=0$ VENDOR I	-2.4 ③⑤	-5.9 / 1250	-4.1 ⑴⑧	-2.5 ③④	1250
$R_{II}=1.7$ VENDOR II	-1.8 ②④	-4.2 / 2000	-3.1 ⑴⑴	-1.8 ②④	2000
$R_{III}=5.4$ VENDOR III	-0.5 / 1560	-0.1 ⓪④	-0.5 / 1940	-0.0 ⓪⑤	3500
$R_d=5.9$ DUMMY	0 ⓪	0 / 825	0 / 110	0 / 1065	2000
DEMAND	1560	4075	2050	1065	8750

Table 5–26

This is the situation where all sources may not have the same "kind" of supply. There might be a difference in the quality of the units from the different sources, equipment (as sources of capacity) might not all operate at the same efficiency, and so on. The procedure assumes that supply from each source is "equivalent" to that from any other, and if at the start we do not have this, then we may or may not be able to make the needed conversion; when we cannot the simplex method may have to be used. Normally, we select one of the sources and use this as a "standard," against which we measure the other sources. To illustrate, let us suppose that we have two machines as our sources and suppose that the characteristics of these are as follows:

Machine	Relative Efficiency	Hours Available	Percent Downtime
I	100%	200	2%
II	85%	150	6%

We must adjust the total available hours, $200 + 150 = 350$, to reflect both the downtime as well as the relative efficiencies. Selecting Machine I as the standard we could develop the following information:

Machine	Gross Available Hours	Percent Downtime	Hours Downtime	Net Available Hours	Relative Efficiency	Adjusted Available Hours
I	200	2%	4.0	196	100%	196.00
II	150	6%	9.0	141	85%	119.85
Totals:	350		13.0	337		315.85

The adjusted available hours figures are those used as the "supply" figures for these machines in the table for the problem.

A general flowchart for the distribution method is provided in Figure 5–2 where again this starts with the formulation of the problem into the proper format. Using the source-to-destination interpretation is most helpful in this phase.

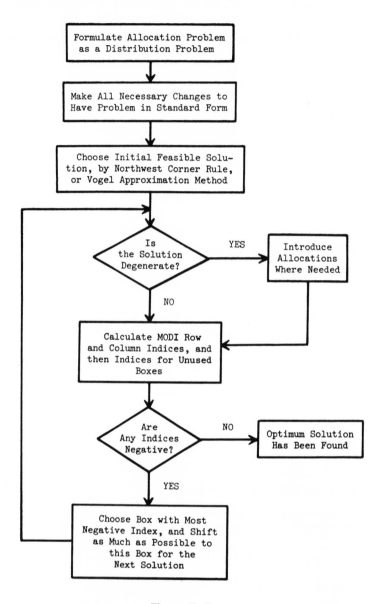

Figure 5–2

Assignment Solution of Linear Programming Problems

As the distribution method is used for a special type of simplex allocation problem, the so-called *assignment method* of solution is specific to a special type of distribution problem. When our problem has the necessary characteristics for this solution method, the method will be the most efficient one we can use. The basic parts of the assignment problem are the following:

1. There are n "facilities" to which we are to assign n "jobs," assigning one and only one job to each facility.
2. For each job-to-facility assignment there is a "cost" of performing this job on this facility.
3. Our objective is to assign jobs to facilities so as to minimize the overall cost of performing all n jobs.

The distinguishing characteristic of this problem is that each job-to-facility variable will be either 0 or 1 (0 meaning "no assignment," 1 meaning an assignment), and this is because two jobs cannot be assigned to one facility and also two facilities cannot perform the same job. Therefore, our solution will always have exactly n variables in it, each of which will have the value 1.

An example will be used to present the technique and in this we will use production orders as the "jobs" and production lines as the "facilities." There are four production orders, 1, 2, 3, 4 to be assigned to four lines A, B, C, D. Each line is capable of doing any of the jobs and the production hours required for each assignment are as follows:

		Production Lines		
	A	B	C	D
#1	10	5	4	10
#2	20	1	15	20
#3	10	3	6	30
#4	9	3	5	10

Production Orders

Thus, for example, if we were to assign orders #1, #2, #3, and #4 respectively to lines A, B, C, and D, this assignment would require a total of $10 + 1 + 6 + 10 = 27$ hours of production time.

Any assignment problem may be set up as a distribution problem, and the table we would have for our particular example would be the following:

LINE \ ORDER	A	B	C	D	ROW TOTALS
#1	10	5	4	10	1
#2	20	1	15	20	1
#3	10	3	6	30	1
#4	9	3	5	10	1
COLUMN TOTALS	1	1	1	1	

This is as far as we will go in this direction, turning now to the assignment method itself. For this our worksheet table is the original table listing the production time values for the assignment possibilities.

The method provides a way for constructing a possible solution and then a test to see if this solution developed is feasible; that is, if it assigns one and only one order to every line. *If the solution is feasible, it is also the optimum solution.* If the solution is not feasible, then another possible solution is developed from the present one and again we test this for feasibility. The very first step we perform, on the original table, is the following:

Step 1. Subtract the smallest element in the first row from all elements in this row, then do this for all rows in the table. Then, working with the resulting table, subtract the smallest element in the first column from all elements in this same column, and continue this for all columns.

This operation will put a 0 (at least one) in every row and in every column, and for our present example we would obtain the following table:

	A	B	C	D
#1	0	1	0	0
#2	13	0	14	13
#3	1	0	3	21
#4	0	0	2	1

To be consistent with the objective of minimization, we can assign a production order to a production line only if there is a 0 in the row corresponding to this order in the column corresponding to this line. At our present state with the above table, we could assign order #1 to lines A, C, or D, but order #3 could only be assigned to line B.

Do we have a feasible solution indicated by the pattern of 0's in the above table? One way to find out is to make the assignments. Since order #3 must be assigned to line B, we would do this first and thereby eliminate line B from any further consideration. This will mean that order #4 must be assigned to line A, since this is the only column of this row where a 0 will appear because line B cannot be considered. In turn this will mean that we can assign order #1 to either line C or D. We will not be able to assign order #2 to any line, and so the solution indicated by this table is not feasible.

A more systematic, as well as expedient, way to test our indicated solution for feasibility is the following:

Step 2. Using the present table determine the fewest number of rows and/or columns which contain all the 0 elements of the table. We can indicate these by drawing a line through them. We then count the number of lines thus used and if this number is equal to the total number of rows in the table, the problem is solved; that is, the pattern of zeros in this table specifies a feasible, and thus the optimum, solution. If the number of lines used is fewer than the number of rows, we go to the next step.

In our present table we can cover all the 0 elements with three lines—one through the first row and the fourth row, and one through the second column. Our table would look as follows:

	A	B	C	D
#1	0	1	0	0
#2	13	0	14	13
#3	1	0	3	21
#4	0	0	2	1

Since we have four rows in the table, but only used three lines to cover the 0 elements, the solution specified by this table is not feasible, which was our previous conclusion. In covering zeros we may find more than one set of lines that will do it, but each set will always use the same "number" of lines.

Our next step modifies our present table into one which specifies a different possible solution. Explicitly, we do the following:

Step 3: Working with the table with the covering lines drawn in, we find the smallest element not covered by any of the lines. We subtract this value from *all* of the elements not covered by lines and add it to all elements at the intersection of two lines. Then we return to Step 2 to test for feasibility.

We will continue cycling between Steps 2 and 3 until we find a solution which is feasible.

Applying Step 3 to our lined table we first find that the smallest element not covered by any line is the "1" in the #3 row, A column position. We are to subtract this amount from every uncovered element, including itself, and add it to those elements at the intersections of two lines. We have two of these latter type elements: the "1" in the #1 row, B column position, and the "0" in the #4 row, B column position. The resulting table would be the following:

	A	B	C	D
#1	0	2	0	0
#2	12	0	13	12
#3	0	0	2	20
#4	0	1	2	1

Returning to Step 2 we find that we can still cover all the 0 elements in this table with just three lines; for instance, one through the #1 row, the A column, and the B column. The table would look as follows:

	A	B	C	D
#1	0	2	0	0
#2	12	0	13	12
#3	0	0	2	20
#4	0	1	2	1

So, we must again perform Step 3 of the procedure. The "1" in the #4 row, D column position is the smallest element not covered by a line, and adding and subtracting this value as required we would develop this table:

	A	B	C	D
#1	1	3	0	0
#2	12	0	12	11
#3	0	0	1	19
#4	0	1	1	0

Returning to Step 2 we would find that we need four lines to cover all the 0 elements of this last table, thus we have a feasible solution specified by the pattern of 0's in the table, and it is the optimum solution as well.

In selecting the actual solution (and there may be more than one specified by a single table), we start by assigning that production order which has but one zero in its row. We assign this to the production line in the column of which this single 0 element appears. Once we make an assignment, we cross out this row and column before we make the next assignment.

Looking at our last table we find that order #2 has but one 0, under the B line column, and so we assign this order to production line B. By doing this we will be left with one 0 element in the #3 row, under the A heading, thus we assign order #3 to line A, and cross out these. The #4 row is left with a single 0 under D, thus order #4 goes to line D, meaning that order #1 goes to line C. Referring back to our first table we find that the total hours required for these assignments is: $4 + 1 + 10 + 10 = 25$ hours.

Modifications in the Assignment Method

The three types of complications which may arise, and which will make the problem differ from the standard form described in the previous section, are now listed along with the necessary modifications we must make.

1. If we want to maximize rather than minimize the total effect of our assignment, and let's assume we are working with profit margins instead of production times, then we find the *largest* of these profit margins and replace every element in the table with the result of subtracting the element from this largest value.
2. If we have fewer assignees (fewer production orders in our previous illustration) than assignments (production lines in our example), then we add as many fictitious assignees as needed to make the table square; that is, the same number of assignees as assignments. All elements in these "dummy" rows are zeros. Similarly, we add on dummy columns if we have fewer assignments than assignees; also, of zeros.
3. If certain assignee-to-assignment pairs are prohibited, we cross out these locations in our table by placing an "X" in these. This X remains in this location regardless of what arithmetic we perform; thus, it can never go to 0, and, if we would normally add a value to it or subtract a value from it, the same X remains. If a calculator is being used in the process, we could assign an extremely large value in these prohibited locations, as is done in the simplex method for artificial variables.

It is necessary to apply these modifications in the same order as given here. That is, starting with the initial table we carry out whatever modifications are needed to meet our particular circumstances, performing these in the order: first 1, then 2, and lastly 3. The resulting fully modified table is the one on which we start the assignment procedure described in the previous section.

Figure 5–3 presents a flowchart for the assignment method, where again we assume that the problem has been cast correctly as an assignment problem. Other potential problems suitable for the assignment method are shown in Table 5–27.

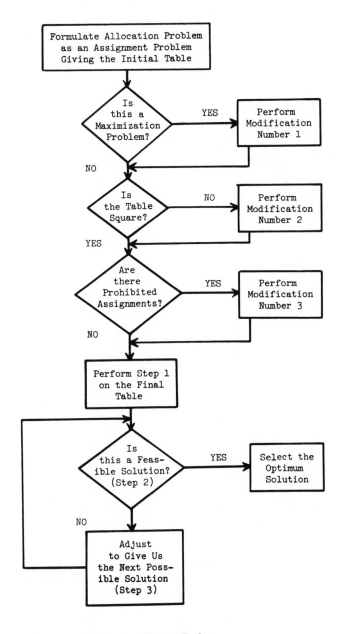

Figure 5–3

The "Jobs"	The "Facilities"	The Measure of Effectiveness of Each Assignment	Objective of Optimality
Machines, equipment, or departments	Area locations	Distance between work areas and the locations	Minimize total distance traveled on the average; during a certain period of time
Machines, equipment, tools, or operators	Production lines, operations, machines or jobs	Cost, productivity, profit, efficiency, or time	Minimize total cost, or time; or, maximize total productivity, or profit, or efficiency
Work jobs, or work orders	Production facilities	Cost of production, or time to complete	Minimize total cost, or total time
Job applicants	Open job assignments, or training programs, or senior men	Rating of applicant for job, potential for training, "suitability" with man	Maximize total rating, potential, or "suitability"
Capital	R&D projects	Expected return	Maximize total return on all projects
Salesmen	Sales areas	Effectiveness, or expected sales	Maximize total effectiveness, or sales expected

Table 5–27

190

CONCLUSION

In this chapter we have attempted to supply the reader with a method for analyzing any system of linear equations. Our main interest was, however, with the linear programming problem, and for this we have demonstrated the simplex, the distribution, and the assignment methods of solution. It has also been our aim to indicate the basic parts of such problems so as to provide the reader with the necessary concepts he will need to recognize and formulate a problem of allocation as a linear programming problem, as well as to select which method of solution will be most efficient.

REFERENCES

Bowman, E.H., and R.B. Fetter. *Analysis for Production and Operations Management.* Homewood, Illinois: Richard D. Irwin, Inc., 1967.

Buffa, E.S. *Models for Production and Operations Management.* New York, N.Y.: John Wiley & Sons, Inc., 1963.

Cochran, E. "Linear Programming Without the Math," *Industrial Engineering,* November, 1970.

Garvin, W.W. *Introduction to Linear Programming.* New York, N.Y.: McGraw-Hill Book Co., 1960

Hillier, F.S. and G.J. Lieberman. *Introduction to Operations Research.* San Francisco, California: Holden-Day, Inc., 1967.

Metzger, R.W. *Elementary Mathematical Programming.* New York, N.Y.: John Wiley & Sons, Inc., 1958.

Parsons, J.A. "The Assignment Algorithm," *Systems and Procedures Journal,* July-August, 1967.

Teichroew, D. *An Introduction to Management Science: Deterministic Models.* New York, N.Y.: John Wiley & Sons, Inc., 1964.

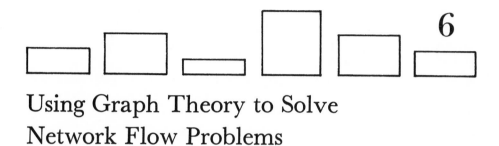

Using Graph Theory to Solve
Network Flow Problems

Network planning and analysis techniques such as PERT (Program Evaluation and Review Technique), and CPM (Critical Path Method), are used to measure and control the development of special, one-time projects. Both start with the construction of a network representation of the project plan, such as that shown in Figure 6–1. In this display circles,

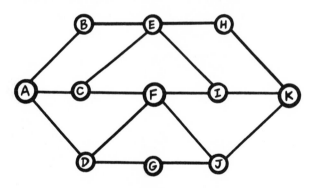

Figure 6–1

or *nodes* as they are called, represent specific and definable events or milestones reached in the course of the project, while lines, or *arcs,* represent the activities or work tasks which take us from one event to another. The pattern in which nodes are connected is in accordance with the precedence constraints existing among the activities. For instance, the activity A-B must be completed before activity B-E can begin.

Many other problems have a basic structure which may be portrayed as a network, and through the analysis of the networks the original problems may be resolved. Underlying such analyses is the mathematical discipline of *graph theory,* where a "graph" is just another name for a network. Thus, Figure 6–1 might be the layout of a distribution system with the nodes representing warehouses, and lines representing roads or highways over which shipments are sent. It could also be the representation of a communications network, a gas pipeline system, or a materials handling route between workcenters. In such cases we have some sort of commodity which can be imagined as "flowing" through the system, and, depending upon the original system, we might have messages, shipments, vehicles, or jobs. In these instances the network shows all the alternative routes we can take from one node to another, and usually we are interested in finding that particular route which will allow us to achieve some stated objective.

If we can associate a measure of "length" with each arc of the network, then our objective might be to find that route through the network which has the minimum overall length. This is the *shortest route problem* in the literature. In another situation we might associate a "capacity" with each arc which limits the amount of flow which can pass over the arc per unit time. In this case we would naturally be interested in determining how flow should be directed through the network, starting and ending at specified nodes, so as to obtain the maximum amount of flow out of the exit node. This is called the *maximum flow problem*.

These problems along with certain others will be interpreted for networks and solution procedures demonstrated for each. These solution methods are iterative, and, for the most part, are quite easily applied by hand.

The Minimal Spanning Tree Problem

For definiteness this problem will be described in the context of a communications system, where nodes will be used to represent communication centers and arcs represent transmission lines. For this problem we do not start with an established network, but rather just the physical disposition of the nodes. Thus, for instance, we might start with Figure 6–2

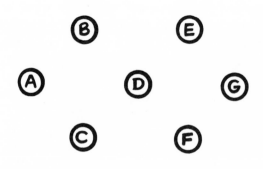

Figure 6–2

showing the relative geographical positions of these centers. A communication center is capable of receiving, sending, and "passing on" messages, and our design problem is to link up the nodes so that a message originating from any center will be able to reach any other center, but with the objective of using the least possible amount of transmission line. Since the cost associated with a transmission line is normally directly proportional to its length, it is logical for us to have this minimization objective.

A network is said to be *connected* if it is possible to start from any node and bypassing over arcs and through nodes reach any other node in the network. Figure 6–1 is an example of such a network. A string of arcs and nodes starting from one node and ending with another is termed a *path,* and if this path starts and ends at the same node, it is termed a *cycle.* A network which is connected but has no cycles is termed a *tree* and this is the type of network we are looking for in the design of our communications network. A tree for which the sum of the lengths of its arcs is minimum is the *minimal spanning tree,* and is the final objective in our problem. How we can find this will be shown below, but first we must introduce the necessary data for our example.

Those arcs which are allowed as well as their lengths are indicated in the following table. In this the notation "AB–6," for example, indicates that the arc from node A to node B is physically possible and will have a length of 6 units. For every arc there is a "reverse arc," and these are also listed. Thus, along with "AB–6," we show "BA–6."

A	B	C	D	E	F	G
AD–4	BE–3	CD–2	DC–2	EB–3	FD–4	GE–3
AC–5	BD–4	CA–5	DE–3	ED–3	FC–6	GD–5
AB–6	BA–6	CF–6	DA–4	EG–3	FG–7	GF–7
			DB–4			
			DF–4			
			DG–5			

To simplify the procedure somewhat it is convenient to organize the table showing the arcs in each column in order of increasing length from top to bottom. Also we label each column with the node with which each arc in this column starts.

In the procedure we will select an arc and refer to the two nodes of it as being "connected." All nodes which are as yet not connected at a stage will be referred to as "unconnected nodes." The procedure starts as follows:

Step 1. *Selecting the first arc.* Select any node with which to begin (it makes no difference which we choose), and from those arcs in this node's column select the one with the shortest length (the top one in the column). This is our first arc and we indicate this selection by drawing a circle around it in the table. We cross off the reverse of this selected arc, and place an "X" above the columns of those nodes which have thus been connected.

Thus, starting with node A, we would simply select the arc at the top of the A column, giving us the arc (A,D), with length 4. We encircle "AD–4" and cross off the term "DA–4," and also place an "X" over the A and D columns. Our table would look as follows at this point:

X			X			
A	B	C	D	E	F	G
(AD–4)	BE–3	CD–2	DC–2	EB–3	FD–4	GE–3
AC–5	BD–4	CA–5	DE–3	ED–3	FC–6	GD–5
AB–6	BA–6	CF–6	~~DA–4~~	EG–3	FG–7	GF–7
			DB–4			
			DF–4			
			DG–5			

Step 2. *Selecting subsequent arcs.* Looking in the columns corresponding to connected nodes (those which have an "X" above them), look at the uppermost, uncircled arc in each, ignoring crossed-outs. Of these, that arc which has the shortest length is the next to select. Circle it, cross out its reverse, and place an "X" above the node which is thus connected.

After connecting nodes A and D with the arc (A,D), we would look in columns A and D, where we would find the candidates "AC–5" and "DC–2," meaning that the latter is the next one to select. At this point our table would look like the following:

X		X	X			
A	B	C	D	E	F	G
(AD–4)	BE–3	~~CD–2~~	(DC–2)	EB–3	FD–4	GE–3
~~AC–5~~	BD–4	~~CA–5~~	DE–3	ED–3	FC–6	GD–5
AB–6	BA–6	CF–6	~~DA–4~~	EG–3	FG–7	GF–7
			DB–4			
			DF–4			
			DG–5			

We don't want to connect two already connected nodes together and to guard against this we cross out those arcs which would give us this redundant connection. If we draw the selected arcs into the figure as we go, we will easily spot those arcs to be crossed out. At this stage we will thus have to cross out the arcs "CA–5," and its reverse "AC–5," for these, if selected, would produce a cycle between the nodes A, D, and C. These deletions have also been shown in the table above.

We continue by applying Step 2 again, looking in the above table under the A, C, and D columns for our candidates. The arcs "AB–6," "CF–6," and "DE–3" are the candidates we find, with the last one being the one to select. We also cross out the reverse of this arc, but here we do not have any arcs which would produce a cycle so this operation is not needed. The resulting table would be:

X		X	X	X		
A	B	C	D	E	F	G
(AD–4)	BE–3	~~CD–2~~	(DC–2)	EB–3	FD–4	GE–3
~~AC–5~~	BD–4	~~CA–5~~	(DE–3)	~~ED–3~~	FC–6	GD–5
AB–6	BA–6	CF–6	~~DA–4~~	EG–3	FG–7	GF–7
			DB–4			
			DF–4			
			DF–5			

Again applying Step 2, we find the candidates for the next selection to be: "AB–6," "CF–6," "DB–4," and "EB–3." The last of these is the proper one to select. Here we must cross out "AB–6," and "BD–4," as well as their reverses so as not to produce cycles. The resulting table would be:

X	X	X	X	X		
A	B	C	D	E	F	G
(AD–4)	~~BE–3~~	~~CD–2~~	(DC–2)	(EB–3)	FD–4	GE–3
~~AC–5~~	~~BD–4~~	~~CA–5~~	(DE–3)	~~ED–3~~	FC–6	GD–5
~~AB–6~~	~~BA–6~~	CF–6	~~DA–4~~	EG–3	FG–7	GF–7
			~~DB–4~~			
			DF–4			
			DG–5			

The next candidates are "CF–6," "DF–4," and "EG–3," from which we select the last one. The arcs "DG–5," and "GD–5" must be crossed off as well as "GE–3." This will lead us to select "FD–4" (or equivalently "DF–4") as the next and final arc, since with this all nodes have been connected. The final table would be:

X	X	X	X	X	X	X
A	B	C	D	E	F	G
(AD–4)	~~BE–3~~	~~CD–2~~	(DC–2)	(EB–3)	(FD–4)	~~GE–3~~
~~AC–5~~	~~BD–4~~	~~CA–5~~	(DE–3)	~~ED–3~~	~~FC–6~~	~~GD–5~~
~~AB–6~~	~~BA–6~~	~~CF–6~~	~~DA–4~~	(EG–3)	~~FG–7~~	~~GF–7~~
			~~DB–4~~			
			DF–4			
			~~DG–5~~			

The minimal spanning tree thus found would be that shown in Figure 6–3, which has a total length of 19 units found by adding the lengths of the individual arcs in the resulting tree.

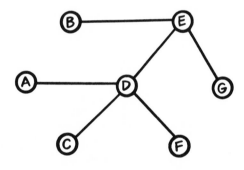

Figure 6–3

It might appear at first glance that the choice we make for the initial node will influence the final minimal spanning tree we find, and its total length. As indicated this is not the case, and to illustrate let's suppose that we had selected node F to begin with as the initial node. If we apply the procedure, we will successively choose the following arcs: (F,D), (D,C), (D, E), (E,B), (E,G), and (D,A). This network is identical to the one obtained by starting with node A. It may easily be shown that we will finish with this same tree regardless of which initial node we choose.

The minimal spanning tree is often helpful in planning a transportation system. Here the nodes in the network would represent shipping and receiving terminals of the system and the arcs the transportation lanes which could be highways, railroad tracks, or air lanes. In this particular context the minimal spanning tree would represent those transportation lanes which can be used to service all terminals using a minimum total distance. This is our normal objective when we must in fact construct these lanes or pay rental on them.

It is also possible to use a different measure instead of arc length. For instance, we might use costs or travel times which are associated with the arcs. In those situations where the arcs will be used with different frequencies, we might wish to introduce an appropriate set of weights in calculating the "lengths" associated with the arcs. In all cases we would have to be seeking the tree whose overall measure is a minimum in order that the procedure is applicable.

It should also be noted that our arcs are symmetrical with respect to their length, that is, each arc and its reverse have the same length. Furthermore, for each arc there is a reverse arc.

The Shortest Route Problem

This problem is concerned with an established network for which lengths, or distances, are associated with each of its arcs. The objective is to find that path through the network, starting at a given origin node and leading to a specified destination node, which will have the shortest overall length. Again, costs, travel times, or some other measure could be used in place of arc lengths.

Figure 6–4 presents a network for which the procedure will be demonstrated. The length of each arc is indicated alongside of it and our objective is to find the path from node

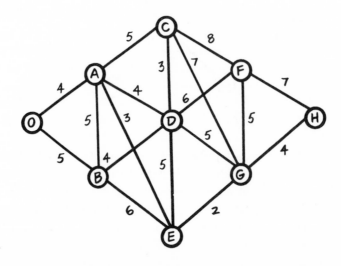

Figure 6–4

O to node H with the shortest length. Again, we work directly on the same table format as used in the previous section, and for our illustration the initial table is as follows:

O	A	B	C	D	E	F	G	H
OA–4	AE–3	BD–4	CD–3	DC–3	EG–2	FG–5	GE–2	
OB–5	AD–4	BA–5	CA–5	DA–4	EA–3	FD–6	GH–4	
	AC–5	BE–6	CG–7	DB–4	ED–5	FH–7	GF–5	
	AB–5		CF–8	DE–5	EB–6	FC–8	GD–5	
				DG–5			GC–7	
				DF–6				

The procedure for finding the shortest route progresses in stages. At each stage a node, and an arc emanating from it will be "committed" to the solution; these are termed *committed nodes* and *committed arcs*. All other nodes and arcs are referred to as *uncommitted*. Eventually the destination node will be committed to the solution, which will terminate the procedure. The arcs committed will indicate the shortest route, and furthermore, they indicate the shortest route from the origin to any other node in the network. The procedure consists of the following steps:

Step 1. *Selecting candidates for the next node to commit.* At any stage of the procedure we look in the columns for those nodes which are already committed to the solution at this stage. The arcs we find will be those which emanate from the committed node corresponding to the column. Ignoring those arcs which are crossed out in these columns, we select the uppermost uncircled arcs, one from each committed node's column, as potential candidates for the next arc to be committed.

Thus, if at some stage of the process nodes O and A have been committed to the solution, we will look in the O column for a candidate and in the A column for the second candidate. The next step determines which from among all the candidates we actually commit.

Step 2. *Selecting the candidate to commit.* At this point we have a list of candidate arcs each of which is located in a different column. For each candidate we calculate a sum of distances and that one with the smallest sum is the one to next commit to the solution. For each committed node we will know (from previous stages) the shortest distance from the origin to it, and to this distance we add the arc distance of the candidate we have located in this committed node's column. The sum we thus find for the selected candidate is the shortest distance from the origin to it which we need for this node in the next part of this step. As an aid it is helpful to shade in nodes as we commit them directly on the network. Also as part of this step we cross out all arcs which end with the node which has just been committed.

At the start of our present solution the only node which is committed to the solution is node O, the origin. The shortest distance from the origin to this node is 0. Thus, according to Step 1 we simply have to look into column O to find the candidate which will be the arc "OA–4," since this is the uppermost uncircled arc in this column. Following Step 2 we would calculate the shortest distance to this node, node A is the one being committed here, as (0 +

4) = 4. We circle "OA–4" in our table, cross out all arcs ending at node A, and place the shortest distance just calculated above the A column. Our table would now have this form:

	0	4						
	O	A	B	C	D	E	F	G	H
(OA–4)	AE–3	BD–4	CD–3	DC–3	EG–2	FG–5	GE–2	
OB–5	AD–4	~~BA–5~~	~~CA–5~~	~~DA–4~~	~~EA–3~~	FD–6	GH–4	
	AC–5	BE–6	CG–7	DB–4	ED–5	FH–7	GF–5	
	AB–5		CF–8	DE–5	EB–6	FC–8	GD–5	
				DG–5			GC–7	
				DF–6				

Returning to Step 1 we look into the O and A columns for our next candidates; from the former we select "OB–5" while from the latter we choose as candidate "AE–3." Going next to Step 2 we calculate the distance (0 + 5) = 5 for node B (from our candidate "OB–5"), and (4 + 3) = 7 for node E (from our candidate "AE–3"). The node with the smallest sum is node B, and so this is the next node to be committed, and "OB–5" is the arc to be committed along with it. We put the value 5 over the B column, circle "OB–5," and cross out all arcs ending with node B. The resulting table would be:

	0	4	5					
	O	A	B	C	D	E	F	G	H
(OA–4)	AE–3	BD–4	CD–3	DC–3	EG–2	FG–5	GE–2	
(OB–5)	AD–4	~~BA–5~~	~~CA–5~~	~~DA–4~~	~~EA–3~~	FD–6	GH–4	
	AC–5	BE–6	CG–7	~~DB–4~~	ED–5	FH–7	GF–5	
	~~AB–5~~		CF–8	DE–5	~~EB–6~~	FC–8	GD–5	
				DG–5			GC–7	
				DF–6				

Again returning to Step 1, we would look into the O, A, and B columns to find our candidates, and there are none in the O column. From the A column we would select "AE–3," and from the B column "BD–4." In Step 2 we would compare the distances (4 + 3) = 7 for node E and (5 + 4) = 9 for node D, thus leading us to next commit node E and "AE–3." It should be noted that to find the distance associated with a candidate we simply add its arc distance to the shortest distance figure over the column in which it is located.

If we encircle "AE–3," cross off those arcs ending with node E, and place the value 7 over the E column, we would produce this table:

	0	4	5			7		
	O	A	B	C	D	E	F	G	H
(OA–4)	(AE–3)	BD–4	CD–3	DC–3	EG–2	FG–5	~~GE–2~~	
(OB–5)	AD–4	~~BA–5~~	~~CA–5~~	~~DA–4~~	~~EA–3~~	FD–6	GH–4	
	AC–5	~~BE–6~~	CG–7	~~DB–4~~	ED–5	FH–7	GF–5	
	~~AB–5~~		CF–8	~~DE–5~~	~~EB–6~~	FC–8	GD–5	
				DG–5			GC–7	
				DF–6				

Continuing in this way, first applying the selection of candidates as given in Step 1, and then the final selection procedure as in Step 2, we would continue until the destination node, node H, has been committed. The final table would be:

0	4	5	9	8	7		9	13
O	A	B	C	D	E	F	G	H
(OA–4)	(AE–3)	~~BD–4~~	~~CD–3~~	~~DC–3~~	(EG–2)	~~FG–5~~	~~GE–2~~	
(OB–5)	(AD–4)	~~BA–5~~	~~CA–5~~	~~DA–4~~	~~EA–3~~	~~FD–6~~	(GH–4)	
(AC–5)	~~BE–6~~	~~CG–7~~	~~DB–4~~	~~ED–5~~	~~FH–7~~	GF–5		
~~AB–5~~		CF–8	~~DE–5~~	~~EB–6~~	~~FC–8~~	~~GD–5~~		
			~~DG–5~~			~~GC–7~~		
			DF–6					

From the H column we interpret that the shortest distance from the origin to node H is 13 units. To find the actual shortest route we trace backwards through the circled arcs, starting at node H. Tracing backwards we have: (H to G) to (G to E) to (E to A) to (A to O), thus the arcs of the shortest route are (O, A), (A, E), (E, G), and (G, H). To find the shortest route to any other node we trace backwards from this node again using circles arcs. So the shortest route to node G has arcs: (O, A), (A, E), and (E, G) with shortest distance of 9 units.

We notice in this last table that node F is not committed to the final solution. If we wanted to find the shortest route to this node we would simply have to find that arc with the shortest length which reaches F from one of the already committed nodes; we choose from those arcs which are neither circled nor crossed out. Here the choice is "DF–6," and adding this distance to the shortest distance to node D we would find $(8 + 6) = 14$ as the shortest distance to node F.

This solution process may also be used to find the "most reliable" path through a network whose arcs now represent "components" which are subject to failure or breakdown. We again start with a network which represents the structural relationships between the components, and now associated with the arc, say (i, j), we have the probability $p_{i,j}$ that the corresponding component will be operational when called into use. This $p_{i,j}$ is thus the reliability of the associated component, and we require that these be independent of one another.

Maximizing the reliability of a path is our objective and this is equivalent to maximizing the value of the product of the $p_{i,j}$'s for the arcs on the path. This, in turn, is equivalent to maximizing the sum of the values of the log $(p_{i,j})$ for the arcs on the path (these are the natural logarithms of the the arc reliabilities), and this is the same as minimizing the value of the sum of the terms $-\log (p_{i,j})$ for the arcs on the path. From this statement we see that we simply have to construct the network and associate a "distance" with each arc, and for arc (i,j) this value would be: $-\log(p_{i,j})$. Using these distances, and the above procedure, the shortest route through the network will be the most reliable route since it will have the smallest value of the sum of these distances. If D is the total length of this shortest route then antilog $(-D)$, which is 10^{-D}, is the overall reliability of the corresponding component configuration.

We might also have a reliability associated with the nodes of the network as well as with the arcs. To handle this we simply split each node into two new nodes, connect these with an arc and associate with this arc the reliability of the original node we have just split. Applying the procedure will find the most reliable component configuration.

In applying Step 2 of the procedure we might find two or more candidates with the same value for the calculated distance. In such cases we might have some additional characteristic which will enable us to break the tie, but if not we can commit all the tied arcs to the solution simultaneously, as well as the nodes which each indicates. In doing this we will build in alternative routes from the origin to the destination nodes, each with the same shortest distance value.

The Maximum Flow Problem

This problem starts with a network for which a maximum flow capacity is associated with each of its arcs. These capacities limit the flow through the arcs per unit of time, and these can be different depending upon the direction of flow along the arcs. Normally, we designate an "entrance" node and an "exit" node, where all flow enters the network at the former and leaves at the latter. Thus, in Figure 6–5, node A is the entrance node while node H is the exit.

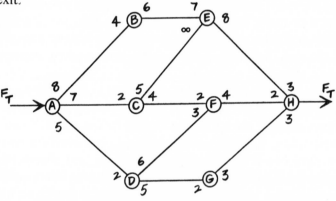

Figure 6–5

The problem is to determine how much flow to assign across each arc so that we will have a maximum total flow out of the exit node, while not violating any of the capacity limitations of any arcs. It is assumed that the sum of the flows out of any node equals the sum of the flows into this same node, and it is also taken that we have no limit on the flow entering the entrance node. Perhaps the most natural setting for this problem is in the area of communications systems; however, it also arises in chemical processes, transportation networks, and in work flow situations.

This problem may be easily formulated as a linear programming problem, but the following solution procedure is much more efficient. To illustrate it we will use the network of Figure 6–5 where the flow capacities of an arc are written alongside of its "initial" nodes. Thus, for example, the capacity of the arc (B,E) is 6, while that of the reverse arc (E,B) is 7. The capacity of the arc (E,C) is shown as infinite, "∞," which means that flow is unlimited in this direction over this particular arc.

The solution procedure consists of the following steps:

Step 1.   Find a path from the entrance node to the exit node, all of whose arcs have positive flow capacity in the direction of the path. If a path has a zero capacity on one of the arcs in its direction of flow, we cannot use it. If no such path can be found then the net flows already set up by the procedure constitute the optimal solution; that is, the maximum flow has been found.

Step 2.   Find from among the arcs of the path found in Step 1 the smallest flow capacity which will be met in the direction of flow on the path; denote this value by K. Assign a flow of K units along this path, that is, along each of its arcs.

Step 3.   All flow capacities of arcs on our path, in its direction, are decreased by the amount K, while all capacities of these arcs in the opposite direction are increased by K units.

For small problems the procedure can be applied directly on the original network for the problem. For our example we begin by selecting as our first path the one using the arcs (A,B), (B,E), and (E,H). The smallest arc capacity on this path is 6 for the arc (B,E), and so we assign a flow of this many units along this path. We also decrease the flow capacities by 6 on all arcs for flow in the direction of the path, but increase by 6 the capacities on these three arcs in the opposite flow direction. The resulting network would be that shown in Figure 6–6, where the path is shown as the heavier lines. We note that the capacity of flow from node B to node E is now zero, and so (B,E) cannot be used for subsequent paths.

Working with the network in Figure 6–6, we return to Step 1 of the procedure and as the next path we may choose the arcs (A,D), (D,F), and (F,H), with the smallest flow capacity in this direction being the 4 units for arc (F,H). We assign this many units of flow for this path, decrease flow capacities in this direction, increase them on these arcs in the opposite direction, and our resulting network would be that shown in Figure 6–7. In this figure we see that arc (F,H) has been cut off for subsequent flow assignments.

Working with this latest network and returning again to Step 1 we find the path with arcs (A,C), (C,F), (F,D), (D,G), and (G,H). The smallest arc capacity on this path is 3 units, for arc (G,H), and after making the necessary increases and decreases we produce the network shown in Figure 6–8.

The last path we are able to form has arcs (A,C), (C,E), and (E,H), with smallest arc capacity of 2 units for the arc (E,H), and we have the results posted in Figure 6–9.

The quantity of flow which has been assigned to any arc, in a specified direction, is calculated as the original arc capacity minus the final capacity (as shown in the final network). Thus, the flow assigned by the procedure to the arc (E,H), is $(8 - 0) = 8$ units. In the same way we determine that the flows along arcs (F,H), and (G,H) are respectively 4 and 3 units. The flow entering the exit node, node H in our example, is simply the total of the flows along arcs ending at this node. From the flows just cited we find that the total flow into node H is $(8 + 4 + 3) = 15$ units, which is the maximum flow we can obtain for this network.

As a check, 15 units must also be the sum of the flows emanating from our entrance node, node A, along the arcs (A,B), (A,C), and (A,D), which it is in our case.

It may arise that in finding a path with a positive flow capacity we will have to travel across an arc one of whose flow capacities we have zeroed-out—in the opposite direction naturally. Doing this will require that we increase this zero capacity, which may then make it usable in a subsequent path. Usually, when looking at the network, finding paths is a straightforward operation.

Looking at the final network will indicate where "extra" flow capacity is still available. Thus, looking at Figure 6-9, we see that we could still assign a flow of 2 units from node A to node E along the arcs (A,C) and (C,E). Depending upon the physical system underlying our network, this may or may not be useful information. We can also see where additional capacity is needed if we wish to increase the maximum flow out of the exit node, and where

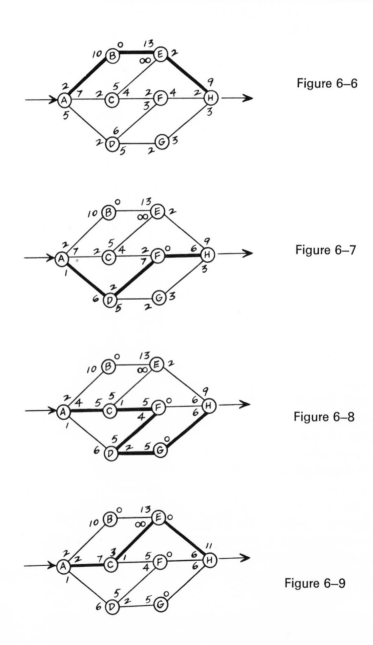

Figure 6–6

Figure 6–7

Figure 6–8

Figure 6–9

increases in capacity would be wasted in this respect. Thus, if we were to only increase the capacity along the arc (D,G), we would be wasting this since we cannot continue along the arc (G,H).

The Graph Coloring Problem

A type of scheduling problem involves a number of events, all of which require the same completion time, and some of which may be performed concurrently. Certain combinations of events are not allowed to run concurrently, and the problem is to find the fewest number of groups of events with no conflicts within any of these. For instance, the events might be final exams in different courses with each of them requiring a full test period. If at least one student is taking two (or more) courses and if these were scheduled for the same test period we would have a conflict. The objective here is to set up the fewest possible test periods so that there are no conflicts.

We need a procedure that will put the different events into distinct groups, and then all events in a given group will be scheduled to run concurrently in a single time period, while different groups will be scheduled for different periods. Finding the fewest number of groups may be identified with the so-called *graph coloring problem* of graph theory. To start, each event is represented by a node of a network and two nodes are connected by an arc if and only if the corresponding events *cannot* take place concurrently. Nodes which are thus connected are referred to as *adjacent nodes* in the procedure.

In Figure 6–10 we have shown such a network involving fifteen "events." This network will used to demonstrate the coloring procedure.

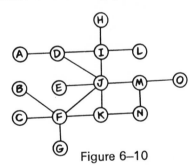

Figure 6–10

We imagine that each node may be "colored," where the color of any node may be selected independently of all others. The constraints of the scheduling problem are translated to our not coloring adjacent nodes with the same color, and our objective now is to use the fewest number of colors. All nodes which have the same color will constitute a group (events scheduled concurrently), and the different color groups specify the different groups of concurrent events.

In graph theory this minimum number of colors used to color a network is termed the *chromatic number* of the network. Determining this for an arbitrary network is as yet an unsolved problem, however, certain approximate procedures may be used to develop quite adequate results. The only drawback with these is that they do not guarantee that the true minimum number of colors will be found.

The so-called *ordering the nodes procedure* is such an approximate method and will be the one demonstrated here. As our worksheet we prepare a table, which, for our example in Figure 6–10, is the following:

From \ To	A	B	C	D	E	F	G	H	I	J	K	L	M	N	O	Row Sum	Order	Color Group
A				×												1	Last	I
B						×										1	Last	I
C						×										1	Last	I
D	×								×	×						3	Fourth	II
E										×						1	Last	II
F		×	×				×		×	×						5	Second	II
G						×										1	Last	I
H									×							1	Last	I
I				×		×		×		×						4	Third	III
J				×	×	×			×		×		×			6	First	I
K										×		×		×		3	Fourth	III
L											×					1	Last	I
M										×				×	×	3	Fourth	II
N											×		×			2	Fifth	I
O													×			1	Last	I

Each arc in our network corresponds to one of the *X* terms in this table; the starting node of the arc specifies the row and the ending node the column in which the *X* is placed. Also the reverse arcs are shown, thus, an *X* appears in the table both at the (A,D) and (D,A) locations. In other words, an *X* indicates adjacency. We add the number of *X*'s in each row and place these sums in the "Row Sum" column. These sums are referred to as the *degrees* which are associated with the nodes corresponding to the rows in which they are found. Thus, the degree of node A is 1, that of node J is 6, and so on. The degree of a node indicates its relative importance for being colored first.

We next arrange the nodes into the particular order in which we will investigate them in the procedure. To do this we arrange the nodes in the decreasing order of their degrees; the nodes we look at *first* will be those with the *largest* degree. This order is indicated in the "Order" column, using word specifications. Here, if two or more nodes have the same degree, they are given the same order position, thus all nodes with degree *1* are *last* in the order. Having nodes tied for an order position is what allows nonoptimality to come into the final solution. We fill in the "Color Group" column in the course of the procedure.

The *first* color group, Group I, is created with the first node we investigate. In our example this will be the J event, or node J. As a means of checking, we could actually color the node in the network. We continue looking at nodes in their prescribed order and any node which is not connected to *any* member of the first color group is added to this first group. We look at all nodes until we have assigned all we can to this first group. From Figure 6–10 we see that we may assign to Group I, along with node J, the following nodes: A, B, C, G, H, L, N, and O. All of these have a "I" in the "Color Group" column for their rows.

The *second* color group, Group II, is started when we find a node not yet colored, but which is next in order and which is connected to a member of the first color group. Again, nodes are inspected in order and any node which is uncolored and not connected to any member of the second color group is assigned to this second group. In our example, we would start Group II with node F with the second order position. Again looking at the figure, we would find that also in this group we can place the nodes: D, E, and M.

We continue assigning nodes to Group II until we have to start a *third* color group, Group III, and proceed as before until all nodes have been assigned to color groups. Here we would start Group III with node I and from the network we would find that the remaining node, node K, can also be assigned to this group.

At this point we have three color groups, which means that we will have to plan on three separate time intervals to complete all events. All events which correspond to nodes in Group I would be run in one interval, all those in Group II would be run concurrently in a second interval, and finally all those in Group III would be scheduled for a third interval.

A type of storage problem which is amenable to this type of analysis is the one where the nodes of our network represent goods, such as chemicals, and an arc between two nodes indicates that the corresponding chemicals cannot (for reasons of safety) be placed in the same compartment together. The problem is then to store the chemicals in the fewest possible number of compartments; each color group we find in the analysis would prescribe a compartment.

Network Planning and Analysis

The most suitable application of such network planning and analysis techniques as PERT and CPM is one where:

1. There are numerous, well-defined activities or tasks which, when completed, mark the end of the overall project.
2. These activities have an order or technological sequence in which they must be performed.
3. Within a given order the activities may be started and stopped independently of each other.

The analysis of the network representing the project plan is aimed at time-scheduling each activity—setting start times for each. Often, this will have to be done to meet a preset completion date on the overall project. In this temporal analysis, certain calculations are required and when the project is "large" some form of machine calculation is needed since the computations would be quite laborious if performed by hand. For even relatively small projects these calculations are tedious unless systematized, and one such procedure will be demonstrated in this section.

The *arrow diagram* is fundamental to all network analysis, and in Figure 6–11 an example of one is shown. The project represented by this diagram ends when node 12 has been reached. Individual activities of the project are represented by arcs which we have labeled with letters and have also indicated their duration times. The nodes of the diagram represent events or milestones of the project and in our particular diagram these merely indicate the start and completion points of the activities. Thus, node 2 represents the start of activity C, while node 4 indicates its completion.

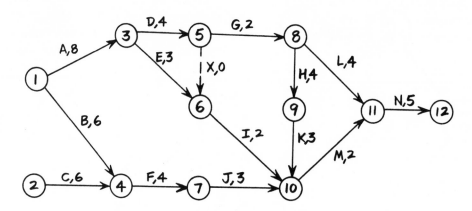

Figure 6–11

In constructing these diagrams certain procedures are used to indicate the precedence relationships between activities. Thus, if two or more activities can be started concurrently, they will have their arcs emanating from a common event node. Activities A and B, for example, can be started concurrently since they both start from the same node, node 1. If an activity can start only after one or more preceding activities have been completed, then all these preceding activities will have their arcs ending at a common event node which is the starting point of this activity. Thus, from our figure, we see that activity M cannot start until activities I, J, and K have all been completed.

At times, to maintain a logical precedence condition, a *dummy activity* will be required in the diagram. In Figure 6–11 activity X is a dummy and as is standard practice its arc is dashed. A dummy activity has all the properties of an activity except that it has zero duration time, and consumes no resources. To illustrate the use of such activities, suppose that activity E is "lath and plaster walls," and activity I "paint walls," with activity D being "install wiring and fixtures." A different crew may work on activities E and I than that working on activity D, and the dummy arc is included since we must have the electrical work completed prior to starting to paint.

Figure 6–11 is an *activity-oriented diagram,* and as such it defines each activity of the project. Another type is the *event-oriented diagram,* shown in Figure 6–12 for the same project represented by Figure 6–11. Here the concern is with specific occurrences or events, and the emphasis is on the identification of the events rather than on the activities which must be completed for that event to occur. Usually, PERT uses an event-oriented diagram while CPM uses the activity-oriented one. The procedure we will demonstrate here requires that we work with the former type, thus if we start with an activity-oriented diagram, our first step is to redraw it as an event-oriented diagram. Each node in Figure 6–12 represents the start, progress, and completion of an activity, with labels and duration times posted inside the nodes. However, if we started with a PERT event-oriented diagram, each node would most likely represent a series of activities, the completion of which would bring us to the indicated event. This will not present a problem to us as long as we continue to view these activities as a collective unit. Also in the conversion we have introduced

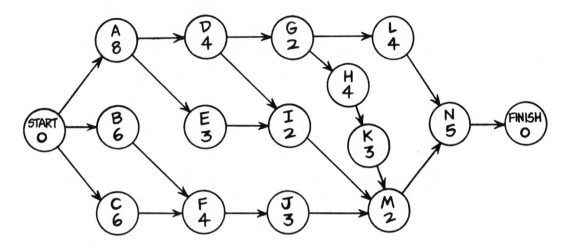

Figure 6–12

two pseudoactivities: "Start," and "Finish." Each of these have zero duration time and are used to give us a single starting event and a single ending event (in a PERT diagram these would already be specified and so need not be used in this situation).

In interpreting event-oriented diagrams, we view each node along with all the arcs emanating from it as a unit. The start of the activity associated with the event node commences upon reaching the node. The arcs are used simply to meet precedence relationships between activities (or events).

The procedure will be illustrated with the diagram in Figure 6–12. How the figures thus developed are used in time scheduling the activities (or PERT events), as well as in the analysis of slacks will then follow. The steps of the procedure are performed in a table, and they are as follows:

Step 1. Construct a table (see Table 6–1) with as many rows and columns as there are events in the diagram (Figure 6–12). Draw a diagonal line and label the rows and columns, in the same order, with the event names. The rows list the preceding events and the columns the succeeding ones, indicated as "To" and "From" in the table. Next, post the duration times of the events. We put the duration time of an event in its designated row and repeat this same value in each column that corresponds to an event which is preceded by this one.

Step 2. Place a "0" in the top-center location in the Start-Start box, enclosing this in a square. All numbers enclosed in squares are termed "squared numbers." Working from left-to-right, column-by-column, bring down the *largest* squared number in a column to the diagonal box in this column, posting this value below the diagonal line in this box and enclosing it in a square. Once a number is posted in the diagonal box, add this value to all the duration times in this same row, posting these sums in the appropriate boxes in squares. We continue posting values in diagonal boxes, and adding these to duration times and then posting these in squares until each diagonal box of the table is filled in.

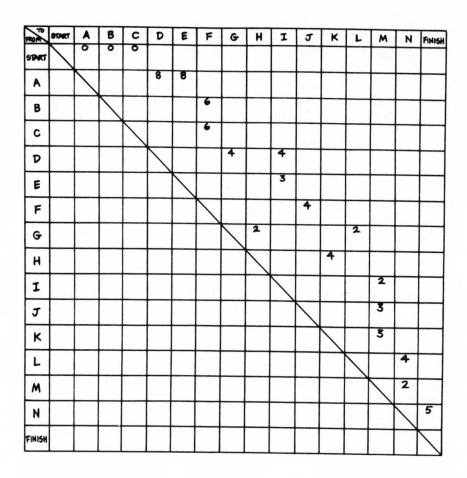

FROM\TO	START	A	B	C	D	E	F	G	H	I	J	K	L	M	N	FINISH
START		⓪	⓪	⓪												
A					8	8										
B							6									
C							6									
D								4		4						
E										3						
F											4					
G									2				2			
H												4				
I														2		
J														3		
K														3		
L															4	
M															2	
N																5
FINISH																

Table 6–1

The finished table at this point, for our example, would be that shown in Table 6–2.

Step 3. Place a "0" in the Finish-Finish box, posting it above the diagonal line here and enclosing it in a circle. Once a circled number is put into a diagonal box we add this value to all duration times in the column corresponding to this box, posting these sums in circles in the appropriate boxes in the table. When a row has all its circled numbers we find the *largest* of these and post this in the diagonal box for this row, locating it in a circle above the diagonal line. We continue in this manner until each diagonal box has been filled in with a circled number. The completed table would be that shown in Table 6–3, and the squared and circled numbers in the diagonal boxes are the figures we need in subsequent analyses.

The *earliest (expected) start time* for an activity is the earliest we could possibly schedule this activity to start. These start times are the squared numbers found in the diagon-

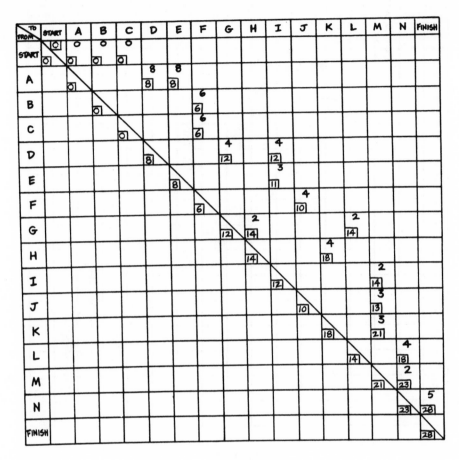

Table 6–2

al boxes in the rows corresponding to the activities. Thus, for example, the earliest start time for activity D is 8 time units (days, weeks, months, etc.) after the project has started, since this is the squared number in the diagonal box in the D row. The procedure develops these start times in recognition of the existing precedence relationships existing between the activities of the network diagram.

The *earliest (expected) finish time* for an activity is the earliest we can expect to finish this activity if we started it at the earliest possible moment; therefore, this is simply the earliest start time for the activity plus its duration time. Activity D has an earliest finish time of 12 time units after the project has started, since its earliest start time is 8 and its duration is 4 time units. The earliest start and finish times are listed in Table 6–4 for our example.

The *latest allowable start time* for an activity is that time by which this activity *must be started* so as not to delay the completion time of the *overall project*. The *latest allowable finish time* is simply this start time plus the duration time of the activity. The *total expected time to complete the project* is found in Table 6–3 as the squared number in the last box (the

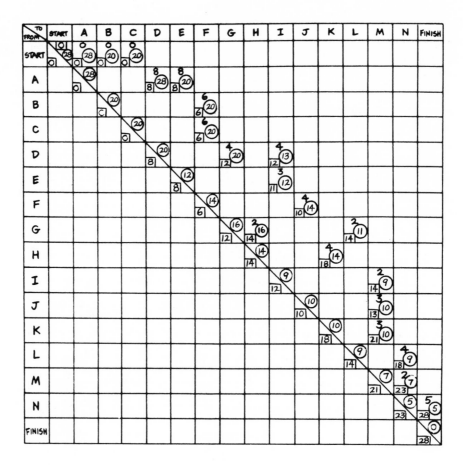

Table 6-3

Finish–Finish box), and this is 28 time units. If we use this value, we are assuming that all activities start at their earliest start times, and so in a sense this 28 is the minimum length of time needed to complete the project.

If we subtract the circled number for an activity from the total expected time to complete the project, the result will be the latest allowable start time for this same activity. Thus, from Table 6–3 we find that this latest start time for activity D is (28 – 20) = 8 time units after project start. The latest allowable start and finish times for the activities in our example are also shown in Table 6-4. Looking at this table we see that the following activities have equal earliest and latest allowable start times: Start, A, D, G, H, K, M, N, and Finish. These are the so-called *critical activities* of the project and together they constitute the *critical path* in the network.

The critical path of the network is the chain of activities which has the greatest overall duration, and so these determine the completion time of the project. If any of these critical activities slip from their scheduled completion dates, we may expect that the overall project will also slip by this same amount which is what makes them "critical." If it is necessary to complete the project sooner than its calculated expected completion date, say in our example we must finish in 24 rather than 28 time units, then one or more of these critical activities will have to be finished sooner. In order to shorten an activity's duration, we usually have to expend additional resources, and, if we were to do this for any but the critical activities, we would be wasting our effort since these will not shorten the overall project time. If we do in fact shorten the duration of a critical activity, we must re-analyze the network with this new time value since we may now have a new and different critical path—a previously noncritical activity may become critical.

In Table 6–4 the critical activities are those with asterisks alongside their symbols. Having these activities isolated, management can now apply the Management by Exception principle to the control of the project, wherein it devotes its attention only to the critical activities.

Activity	Earliest		Latest Allowable	
	Start Times	Finish Times	Start Times	Finish Times
Start*	0	0	0	0
A*	0	8	0	8
B	0	6	8	14
C	0	6	8	14
D*	8	12	8	12
E	8	11	16	19
F	6	10	14	18
G*	12	14	12	14
H*	14	18	14	18
I	12	14	19	21
J	10	13	18	21
K*	18	21	18	21
L	14	18	19	23
M*	21	23	21	23
N*	23	28	23	28
Finish*	28	28	28	28

*Critical activities

Table 6–4

When we prepare the schedule for the project activities we must start each critical activity at its earliest start time, that is, if we want to finish the project in the shortest time possible. We have a certain amount of flexibility in scheduling noncritical activity start dates and to determine this we next perform a *slack analysis*.

The first slack we can associate with an activity is *total slack*. This is that length of time by which an activity duration time may be increased without delaying the completion of the overall project. This slack is calculated by subtracting the earliest start time for the activity from its latest allowable start time. Critical path activities will have zero total slack.

The total slacks for our example are shown in Table 6–5 and from these figures we see that, for example, activity B can be increased by 8 units of time without delaying the overall project.

A convenient device used in analyzing slacks, as well as in scheduling, balancing workloads, and allocating manpower, is the construction of a bar chart representation of the network. Figure 6–13 is this chart prepared for our example. To construct it we lay out the critical path activities in a straight line bar against an appropriate time scale; the length of each bar is equal to the duration time of the corresponding activity. Secondary portions of the network are drawn above and below the critical path positioned at their earliest start times. These secondary bars have lengths equal to the duration times plus the total slacks of the corresponding activities; the slack portions of these are shown shaded in the figure. The unshaded portion of these bars represent the duration times of the activities and these may be shifted within the overall confines of the total bar.

We may postpone the start of an activity with total slack any length of time we may choose up to the latest allowable start time. But, in so doing we will delay the starts of all activities which have a precedence relationship with this activity. This bar chart is very useful in seeing where shifts can be made and what effects these will produce on other related activities. Thus, from the figure, we see that if we choose to delay the start of activity B by 2 time units (not as far as we can delay this activity since the latest allowable start position for it is at 8 time units after project start which in turn means we could delay B up to 8 time units) we will use this many units of B's total slack. This delay will mean that activity F cannot start at its earliest start time, but rather 2 time units after this—starting at

Activity	Total Slack	Free Slack
Start*	0	0
A*	0	0
B	8	0
C	8	0
D*	0	0
E	8	1
F	8	0
G*	0	0
H*	0	0
I	7	7
J	8	8
K*	0	0
L	5	5
M*	0	0
N*	0	0
Finish*	0	0

*Critical activities

Table 6–5

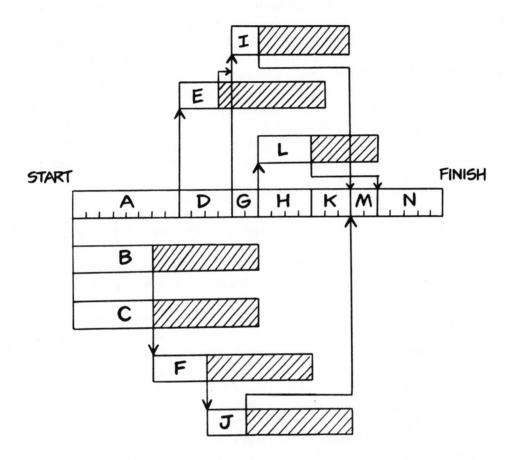

Figure 6–13

the point 8 units after project start. Therefore, F now has only 6 units of total slack instead of its previous 8 units.

The bar chart for the network is often useful in leveling the use of resources in the project, whereby noncritical activities are scheduled to start so as to level the demands of these resources. Figure 6–14 will be used to illustrate this. In the upper diagram we have drawn the critical path bar along with the bars for activities B, E, and F, which are shown at their earliest start times and repositioned to simplify the presentation here. We suppose that activities A, E, and F each require two workers (this could be any other common resource), and we specify these as carpenters. Above the critical path bar we have plotted vertical bars to indicate the number of carpenters which will have to be made available if these activities (A, E, and F) are scheduled to start at their earliest start times as shown. The letters in these vertical bars indicate to which activity the carpenters will be assigned. Thus, we need 2 men over the course of activity A until F is started where we will need 4 in total. When A stops, we can reassign its men to activity E, but in total we still have 4 until F stops at which point we need only 2 men working on activity E until it is completed. The peaking in this "workforce" bar chart indicates that demands are nonlevel.

In the lower diagram of Figure 6–14 we have the same basic figure as in the above, but here we have delayed activity B by 2 units of time, which means that F cannot start until 8 units of time after project start, this being where activity A terminates. In addition, we have scheduled activity E to start at a point 12 units of time after project start, which means we have delayed the start of this activity by 4 units of time (still before its latest allowable start time of 16). By so doing, E will start after F has been completed, and the net effect of these delays is seen in the workforce bar chart which is now level at 2 carpenters. We will now have to make available only 2 carpenters and these men will be continually utilized through the first 15 periods of time in the project.

On the larger scale we could lay out the different resource requirements for the different activities, doing this over the complete bar chart for the project. Through the use of delayed starts we would then attempt to level (or as nearly as possible) these requirements over the course of the project.

The longest length of time by which an activity may have its duration time extended without forcing any succeeding activities to be delayed from their respective earliest start times is known as the *free slack* of the activity. This type of slack is used on the operating level where some unforeseen occurrence requires that we lengthen a duration time. An activity may have a total slack without having a free slack, and in any case the latter is always less than or equal to the former. To calculate the free slack of an activity, we subtract the earliest finish time of this activity from the smallest earliest start time for the immediate successors of it. Thus, for activity E, we have a free slack of 1 unit of time since its earliest finish time is 11 and the earliest start time of I (its only immediate successor) is 12. Table 6–5 lists the free slacks for the activities in our example. Again, the bar chart of the network is useful in spotting free slacks as well as seeing the effects of using them.

It is important to keep in mind the fact that the way total and free slacks have been calculated assumes that all activities preceding the one with which we are working start at their earliest start times. If this is not the case, these slacks are best found from the bar chart of the network. This is a feasible way of working for small projects, but then this is the type of situation for which this section was prepared.

CONCLUSION

This chapter has focussed on problems which may be structured in the form of networks, through the analysis of which solutions may be found. Iterative solution procedures have been provided for four of the most basic types of network problems: minimum spanning tree, shortest route, maximum flow, and graph coloring problem. There are many manufacturing problems which can be framed as one of these network problems. In addition, some basic concepts from the area of network planning and analysis have been introduced, along with a tabular procedure for deriving the necessary figures for the actual analyses. The objective here has been to provide the reader with a practical procedure for handling relatively small projects.

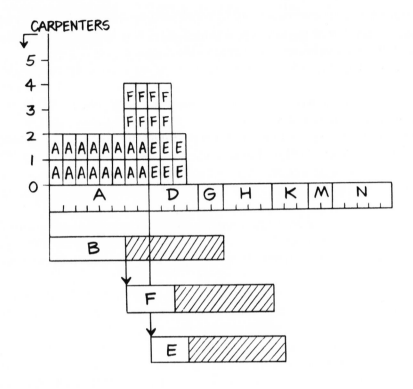

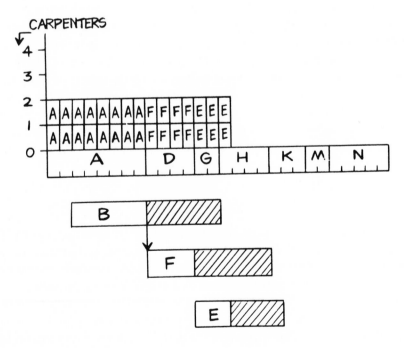

Figure 6–14

REFERENCES

Ford, L.R., Jr. and D.R. Fulkerson. *Flows in Networks*. Princeton, N. J.: Princeton University Press, 1962.

Hillier, F. S., and G.J. Lieberman. *Introduction to Operations Research*. San Francisco, California: Holden-Day, Inc., 1967.

Moder, J.J., and C.R. Phillips. *Project Management with CPM and PERT*. New York, N.Y.: Reinhold Publishing Corporation, 1966.

Wood, D.C. "A Technique for Coloring a Graph Applicable to Large Scale Timetabling Problems," *The Computer Journal,* Vol. 12, page 317.

Index